ADVANCE PRAISE

"*How To Build A* ... has ever wondered what next ... Honest, witty, passionate, an ... proach to life shows that you don't have ... ney business degree to succeed. You just have to take the next step. The rest will take care of itself. Ruthi's philosophy is profound yet simple. I loved this book!"

—*Ilene Rosenthal, CEO, Footsteps2Brilliance*

"Through honest, warm stories about her past, Ruthi paints a picture of a strong, driven young woman who found lessons in all that came her way. Her experiences demonstrate her grit and determination. From the book's enticing title to the final messages, this is an entertaining and important work."

—*Randy A. Ehrenberg, retired school superintendent, North Colonie Central School District*

"From the small paper mill town of Prichard, Alabama to Washington, DC, *How to Build a Piano Bench* is a heartwarming story about Ruthi Postow Birch's simple upbringing and how it prepared her to survive and succeed in one of the most competitive cities in the world. Her stories, sweet and sometimes downright outrageous, demonstrate that aha moment we so desperately seek. A good read for anyone who works with people, this book is a gentle and kind reminder that the lessons we learn as a child can and will serve us well in adulthood."

—*Nancy Lilja, CEO, National Institute of Transition Planning, Inc.*

HOW *to* BUILD *a* PIANO BENCH

HOW *to* BUILD *a* PIANO BENCH

Lessons for Success from a
Red-Dirt Road in Alabama

RUTHI POSTOW BIRCH

RIVER GROVE
BOOKS

Published by River Grove Books
Austin, TX
www.rivergrovebooks.com

Distributed by River Grove Books

Design and composition by Greenleaf Book Group
Cover design by Greenleaf Book Group
©iStockphoto.com/horiyan

Cataloging-in-Publication data is available.

Print ISBN: 978-1-63299-108-9

eBook ISBN: 978-1-63299-109-6

First Edition

DEDICATION

This book is dedicated to people with dreams—dreams that will take them far from where they started. It's for people who are determined to follow those dreams in spite of the obstacles in their way, who won't accept the limits other people try to impose or listen to the voices that tell them, "You can't." Its message is to accept yourself and appreciate what makes you special—including your flaws—and to lighten up and laugh at yourself, because a lot of success in life is about getting past the scary parts.

Nobody wants me down like I wants me up! . . . Oh, I hate that word 'down'! But, I love that word 'up'! 'Cuz 'up' means 'hope' an' that's just what I got! Hope!

—from The Unsinkable Molly Brown by Richard Morris

INTRODUCTION

Thirteen East Petain Street, Prichard, Alabama—that's an important address for me. It's where I learned everything I needed to know to succeed in life and in business—lessons passed on to me by the people who lived in this neighborhood that straddled the poverty line. I learned I'd have to be independent enough to do things for myself. I would have to be brave enough to take on things I'd never done before and didn't know how to do—and would have to figure out as I went along. Not knowing how to do something never stopped my daddy from doing it. He didn't know how to build a piano bench till mine broke.

I wasn't sorry the piano bench broke. I was hoping it meant I'd get to stop taking the piano lessons I had been taking since I was seven. Mama wouldn't let me quit. She said I'd be glad someday when it would make me popular at parties. I never found out how that would feel because, in five years of lessons, I never got good enough that people would want to listen. To do that I would have to play with my right and left hands simultaneously. I couldn't do that—no eye-hand coordination. I also couldn't master any key that had more than one sharp or flat. More than that and it was multiplication tables all over again.

One of my friends took lessons, and she said she couldn't wait to get home every day to practice. I thought she was just saying it to sound uppity, and I didn't believe her. I didn't want to spend my afternoons practicing the piano any more than I wanted to spend them doing multiplication tables. But I couldn't quit, so I needed a new piano bench.

Daddy didn't know how to build a bench, but he knew where he had to start. He bought some wood. That was the way Daddy did things. He said when something *had* to be done, it had to be done, whether he knew how to do it or not.

"There is always just one right next step—and you know it because it's the only one that makes sense. Find that and do it. Then look for the next. If there is something you can't do, figure out who can do it for you." So that's how Daddy built the piano bench—by doing the next thing that made sense. It made sense that he needed wood and nails and varnish, so he went out and bought them. He wanted round legs but didn't have a machine to turn them, so he cut blocks of wood for the legs and took them to his friend who did.

He made a sturdy box for the bench's seat, then he built a frame for the lid. But Daddy wouldn't just slap together any old bench. It would be the best bench. After he had the top framed, he decided he wouldn't finish it with one piece of wood. No, sir. He spent every day after work for months inlaying the top with little pieces of wood of different colors in a geometric pattern because, "If I'm building it anyway, I might as well build something you'll want to have when you're grown." Daddy worked on the bench for two years, gluing tiny brown, blond, and gray strips into a design, then applying coat after coat of varnish. He finished my piano bench not long after Mama admitted I wasn't going to make it as a pianist and I got to quit taking lessons.

Today I can't play an instrument to charm people at parties, and the piano is long gone. But in the sitting room beside my bedroom sits a work of art Daddy built when he didn't know how to build it.

How to build a business—or a piano bench—is just one of the lessons for success that I took from Petain Street.

1

A STREET PAVED *with* ALABAMA RED CLAY

Growing Up with Advantages

"You're going to get off Petain Street. You'll get your education, and you're going to amount to something." That was the commandment Daddy gave me. And I did it. I amounted to something—but only because of the lessons I took with me from the street he made sure I would leave.

Paved with Alabama red clay and lined with the old yellow houses built for the paper mills' workers in the early 1900s, Petain Street was in Prichard, a blue-collar town in Mobile County. I grew up there in the '50s with all the advantages a child could have—the freedom of safety, working-class people with working-class values, and time to waste. Everybody knew everybody on Petain Street and watched out for each other, so I was free to go about and talk to neighbors, mostly laborers, factory workers, and lots of old people who were retired and had time to spend on a child. And Mama and Daddy worked long days, so I had time to waste.

I had time to spend learning people. As far back as I remember, and I remember just about everything, I was a watcher, a listener, and a gatherer. I soaked up everything I saw on Petain Street—the people, stories, feelings, and scenes of worn, lived-in landscapes in colors running from dusty taupe and khaki to bright orange and red—even the different ways the air felt and smelled, and I held on to it to use whenever I'd need to. The street was full of storytellers, not just Daddy, Mama, and Grandmama, but all of the old folks who lived in the other mill houses. I listened and gathered up their stories and saved them for later. I was a kid, so I listened like a kid—just heard them and accepted them at face value, without passing judgment.

That was one of my first and most important lessons. People have stories to tell and they love to tell them—and will do most anything for a person who listens and doesn't judge them. I listened, so they talked. They told me about funerals and weddings, happy times, things that hurt them, things they were ashamed of.

What I didn't know then, and wouldn't figure out for what seemed a whole lot of years, was that at eight years old I was already training for the career that would keep me off of Petain Street. I was going to be a gatherer of images and words, and a listener to people who would tell me all I needed to know so I could amount to something.

But then I found out the world wasn't just made up of people. It was made up of groups of people. And when they got together, they weren't people anymore. They were a group, and I was the little girl who was on the outside, looking in, and scared to join in. I was five years old the first time I met one of these impenetrable groups.

Right after I graduated from kindergarten, Mama and Daddy packed up and moved me away from Grandmama's house on Petain Street to an apartment in Wharton, Texas. My brother had moved to Houston after he married Leona, and Mama and Daddy wanted to be near them and their new baby, Will.

Our apartment was over a feed store that sold chickens and all kinds of farm tools. Mama and Daddy worked six days a week, and there were no other children living in the building, so I spent my time watching the chickens or playing by myself on the little grass strip beside the store. I was so happy when I met a little girl who lived in a house on the street that backed up to our apartment building. We played together all afternoon. As she was leaving to go home, she said she was having a birthday party on Saturday and I was invited. Mama had to work on Saturday, but that was okay, I could walk there by myself.

Saturday afternoon I got dressed and went to her house. I climbed the steps to her porch. The party had started. I could hear children laughing inside. But I didn't knock on the door. I just stood there, frozen on the porch, for a long time, scared and sad, wanting her mother to find me and yet afraid she would at the same time. Then I went home.

I didn't know it then, but I'd never be comfortable in a group. People were fine one at a time. But groups judged you for being poor, for being dumb, for being from the wrong town—for everything. When I was in a group, I'd get a strange feeling of being apart—not fully part of the scene, but standing just outside, looking in at the other people and at myself, too. It was weird to be outside of myself, watching me and seeing myself wanting to be part of it, but unable to cross the barrier.

After first grade, we moved back to 13 East Petain Street and to Grandmama and the people I knew on the street that I'd someday be successful enough to get off, which meant finding a career. But with a world full of groups that I was pretty sure wouldn't like me and would judge me, if I was going to get off of Petain Street, it would have to be in a career that didn't put me in the middle of a group. I'd have to find one that would let me be with people, like the ordinary people on Petain Street, who appreciated having me there to listen—one at a time. I would finally find that career in sales at a staffing business (called a personnel agency back then), selling to clients and interviewing candidates one-on-one.

Another lesson I learned from my story gathering was that people who didn't look as though their lives would be all that interesting actually had exciting, funny, or poignant stories to tell. The people who I grew up around sent me into the world expecting people, all kinds of people, to have stories to tell me and expecting them to value me for listening.

One of the biggest advantages to growing up on Petain Street was that I had time to waste. This was a time and a place when parents were too busy supporting us children to worry about entertaining us. I had time enough to be bored, bored enough to become creative in ways to fill the time. We weren't the poorest on the street. At least we never had to eat Spam—that's where Daddy drew the poverty line. But we still couldn't afford to waste money on a lot of extras or after-school activities like tap dance lessons, which Mama couldn't have gotten time off work to take me to anyway. And besides that, it was against her religion. So, except for the thirty minutes a week I spent taking piano lessons (that Mama would put aside five dollars to pay for), and aside from the ten or fifteen minutes a day I practiced (and stretched to "an hour" when I told Mama), I had time to waste, time to wonder, time to figure things out for myself.

I had time to develop curiosity about the things I saw and the things I read in books. When I was six we got a television. We had two channels (5 and 10) to choose from, and sometimes we watched channel 3, but it had either a picture or sound, never both at once, because it was broadcast all the way from Pensacola, Florida. Television gave me a view of all kinds of fascinating places where different people lived exciting lives. I wanted to be a part of that world.

I spent a lot of my time alone. I didn't mind. That's when I did my dreaming, and the dreams became the goals I'd shoot for. I imagined how it would be someday, when I'd be rich and successful and popular. I dreamed of myself with a brilliant and elegant man. He would be rich, but I'd not be supported by him, or any man, or bossed by one. No, someday I'd have a career that would make me independent, so I could do whatever I wanted. Someday I'd buy clothes from stores I was afraid to even walk into then. Someday vacations wouldn't mean just going to visit kinfolks. I'd go all kinds of exciting places and I'd stay in hotels. I'd meet fantastic people. I'd be somebody, and I'd be a long, long way from Petain Street—just like Daddy said.

From the time I could understand, Daddy told me I had to get my education and get away from Petain Street and be *somebody*. I figured that meant have money and live in a fine house like the ones I saw in Mobile when we drove down the streets through the rich people's neighborhoods every spring to see the azaleas. Even our very street was dirt-poor—too poor to have cement the way Paper Mill Road, Wilson Avenue, and every other street did, even in Prichard. Petain Street was paved with red clay—Alabama red clay they called it, and seemed real proud of it. But I thought the only reason they gave our street the clay was because they couldn't do anything else with it. They sure couldn't farm it. I never saw a weed or blade work its way up through that clay. It turned to thick mud when it rained and squished up through my toes when I walked barefoot. Cars carved the mud into deep ruts that baked hard in the sun and gave off a fine red dust that every little breeze picked up and carried around the street, to turn the white houses, the curtains, the porch rockers, and my shorts a red-orange that Mama could never wash out. Every month or so the city sent an oil truck to slick down the road. That was supposed to hold down the red dust, but it only lasted till the next rain.

I looked up and down the street and saw two kinds of poor people. We were poor, but other people were really poor. I could tell the difference just by looking at the yards. Really poor yards didn't have grass, not even weeds, just dusty gray dirt, and sometimes a skinny dog or two. Most of the really poor on Petain Street lived down below the ditch, on the end of the street closest to the paper mills.

In the yards on our end of the street, things grew—grass, crepe myrtle trees, and me. I was happy on Petain Street. Funny, I thought, our street was dirt, but it had a curb made of cement, and a cement sidewalk too. I was happy sitting on the curb making animal figures out of the mud, happy sitting in the chinaberry in our backyard thinking, and happy listening to the old people tell stories about the little and big things in their lives that were important enough for them to tell to a little girl.

Eva May Simmons was my mother and the most important person in my life. Mama didn't think she was beautiful. And she wasn't beautiful in the Hollywood sense, but she had a face that never blemished and never aged, and she was proud of that. Every year at Mardi Gras and at the Mobile County Fair, they had a man who claimed he could guess your age or your weight, or you'd win a prize. Mama always let him try to guess her age. He never came close, but guessed ten or fifteen years too young. I always walked away with her prize.

Five feet two inches tall with brown eyes that laughed and a quick, sometimes mischievous smile, she didn't appear formidable, but she was. Mama had the strongest character and the most integrity of anybody I ever knew. She knew what she believed and fought for what she thought was right, whether it was a union for the workers in her grocery store, or to get a credit card in her own name when they were supposed to be issued to husbands only.

Mama set an example so high I would spend my life trying to live up to it. She didn't believe in excuses. She got things done and expected I would too. "Other children have excuses," she told me. "Other children don't have enough to eat and have to work after school or take care of little brothers and sisters. You don't have excuses." Mama gave me the drive that made me successful and took away any excuse to stop driving. That was a tough combination to live with because it never let me get to good *enough*.

I knew I had plenty of flaws, and I knew most of my flaws came from Daddy. He gave me the big personality I was never comfortable with and was part of what made me afraid of people. Daddy was a character. He was a tugboat captain who had done some prize fighting when he was young. Most anybody who knew him could have told you Norvelle G. Simmons's faults. He had been a womanizer until he got caught. He cussed, and chewed tobacco, and spit, and never went to church with Mama and me. I used to hate it when anyone said I was like him.

With all his flaws, Daddy was something special. He was smart and he was quick. And he was down-home, dirt-plain wise about people. He knew people and how they thought, and he taught me a lot of things I'd need later in my business and life. Maybe he didn't lead his life as well as he could have, and sometimes I resented his advice; but he never once told me a wrong thing to do.

Daddy was something else too. He was magnetic. He walked into a room and lit it up. People took notice. He had a movie-star handsome face with its strong chin and a nose inherited from his Native American ancestors. But it wasn't just his face, which was handsome enough to set women to touching up their rouge, or the sky-blue eyes that I'm glad were passed down to my children. He had wit, a bearing, and a huge personality that grabbed people. But the problem was he couldn't stop it. He never faded into a crowd. That's something else he passed on to me, and it's intimidated me all my life—the feeling that I could never blend in, that people were always watching me, judging me.

By the time I was eight years old, I had a clear picture of the life I wanted when I grew up. I drew it from the old movies on channel 5 that showed me how people lived in other places, exciting places, like New York City. They lived in elegant penthouses, rode in limousines, and wore beautiful clothes. That's what I'd do. The people on Petain Street wore the uniforms from their jobs, khakis in the garages, the mills, and the Alabama State Docks in Mobile, and nylon dresses in the grocery stores. I was going to wear clothes from the finest stores!

But those people in uniforms taught me what I'd need to know if I was going to get those fancy clothes. I was taught to run a business by people who never ran businesses. I learned to love the game and competition from people who never got to compete for the world's big prizes. Time after time, their words came back to me—their lessons made the difference between success and failure, and now, now I want to pass their lessons on.

One of the most valuable things they taught me was how to simplify. I built my career in a complex and fast-moving business. I spent most of the day on the phone, cold-calling and selling the company's recruiting service to employers at a pace you might see in a movie about Wall Street. When I wasn't on the phone, I was managing the process to get the jobs filled, which meant interviewing candidates, screening them, coordinating interviews for them, teaching them to interview, and closing deals. While I was balancing all of this and building my reputation in business, I had my share of life's complications crashing in at the same time. There were times I felt I was being dragged down into a whirlpool, but I was able to stop and take control because I'd learned the secret—from Daddy when he was building my piano bench. No matter how serious the problem, I can look back and remember what Daddy said: "There is always just one right next step. Find that and it's simple."

Life was simple for the people who lived in the old mill houses. They were clear about what was important—steady work, plenty to eat, school shoes for Billy and Gloria, to go to Heaven when they died. They couldn't afford to complicate things or borrow trouble by worrying about what might happen. They had to live in the moment, face their problems, solve them or mourn them, then go to bed and get some sleep so they could get up and go to work in the morning.

The lessons from my childhood were simple and clear—work hard, make no excuses, stay a steady course, live in the moment. And those lessons worked for me. I got off of Petain Street. But no matter how far I went, I never got far enough to be out of danger. It was always there, just behind me, chasing me, daring me to believe I was finally safe. But, if I looked back over my shoulder, I'd see it, gaining. On the heels of any success, it came, whispering, "Was it a fluke? Can you do it again?"

As afraid as I was of failing, I was equally afraid I'd slip up and show my flaws to the new people I met along the way. How could they miss them? They seemed to blaze like neon signs to me. I worked to hide them, or just hide me altogether, but that wasn't possible for my daddy's daughter. I could never be invisible and I could never be secure enough to fit in.

Why were people always telling me to "Just be yourself"? That was a ridiculous piece of advice as far as I was concerned. I didn't know who I was when other people were around, or how to control the personality that made my teenage years a nightmare and followed me into adulthood. And I certainly didn't think "myself" was something I'd even want to be—an insecure girl who talked too much and tried too hard to impress.

If someone had told me the big fat personality I hated so much would be an advantage someday, or that my fate was to be in a business totally dependent on developing relationships with other people, I wouldn't have believed it. But that's where I would end up—in a job where I had to approach strangers, win their time and their trust, listen to them, understand them, and counsel them. It was the career I'd spent my childhood training for.

I hadn't changed, by either counseling or magic. I was still uncomfortable at social events. One day I just realized that it was okay that I felt uncomfortable. I wasn't meant to be in the crowd. I was meant to stand back from it and watch, and I was wonderful at that. I was meant to focus on one person at a time and listen. I was meant to adsorb the scenes I saw and the stories I heard, and save them. I was meant to be the gatherer.

Other traits that I had never thought of as sellable in the job market turned out to be the ones that brought me success: I was funny. I was quick. I was curious. I could listen. The world needed me! People were aching to tell their stories to someone who wanted to listen. And they would line up to give their trust, their business, and their money to the listener.

They were also longing to be saved from the humdrum of everyday working life and laugh or be entertained. I was meant to make people laugh—and I did. I tried new ideas and I made mistakes. They were funny—at least in retrospect. My clients laughed too. Why? It could be that they just liked to take the focus off themselves and laugh at me. But I think it was more than that. When they saw me admit mistakes and laugh at myself, it made it okay for them to make mistakes too.

One thing my story proves is that success is not created by just your assets. Success is created by the whole person, with all of the experiences and all the irony, sadness, or silliness that went into making that person.

It's not only the dreams, the strengths, the ideals, the laughter, and the wisdom you've gained that develop your drive and character, but also the fears, sorrows, sensitivities, and weaknesses. The terrors that wake you up at three o'clock in the morning are as essential to your success as your talents and gifts. It took all of my traits to bring me here, with a life pretty close to the one I dreamed of, the one I played out and perfected in my backyard.

I've come a long way to arrive at my own company's corner office overlooking what has been called the nation's most powerful street. I'm a long way from Petain Street and, ironically, as close to it as ever.

I saw just how close as I conjured up memories to write this book. An image formed in my mind of my life, folded over so the two ends meet. On one side is the child on Petain Street. On the other is me as I am today—pretty much the same. I've grown and learned more than I could have imagined, but not one piece of me was changed or left behind, and that's the point. All of our parts have value. The trick is to learn how and where to use them. The flaws we would love to be rid of, or at least hide, are as valuable to us as our strengths. Mistakes might be signs you are stretching and growing—and they will probably be good for a laugh someday.

2

THE SMART ONE

Who Believed Love Had to Be Earned

I was born in an orphanage. I had a brother and a sister. I was an only child.

"Look . . . That's where you were born—in an orphanage." That's what Mama joked every time we drove past the Allen Memorial Home in Mobile. It was true. On September 18, sometime before dawn, I was born there, but that was before it became an orphanage and was still a maternity hospital. Wherever I was born, I was anything but an orphan. I was the center of my family's world every minute of every day, the child they had waited over fifteen years for, and they showered me with love.

I learned three things about love very early, and the things I learned scared me. I learned people could love me more than anything and still go away and leave me, or they might even stop loving me so they could love somebody else. I learned there was a connection between how much I was loved and how I looked. Finally, I learned I could win love by doing and by being smart and clever.

I had a brother and a sister. They were seventeen and fifteen when I was born, so in a way I was, for a while anyway, the best toy they ever had. My early recollections of them are a patchwork quilt of memories and things my family told me later. They loved me and they fought over me. At the hospital, when I was just hours old, my brother, Buddy, asked Mama if he could have me—that was after he asked if he could trade me for the chubby baby boy next to me in the nursery. Mama wouldn't trade, but she went along with his other joke. I could be his. I don't think Mama ever understood how that little joke hurt my sister.

I came home to this family who adored me. Brother and Sister loved playing with me, teaching me, and showing me off. Both were certain I was the most remarkable baby ever, and the most beautiful. One of my favorite pictures is a tiny black-and-white shot of Buddy and me. I was about a year old and smiling. Buddy, so handsome, was beaming and holding me by my hand as I walked unsteadily through some flowers. I looked at it often as I was growing up, this boy who looked like a high school heartthrob, and he was beaming with love at a happy baby, and that baby was me. And when I looked, I wished I could remember the Buddy of that picture. But before I was old enough to have clear memories, he left me.

I didn't understand. If he loved me so much, what happened? The answer was he joined the Navy. When I was older, Mama told me he did it for me because we were really poor then. He worked and he sent home every paycheck to make sure I had what I needed. He loved me and sacrificed to give me nice things.

But he did come back, and when he did, things were different. He already had his own family. He didn't seem to care about me anymore, or even to like having me around. His children were still cute babies, and I was five. He got mad at me all of the time, and said I made too much noise or ran around the house too much. I was spoiled and bad, and my brother didn't like me.

From that time, I tried to win my brother back. Every time I knew I was going to see him, I hoped it would be different, that he would notice something good about me instead of thinking everything I did was wrong.

Finally, when I was fourteen, I did something that made Buddy proud of me. I took an IQ test. Buddy was finishing his PhD in psychology and practiced his IQ tests on me. I liked taking the tests. I loved testing days at school. It was a game for me to race the clock and answer more questions than the other kids. Buddy gave me his tests, and they said I was already at college level. He was proud of me, and it felt wonderful. I wished he would give me tests every time he saw me.

After Buddy left for the navy, I still had Mama and Daddy and Grandmama, and I had Sister. I never called her anything but Sister—except for when I was a baby. She was the first person I called Mama, but my mama put an end to that right quick. "I'm your mama. She's your sister."

Sister took me everywhere, to school functions and even on dates. She wouldn't go unless the boys would take me too. Sister was beautiful, fun, and popular, so the boys went along. I think I may have gone to more parties and sock hops as a baby than I did in high school.

Then, when I was three, and I remember this, Sister started being too busy to play with me. I remember the first time I jumped onto her bed in the morning to wake her up, and she didn't smile. She got mad at me. Then one day she went away too, and left me with a fear that would plague me in some form for my whole life: People who loved me could still leave me. Could Mama leave me too?

The thought of losing Mama terrified me. I knew that she wouldn't just go away as Sister and Buddy had; but she could die. What if she died?

This new fear was more terrible than all the others a three-year-old could have, so serious that I started praying to God about it every night and continued to pray through most of my school years. But I didn't pray to God to not let her die. I was afraid if I asked God to not let Mama die, it might give Him the idea, so I tricked Him. I prayed, "Dear God, please let Mama wake up feeling good in the morning."

When Sister left, she went into the US Army. Daddy and Buddy were mad at her for doing that and tried to talk her out of it, but she did it anyway. The army sent her far away, so she didn't get to come home for a long time because it cost a lot of money, and she didn't have much money because she hadn't gone to college to get her education so she could amount to something. That, Daddy said, for sure wasn't his fault. He'd tried to get her to go.

Before Sister joined the army, Daddy had paid for her to go to nursing school. But she quit. Later she told me she stayed until they told her she had to brush a patient's teeth. That was it for her! She walked out and went straight to the army recruiting office and joined that very day. Buddy said, "Decent girls don't join the army." I saw a picture Mama had cut out of the newspaper of my sister with two other girls taking their army oath. I knew Buddy meant the other girls were the ones who weren't decent, not Sister, but I wondered and worried about it anyway. I wanted my sister to be decent.

The army sent Sister all the way to France. Then she married a man we never even met until after they got married. He was from New York City, and he was Italian! And he was Catholic! And sometimes he drank beer!

Finally she was coming home again. It was five days before Christmas. I was too excited to go to sleep, and Santa Claus wasn't the reason. It was Sister. I was going to be with her for the first time in two years. It felt like more than two, but I was little and years were longer then.

I was expecting to show my sister off, like a prize, to everybody. Everybody in the family and all of Petain Street loved her, but I knew I was the one she loved most, and I was the one she had missed most, the one she would play with now that she was coming home again.

Finally it was morning. Daddy picked her up at the train station and brought her home. But it wasn't like I thought it would be. Sister just wanted to sleep all day because they'd come so far, and when she woke up, she had to tend to her baby. It wasn't as much fun with him—her baby—there. It wasn't that I didn't like him. I just didn't want him around. He was cute enough, I guessed. He had red hair like Sister, but I wasn't sure I liked it on a boy. I held him and played with him a little when he wasn't crying—and he cried a lot. Every time I asked Sister to play with me, or look at pictures I drew for her, he cried, and she had to tend to him. I'd gotten used to being an only child, and now this screaming baby was taking everybody's attention. I was sure Sister wanted to play with me. He just didn't let her. I knew she didn't like him more than she liked me.

The best day we had was when Mama watched the baby, and Sister and I went to Prichard all by ourselves. Nobody was as much fun as Sister. She made going to Kress's for sodas an adventure. We tried on hats and earbobs, and she bought me a Tangee natural lipstick, but Daddy took it and threw it away. After we had sundaes at the soda fountain at Kress's Five and Dime, we stopped at J. C. Penney's and she let me try on high-heel shoes.

If I didn't like her baby all that much, her husband was a different story. I loved him from the minute I saw him, and he had plenty of time for me. I think it was probably scary for him to come to Prichard with all of the new people, especially since he was so different. His name was Richard, and he wasn't like anyone I'd ever met before. Being from New York City, he didn't talk the same as we did. His words sounded harder and some words like "sure" and "worm" didn't sound the same at all, because they didn't have *rs* in them. Even though he was the one who sounded different, he laughed at the way we talked; but I liked listening to him. He told me about New York and places with funny names like the Battery and the Meat Packing District. He grew up in a place called the Bowery. I knew about the Bowery because I'd seen *The Bowery Boys* movies on TV. His stories made me want to go there. New York had all different kinds of people from places as far away as China, and stores where you could get anything from anywhere in the world. Rich was just about the most interesting person I'd ever met, and I wanted to do everything he did, just as he did—including the way he walked around with his shirt unbuttoned and sat straddling the back of the chair—but Mama said I couldn't.

All the aunts and uncles and cousins came to our house for Christmas dinner. After a while I got bored, because nobody was my age. Even my cousins were older than I. Nobody paid me any attention at all. At dinner, they talked about stuff I didn't care about, like cars. Uncle Stanley said he was thinking about buying a used Mercedes Benz car with a diesel engine. He and Daddy got into a big argument about it. Daddy said it was stupid because in some states, they added taxes for truck drivers onto the diesel fuel, and I had no idea what they were talking about. When that was over, they talked about some war in Korea and "the draft."

The talk about the draft led Mama to say something that shocked my aunts and uncles. She declared, "If boys are going to be drafted, then girls should be too." Aunt Pauline said, "You don't mean that, Eva!" But Mama meant it. She always meant the things she said.

When they weren't talking about the news, they talked about baby Ricky, how cute he was, and how lucky he was to have gotten his mother's red hair—and they talked on and on about all the reasons he cried a lot. Maybe he was coming down with croup or maybe it was because of the different weather in Alabama. Babies always changed things—just like with Buddy.

At every family gathering, talk came around to kinfolks who weren't there, those who had gotten married, gotten a raise, died, didn't raise their children right, or who "carried on." There was poor little ugly Katie, "who'd best learn a trade." Katie was mean to me, so I was glad she was the ugly one. One uncle was "crookeder than a barrel of snakes." Another was the dirty one. "Uncle Bruce is so nasty, if Aunt Ernie May ever wanted to kill him, all she'd have to do is wash him."

Aunt Thelma was somebody they all loved because she was so sweet and good, but that didn't keep them from talking about her. Grandmama said, "Thelma Bell is the sweetest person you'd ever want to meet. It's such a shame she's so sickly. She'll never get married and have children. I guess she'll have to live with her brother all her life. Lord help her if anything should happen to him." I thought about that. Thelma wasn't married. I wondered why being sickly meant she couldn't get married. She didn't die. In fact she had already lived to be pretty old, at least as far as I could tell.

Family always says nice things about the people who are home after being gone a long time. That's how it was with Sister. "It's just so good to have that sweet Eva Erline home again. Look at her. Doesn't she just get prettier all the time?" Sister was always referred to as "that sweet Eva Erline." Even when she was a baby, all she had to do was be there to be looked at. I saw her pictures as a baby in a fancy dress—the sweet, pretty red-haired doll that everybody loved.

Daddy chimed right in. He put his arm around her and said he was proud of her. He called her "smart as a whip" and his "smartest child." I stared at him. I thought he must have been trying to make her feel good because I knew he didn't mean it. Sister knew he didn't mean it. Everybody knew. Sister wasn't the smart one. She was the nice one and the pretty one. She was the one who "got all of the personality in the family."

I didn't say it, but I thought, "She's the nice one, but she's not the smart one, and she didn't go to college, and she's never done a thing with her life. Daddy said that. Everybody in the family knows I'm the smart one—and I'll go to college, and I'll amount to something." Daddy would see to it. He had failed with Sister, and he was not going to let that happen to me. I wasn't going to be a doll.

When I was a baby, Daddy and I did all kinds of things together. When I was two or three, he started to take me on car trips, especially Saturday mornings while Mama worked at the grocery store. We took off early in the mornings to go to the country to visit relatives or to "see something." There was always something Daddy wanted to see, a rose farm, or a gristmill, or an old railroad train. Off we'd go, with me standing beside him in the front seat of our old brown Plymouth, no baby seat, no seatbelt, not even sitting, but standing up on the seat next to Daddy. Nobody thought anything about it. It was just the way we did it back then.

I loved our trips. I loved seeing things and listening to the stories Daddy told along the way. He told me about President Roosevelt, Robert E. Lee, Mark Twain, Will Rogers, and the Cherokee Indians. Daddy knew just about everything because he'd read every one of his Compton's Encyclopedias. He never missed a chance to talk about how I'd go to college someday and learn things about the world he never had the chance to learn.

When he got tired of answering my questions he'd say, "All right, I'm talked out." Then we sang songs. We sang "Mares Eat Oats," "Bill Grogan's Goat," "On Moonlight Bay," and "Three Blind Mice" as we traveled over miles of two-lane roads from Prichard to Mobile, or Satsuma, or Saraland, or all the way to Brewton.

After we drove an hour or so, Daddy would look for a little café to stop for breakfast. I got a lot of attention from waitresses. They would pick me up, hold me, or even give me my bottle while Daddy ate. Sometimes they stood me on the counter to sing the songs Daddy taught me, then the whole café would laugh and clap their hands. People always went on about what a beautiful baby I was. Thinking back, it was probably less about the adorable Ruthi and more about the handsome Norvelle that got the attention of the waitresses.

Waitresses weren't my only audience. Petain Street was a stage, and its people sitting on front porch swings and rockers—the housewives, the widows, and the old people whose babies were long grown and gone—were my best audience. Everybody loves a beautiful baby.

Then, almost overnight, I went from adorable baby to self-conscious preteen—one with a weight problem. Until I was eight or nine, I was a skinny little kid. But in that era in the South, thin meant you were poorly or sickly. Grandmama got worried I was too poorly and became determined to fatten me up. She overdid it and I got chubby, just as I was becoming aware of how I looked.

I became uncomfortable with myself, and more sensitive. That was when I started to move away from Daddy. He yelled, and I crumbled when anyone was mad or yelled at me. Worse, he teased me and hurt my feelings, which were pretty easy to hurt. I had heard the mean teases he said to Sister. She was poor because the army didn't pay much. One afternoon when she wanted to take me out for ice cream, she went outside where Daddy was talking to some neighbors and asked if she could borrow five dollars. In front of the neighbors Daddy handed her the money, made a little wave at it, and said, "Goodbye. When she borrows money, I just tell it goodbye. I'll never see it again."

Now he said mean things to me, too, and he did it in front of other people. One day Uncle Stanley and Daddy were sitting on the porch. I was in the front yard playing with my dolls, singing and talking, oblivious to them, until Daddy told me to stop talking to myself. "When you talk to yourself, it's one thing; but when you answer yourself, you're crazy." I can still feel my face turn hot from the humiliation to this day.

The Daddy I'd thought was fun when he was outrageous was actually embarrassing, especially to Mama. Mama didn't want me to grow up to be like him. When I was loud or did something wrong, she would tell me I was just like Daddy. I didn't want to be whatever that was, so I put some distance between us. Our Saturday trips dwindled until I was spending as little time with him as possible. I wanted to spend Saturdays with my friends, for one thing. But the truth is, I didn't like him anymore. I felt guilty about it, and I imagine he could see it and it hurt him. Maybe that's why he got grumpier and more critical with me. Sometimes I forgot he loved me at all, and it surprised me when he made a loving gesture. We were never estranged, but were never as close again.

It wasn't until I was an adult that I realized what a complicated man Daddy was. Then I remembered those old adventures, realized how much he had always cared, and appreciated what he had given me. Saturdays with Daddy added wonder to my life. He gave me the thrill I'd always have at jumping out of bed early in the morning to get going on some adventure—to go off to "see something."

As I grew into a preteen, my problems mounted. My self-consciousness grew along with my weight, and I became aware of another unattractive problem caused by my allergy to mosquito bites. Mosquitoes made up the largest part of the total population of south Alabama, and every one of their bites turned into an ugly sore on me. When people looked at me, I was sure they were staring at the sores on my arms and legs.

Then there was my hair. It was a mess. I wanted to have hair like Freddie Rice. She lived next door, and was beautiful, and her hair was a perfect pageboy. I tried, but I didn't know how to comb my hair into anything. Mama didn't have time or interest in makeup or hair styling. She thought my hair would be easier to handle if I had a permanent, so she gave me a Tonette permanent wave. But she just had time to do the curl part of the process, which left me with a head full of tight little curls like a blond wool cap. Luckily, the lady next door offered to finish the process and loosen the curls. That was it for permanent waves as far as I was concerned. I let my hair grow long—and tangled because I had too many things I wanted to do besides mess with my hair. When I was in the fourth grade, my best friends, Elizabeth and Delilah, brought combs and brushes to school and worked on me. It didn't help.

So I approached my teens chubby, with stringy, unstyled hair, and scarred-up arms and legs—and believing all eyes were on me and judging me.

I hoped I would get better as I got older. Then I heard something terrible. I was playing around the porch where Grandmama sat with a neighbor lady. The lady said, "You know what they say, 'Pretty babies make ugly adults.'" I stopped playing. Everybody said I'd been the most beautiful baby they'd ever seen. I went inside to Mama's dresser and looked in the mirror, dejected. "It must be true," I thought, "but it's not fair. Will I really be ugly when I grow up?"

No longer a beautiful baby, I didn't feel very lovable, but I wanted to be. I wanted to be popular (which I equated to love). I read in *Jack and Jill* magazine you didn't have to be pretty to be popular and make people like you. It said children who were popular were more interested in other people than they were in themselves. When they met other children they focused on them, showed interest in them. I remember just how I felt when I read that—sad, because I didn't know how to do that. When I met someone new, I wanted to see them, but all I could see was me, how I was acting, if I was sounding dumb, if I slouched, if I was hiding the mosquito-bite sores on one leg by crossing my other, less-bitten, leg over it. When I met a new person I felt as though they were normal size and I was as big as a billboard, and probably deformed with my legs crossed and twisted. I wished I could be like Sister and the popular children in the *Jack and Jill* article. I wished I could be the pretty one, the one with all the personality.

People were ever more confusing. They seemed to be able to change how they felt about somebody in an instant. They loved you if you were good, and stopped if you were bad. I knew, because I heard Mama and Daddy talking. Uncle Pete, Mama's cousin, had always been nice to me, but one day I heard them say, "Pete's been hanging around those beer joints again. He's put another car in a ditch." It sounded to me that Pete was bad, and we weren't supposed to love him anymore. Mama and Daddy and Grandmama talked about other aunts, uncles, and cousins who did bad things sometimes too. Then came the part that really confused me. We would go see those same people again, or have them over to Sunday dinner, and Mama and Daddy would still be nice to them. I didn't know if I was supposed to love them or not. And I worried about what this might mean for me too. When I got in trouble and people got mad at me, maybe they would think I was bad and stop loving me too—and then they might act nice and normal so I might not be able to tell. I had to find out. Mama's love was the most important thing in my life. From then on, when I got in trouble for anything, I asked Mama if she still loved me. She hated that.

One Sunday when Aunt Charity and Uncle Van were at our house for dinner, I dropped a plate and it broke into pieces. I started crying, "I'm sorry. I'm so sorry." Mama grabbed my arm and jerked me into the bedroom. "Why are you crying? It doesn't matter about the plate. These people are going to think we beat you. Wash your face and let's go out there and be happy!"

I had girl cousins and constantly compared myself to them, especially to Mary Gayle, who was pretty and had boyfriends who gave her a roomful of stuffed animals. I never saw her break things. She was graceful and elegant and ladylike. I wasn't ladylike. She always kept clean and looked pretty. I got dirty. I played cowboys, and even had my own six-gun and holster until I gave them to Tommy Rice, who lived next door and was handsome, in the hopes that he'd like me. (He still didn't.)

I wished I was graceful like Mary Gayle, but I'd have to slow down to do that and make my thoughts go in a straight line. There were so many things to get excited about that sometimes my ten-year-old head was a jumble. My thoughts were like the balls in a pinball machine—pinging from point to point at lightning speed. And my head was miles away from my feet, so I wasn't aware of a table in front of me until I tripped over it. At those times, if another person came to me with a question or request, my brain might overload. (This still happens to me. Recently someone asked what overload is like. I said it's like my mind is full of white noise and it stays that way until I can find one thing to focus on as an anchor.)

Thinking fast and moving fast, I got in trouble fast. I'd get some "great" idea and jump into it. That's what caused one of the most miserable weeks of my childhood. It started on a rainy day when Mama and Daddy were at work and I decided it would be just the thing to play with my baton in the living room. I tossed the baton up to the ceiling and I didn't catch it. More than half of the time I didn't catch it, but this time it landed on the coffee table and smashed the candy dish Sister had sent to Mama all the way from Paris, France. She would find out. There were too many pieces to glue back together. I knew what Mama would say. She would say I didn't think before I acted. Even if it was true, I didn't want her to say it.

I hid the dish and put some flowers on the table, hoping she wouldn't notice for a while. I was already in enough trouble with her because I'd just told her I'd lost my science book and I had to pay for it. I was afraid she would tell Daddy and I'd be in trouble with him too.

Then the chicken pie mix-up happened and I was going to be in trouble with Grandmama too. It was because I wasn't a good listener. I didn't want to be a bad listener. I did try to listen but it was hard to stay still and listen to every little word without having my mind drift off and back to my other thoughts. The longer the explanation, the less I'd hear. I'd end up with some idea of what she wanted but with some of the pieces missing.

Grandmama's chicken pies were famous. She baked them in a big metal dishpan and one would feed the family, and company too. Grandmama called me in one afternoon and said, "I'm baking a pie for Mrs. Carpenter. She has a load of relatives coming in and she's been down with her back and she's just not up to cooking. Ruthi, tomorrow you come straight home, right after school, and take the pie over to her. Don't forget because Aunt Pauline is coming to take me to the beauty parlor. I'll leave the pie and a plate with extra crust strips [she always made plenty of crust because the crust was the first to go] right here on the table. Take them to her as soon as you're home. Don't forget the extra crust. Now, do you understand?"

I said I understood. I was to take the pie and crusts to Mrs. Carpenter who lived behind us on Haig Street.

The next day I did it. I delivered the pie and I didn't forget the crusts. The only thing I got mixed up was the people. I wasn't good at remembering people's names. We had two neighbors on Haig Street, the Knapps and the Carpenters. One bordered our yard and the other backed up to the Rice's house next door to us. But which backdoor neighbor was Mrs. Carpenter? I stood there looking at the two houses and thought about the problem. I reasoned, Mr. Knapp was a carpenter. I knew because I'd seen him sawing lumber in his backyard. I have no idea how my mind went from the name Carpenter to carpenter work, but it did. So the Knapps got the pie.

I found out I'd given the pie to the wrong people on the way to church the next Sunday. We passed a neighbor and Mama waved and called out, "Good morning, Mrs. Carpenter. It's good to see you up and around." Oh, no! She was the person I had *not* taken the pie to! I crumbled inside. I prayed to God, "Please don't let them find out. Please!"

It seemed I'd been in trouble all week, and when they found out about the pies I'd be in trouble with everybody—forever.

I made up my mind I'd never be bad again, but that very morning I got into a big fight at church and with the son of my favorite Sunday school teacher. That one wasn't my fault. Raymond was picking on me and all I was trying to do was tell him I knew his mother didn't raise him to be so mean. Somehow that's not what came out. He said I'd insulted his mother. I never meant to do that, but he would probably tell her and she'd be mad at me too. I knew Mama wouldn't change churches.

Broken dish, lost book, misplaced chicken pie, insulted teacher! I went home from church, climbed the chinaberry tree in the back yard, and thought about how they'd all feel if I fell out of it and died. They'd be sorry! I decided I'd stay up there and never come down, and when they came looking for me, I'd hide.

But they didn't even come looking for me. I told myself I didn't care about them. I didn't want to come down and see anybody anyway. I'd probably just get in trouble all over again. I'd probably be in trouble with them for the rest of my life.

Finally, I couldn't stand it anymore. I climbed down to face them. First I told Grandmama what I'd done with the chicken pie. She and Mrs. Carpenter and Mrs. Knapp had already figured it out and they thought it was the funniest thing they ever heard. Mama wasn't mad either. She said the flowers were prettier than the old dish anyway.

Then the most surprising thing of all happened. Monday morning I found three dollars on my dresser, with a note, in Daddy's handwriting: "Buy a new science book." Daddy knew, and he hadn't screamed or cussed that I lost the book. I thought about that a long time. Even at the time, I thought it was sad that I felt surprised.

It took me weeks to get up the courage to apologize to Raymond, the Sunday school teacher's son, and he didn't even remember the fight. I couldn't believe it! He hadn't been bothered by it at all. I'd spent weeks in Sunday school feeling miserable, knowing he was looking at me, hating me, when all that time he hadn't even noticed me. I sure suffered for my mistakes back then.

Thank goodness for the old people. That was one group of people I didn't have to worry about. They never thought I was bad. I didn't have to be smart or take tests, and they always told me I was pretty, no matter how I looked. They appreciated their talks with me, and I liked listening to them tell me their secrets. I could make them laugh, and I loved that too. I didn't know then how important those skills would be someday.

After I learned which house was Mrs. Carpenter's, I knew she was the mother of the grown son who never went to work because he was deaf. I never heard anybody call him by his name. Some of the neighbors said he "wasn't right," and even dangerous, because he couldn't talk. But they were wrong. In my whole life I can't remember any person who seemed quite as thrilled as he was just to see me, and I didn't have to do anything. When I passed his house, he always made a loud sound to get my attention. I'd look up, and he would smile, as big as the sun, and wave both arms.

One day he was out in the yard on his knees in the grass. He saw me, and swung his arm round and round for me to come over. I did and he pulled my arm to make me get down on my knees, and pointed for me to look down. He made excited sounds and pointed at the ground, but I couldn't understand what he wanted me to see. I looked up at his face for an answer, but he took my head and turned it to look at the grass, which he pushed apart. Then I saw it—a real four-leaf clover. I knew they were lucky. He let me pick it and take it home. One of Grandmama's friends was there when I came to show off my clover. She said he was strange and I shouldn't go in his yard. But he made me feel good about myself. And I had a four-leaf clover and she didn't.

When I walked to Smith's grocery on the corner or to school, sometimes I stopped and talked with the old ladies when they sat out on their porches. Then, totally on a whim, I did something that taught me good things can come from the littlest thing. It all started with a Christmas present I hadn't intended to buy.

I was Christmas shopping at Kress's Five and Dime in Prichard, all by myself with the allowance I'd saved—four dollars. I bought a fountain pen for Daddy and walked around the store looking for things for Mama and Grandmama. I think that was the year I bought Mama the oversized red glass beads. She didn't like them. She told me, "If you can't afford to buy the best, don't buy anything showy. Buy something plain." It hurt my feelings, but I've remembered her words every time I bought a dress or a piece of jewelry.

I bought all my presents, and had a dollar left. I wandered to the very back of the store where I found a box full of "cut glass" vases and they only cost a dime apiece. The plastic roses were only a dime too. For my dollar, I could get Christmas presents—vases with two red roses—for Mrs. Gates, Mrs. Carpenter, and Mrs. Bailey.

I bought the vases and roses, and wrapped them. Christmas day I went to see the ladies and gave them their presents. They all thanked me, but when I gave Mrs. Gates hers, you'd have thought I gave her a Cadillac car. She traced her finger over every angle of the vase. She held it up to the light and exclaimed, "My! My! Look how it sparkles, just like crystal." Some people just know how to receive a present.

But it didn't stop there. From that day on, whenever I sat on Mrs. Gates's porch and a neighbor passed by, she called for them to stop so she could brag on me, and tell them what a good girl I was. She said I was the best girl there ever was. No other girl in the world had ever been so good to remember every old person on the street. "Ruthi has never missed a Christmas. She always remembered the old folks and brought us a little something." Even if I knew it wasn't true, I never got tired of her saying it, and I wanted to be the girl she told everybody I was. I never got tired of the feeling that came from approval—I still get a little thrill when the credit card machine in the grocery store says "approved."

Actually, I'd only taken presents to three of the neighbor ladies, and I had never brought Mrs. Gates a Christmas present before. But I never failed to again. Every Christmas I went back to see her, and took her a little gift. Even after I moved to Washington, I sent Christmas cards every year until the cards started coming back unopened.

This was something I could do that didn't require "having all the personality." People liked to be thought of, and even very small gifts got attention, especially if they were creative. For Father's Day, I made a card for Daddy. I changed the words of the song "Mother." "F is for the funny stories you tell me. A is for the ashtray by your chair . . ." I attached long ribbons from the words on the card to separate gift boxes that held a pen, an ashtray, a notebook, and a handkerchief, which made the gift awkward to present. Daddy saved the card and kept it in his top drawer for years.

Sister might be loved for just being there and just being herself, but I had some special talents for making people love me too. Just paying attention to a person others were too busy for was something I could do. I could ask them about their lives and listen to them. I could create meaningful gifts, too, and I could take IQ tests.

With my special gifts, I had no idea how to—or even if I could—put them into a career. Going off to college, I had no idea what I should study to make use of them. I thought journalism might fit me. I'd get paid to go out, see the world, meet people, and hear stories. But my family said no. It wasn't a secure career field. Mama, Daddy, and Buddy pushed me to get a teaching degree. "Teaching is a respectable profession for a girl, and it's steady. You'll always have a job." I was pretty sure I didn't want to be all that respectable.

When I played make-believe as a child, I had never, ever played teacher. I never saw anything glamorous about being a teacher—I certainly didn't see any glamour in any of the teachers I ever had. I liked most of them, but I didn't want to be like them. Teaching totally missed the "rich and successful" part of my dreams.

But college was too important to me and courage wasn't my strength. I was afraid to risk too much. I did the "safe" thing. I signed up in the education department, still hoping it would somehow lead me to an entirely different career. It didn't.

Since I hadn't studied for any other kind of career, I graduated unprepared to do anything except teach. So I taught. I taught for two years before I got up the courage to quit and go out to find the right career for me, whatever that would be.

I still hadn't put all the pieces of me together, but I did learn some important things about myself while teaching. I learned getting rich wasn't the only thing I wanted. I learned I was energized by fighting for the kids and winning. I liked making a difference. I also thrived on the recognition. I knew if a help-wanted ad said, "Thankless job but somebody has to do it," I could be sure that wouldn't be the job for me. That made sense when I remembered how I'd sat in church as a kid and imagined myself on Broadway. I'd be up there and everybody would be clapping for me. Unfortunately, I didn't know how to go about getting on Broadway, so I had to keep searching. I had always been good at drawing, and considered it; but that wasn't the same as performing in front of people, and anyway, the charcoal and paints made a mess.

I made lists of the things I wanted in a job and tried to imagine what it could be. I wanted to wear beautiful clothes to work, like the women in the movies, but I never saw ads that asked for candidates with style. What else did I want? I wanted to make people laugh. I wanted a job that would challenge the brain that took IQ tests so well. Finally, I still wanted no end to the money I could make. Was there a job anywhere like that—and one I was qualified for? I had almost decided I would never find it when there it was!

I found it in Washington, DC, in a business I never knew existed—a personnel agency. The company was San-D. The job was sales. It was simple, really. All I had to do was talk to people and convince them to talk to me. First I would interview an applicant from one of the company's help-wanted ads, usually a secretary, clerk, or typist; then I would test her typing (almost always "her" back then) then ask her what she wanted in a job. Then all I had to do was make "cold calls" to strangers (this was the largest part of the job), convince them to talk to me about my applicant, actually meet the applicant, and then hire her. I could do that. I could talk to people. I could call strangers on the phone all day and never get tired of it. I could get them to talk to me, and I didn't have to be the pretty one to do it. I could sell. The baby of the family and practically an only child, I'd been convincing people to do things my way all my life.

Sales and staffing fit me. The phone and cold-calling fit me. The money I'd dreamed of earning rolled in, and I started to create the life I wanted. There were rewards beyond the money, too—applause!

We worked in a bull pen that had a big blackboard on one end with a brass bell sitting on its ledge. The board was divided into columns, where our names were listed by spaces where we wrote in the number of placements and dollars we produced each month. I remember the day I placed my first candidate and made that first walk to the board, ringing the little brass bell, writing a number "1" in the placement column, and $680.00 for the fee. (That was 8 percent of her $8,500 salary, which was top dollar in those days.) Everyone got off the phones and cheered. These days we're too sophisticated for bells, and it's a shame because that walk to the board was incredible. I loved it and wanted more of it. And I knew exactly what I had to do to get it.

Every month my production went higher, until I was the top producer in the office. Finally. I was the star of the show with the highest number on the board. And that wasn't all!

We had company trips, even if they were to places nobody ever heard of or wanted to go—Colombia, South America, for example, where we were strip-searched upon leaving. To get us psyched for contests, the managers held rah-rah meetings. Those meetings were sometimes more exciting than the trips.

In my first meeting, Jim, the vice president and "number two" man in the company, came out in a straw hat and Hawaiian shirt, strumming a ukulele, and announced we were going to have a production contest; the prize was a trip to an island resort off the coast of Spain. A contest! I didn't look around at the others, but stared down at my lap. Only the top producers would win. Could I actually win? Spain! I'd never been out of the United States before. I wanted to go on that trip. What Jim didn't say was the island was second choice; he had originally booked a cruise, but the boat sank. He also didn't say that we weren't actually going to Spain, but to the Canary Islands, which are administered by Spain, but are located more than 700 miles away, closer to the coast of Africa. And that this "tropical paradise" was just beginning to be developed and consisted of only one resort hotel so far—and even that hotel was still a little way from having all of the kinks worked out. But that didn't matter to me. I wanted to win—and I did.

When I got there, I found the Canary Islands had beautiful areas, but I didn't get to see as much of the island as I would have liked. The brochure said the water was purified and safe to drink. What it didn't say was the water was purified with chlorine that not only killed the bacteria in the water, but the bacteria in the digestive tract as well. The "purified water" kept me in the bathroom for three days. And the people in the town hated Americans.

One of the best contests ever was the "3K PDA" ($3,000 per desk average, per office). The contest had the layers of an onion—individual 3K, office 3K PDA, division 3K PDA, and company 3K PDA. I don't even remember the prize. What I do remember is the plywood racetrack that covered two empty desks with little cars representing the different offices as we raced to hit 3K first.

Today, my staff is motivated by flat-screen TVs and gift cards; but back then, we had real prizes. One was a handsome onyx desk pen set with a gold-fill ballpoint pen. The heavy, thick onyx base had a little brass plate that said something like "NRI AE of the Week Award." I won the first week, for placing four people, and was so proud I called home to tell my mama about my victory and my prize. She waited a beat before she said, "You placed four people and they gave you a ballpoint pen?" I told her it was a contest—it was recognition. She responded, "They couldn't recognize you with money?"

The onyx pen contest kept going for a full quarter, with weekly chances to win and no limit to how many you could win. One pen set is a prize, and winning two, still pretty exciting. By the time you got seven, they became a storage issue. You can't use them, there is no market to sell them, and you hate to throw them away.

Management got more and more creative in selection trophies, one of which was a century clock, a fancy gadget with little gears and whistles under a glass dome. It was supposed to run for a hundred years. Mine stopped thirty minutes after I sat it on the mantle. If I picked it up and carried it around, it ran—until thirty minutes after I set it down again. No way was I going to spend my life carrying a clock around. (I hadn't had babies at that time, so I didn't know that babies work on pretty much the same principle as century clocks.) Still, whether the prizes were good or odd, I worked for them because the thrill was in the winning.

Even though the prizes were sometimes coveted—and sometimes odd—the good months brought glory and recognition. But where there are highs, there are also lows. The lows were awful, especially on the heels of the highs. I remember my first bad month. I had just come off of my best months ever. (You don't know you're in a worse month unless you've had a better one to compare it to.) I was sailing along for several months of higher and higher production. It was an exhilarating ride and I never thought it would end. Then I crashed. It was a dismal, bleak, ugly September for me.

From my experience, good things take forever to build, but bad things happen overnight. And that's what happened: Overnight, I went from top of the pile to nothing—nothing on the board, nothing going, and no glimmer of hope for immediate change. I had no candidates and no clients. By the last week of the month, and still at zero on the board, my only applicant cancelled her interview to go back to school, and the one client I worked on all month called to say he was putting the job on hold indefinitely.

Sitting with nothing but emptiness glaring down on me from my space on the board, I felt like a kid again, sent to sit in the corner and certain everybody had nothing better to do than look at me and think how dumb I was.

I wondered if I would ever pull out of it. Maybe all of my success had been mere luck after all. Maybe I couldn't do this job. My self-esteem sank along with my numbers.

Desperate to pull out, I flung myself into a frenzy of activity that felt like work. I called all the employers who *always* had job orders for me—job orders I could never fill. I scheduled interviews with as many applicants— for whom I had absolutely no jobs—as I could squeeze into the day. A couple of years ago I found a quote from writer Stephen Leacock that made me laugh, because it described me perfectly: "Lord Ronald said nothing; he flung himself from the room, flung himself upon his horse, and rode madly off in all directions."

Nothing I did was working. This was my first time experiencing such failure. I was miserable and terrified. That's when Daddy called. I was sitting in my living room, wallowing in self-pity with no immediate plans to stop. As soon as he heard my voice, Daddy said, "What's wrong with you?"

I expected sympathy, and started to cry as I told him about my month. "This is awful. I can't do anything right—everything I touch blows up. Daddy, I can't pull out of it—I don't think I can do it. I hate even going to the office."

He cut me off. "You haven't been carrying on this way in front of those people you work with, have you?" I said no, but he knew I was lying.

"Well, you quit it right now! Never let the folks at your job see you bellyaching like this! You don't want those folks to hear you talking on like this. You'll get back up, but they'll still be wondering about you. They'll be wondering if you've got what it takes. Get yourself together and walk in that office tomorrow morning like you're having the best month you ever had."

"I don't think I can."

He cut me off again. "You can and you better! You remember that old man who runs the haberdashery store on the foot of Government Street in Mobile? He's had that place for over fifty years—through the war—through the Depression. You watch how he acts when business has been good—he'll be out in front of his store, smiling and speaking to everyone who goes by, 'Good morning. Beautiful day, isn't it?' And when he hasn't sold a suit in a month, what does he do? He's out there, big smile, 'Good morning. Beautiful day, isn't it?' Nobody ever sees him scared. You want to make it?—do like him. Don't let anybody see you down."

Daddy wasn't a businessman. He wasn't even a college graduate. In fact he left school before he was twelve to go to work. But he knew. He knew people.

Over a thirty-year career, I've been able to figure out some of the things that caused slumps. In fact, I know one way to guarantee one. Sales is like the circus: One way to ensure failure is to change your act—to stop doing what you're trained to do because some other act looks better. Maybe the tightrope walker can tip-toe through the lion's cage once without harm, but for him to think, "Ah, now I am a lion tamer" spells disaster.

That's what I did somewhere in my second year. With more than a year of success filling administrative positions, I decided I had a better idea. I'd change fields and make even more money. The total fees we charged for placing clerks and secretaries ranged from $180 to $680 (annual salaries ranged from $4,500 to $8,500. The fees were calculated at 1 percent per thousand dollars of salary so the fee at $8,500 was 8 percent). An insurance agent asked me if I could find several "young men" (it was still the 1970s and I confess his request didn't strike me as odd) to train as brokers. It wasn't in our field, but a few days later, by chance, such a young man came in. Steven had the right credentials—he was smart, had a college degree in business, and was interested in a career. Perfect. I called Mr. Jefferson and sent him right over, where he was hired on the spot, and at the unbelievable salary of $12,000. That meant I got a fee of $1,200 for just one placement! It was the first time I'd ever gotten a 10 percent fee, and it happened so fast and easy. It was crystal-clear to me what my new strategy should be. I'd triple my production by dropping secretaries and focusing on young professionals in the insurance business. And that's just what I did, in spite of warnings from my manager.

For the next month, I threw myself into finding candidates for Mr. Jefferson. By the end of the month, I still had just the one placement, and my production was half of what was expected of me. Then, two days before the end of the month, Mr. Jefferson called to say Steven hadn't passed training and they wouldn't be paying the fee, thus ending my career in insurance staffing.

This was worse than just having a bad month. I had to go to my boss, Karen, with the news that my brilliant idea had failed. Just as when I was a child, I was afraid, again, of "getting in trouble." But there was nowhere to hide—I was 1,500 miles and nearly twenty years from Petain Street. I had no chinaberry tree to climb. That was when I started to learn to not only live with my mistakes, but to claim them. I had to learn it sooner or later because I was going to make plenty of them, and now I couldn't get out of trouble by crying and asking a manager if she still loved me.

Daddy's words came back again: "If it's somebody else's fault, you can't fix it." He was right about that, but taking on every action as my fault did something else for me. I hated getting in trouble. Taking responsibility for everything, whether I did it or somebody else did, meant I had control, not trouble. I almost competed—with managers, clients, pretty much anyone— to find my own mistakes before they did. I wanted to not only find them, but learn from them, and sometimes laugh at them—a lot of them were pretty funny. Better they laugh at my mistakes than yell at me. And some of those mistakes were spectacular.

One of the most spectacular happened in 1980 and it involved one of my best and most loyal clients, Jack the human resources manager of a stock brokerage firm. He asked me to locate an accountant to work in his cashier's cage—that's where they kept the bearer bonds and negotiable securities. The candidate had to be professional, personable, polished, and have an accounting degree—all at a salary that wasn't at the top of the market.

I had the entire office working on the search, but after two weeks, we still had no one. I was getting desperate and afraid Jack would find it necessary to go to another firm. Then it happened. A woman came in who not only had the degree, but five years of experience, and she looked impressive in a professional, tailored suit. I interviewed her for less than five minutes and called Jack. "I've got your accountant. May I send her over right now?"

I felt great. Half an hour later, when my receptionist said Jack was on the line, I grabbed the phone and said, "When does she start?"

"Ruthi, Sherry is sitting here with me and, you're right, she is a lovely woman. But did you happen to notice the gap on her application?"

"No. I missed it." I grabbed up her application and scanned the dates of her jobs. There was the gap—three years.

"So you don't know what she was doing during those three years?"

I didn't answer. I was getting sick.

"No? Well, does the word *incarcerated* mean anything to you?"

"I have to go now."

"No, wait. There's more. Would you like to know why she was incarcerated?"

"No."

"Embezzling. So, in answer to your question, Sherry is a charming person and her experience is all I could ask, and she has paid her debt to society. But she and I have discussed it, and we agree that this isn't the position for her, as she might have a problem getting bonded."

"I have to go now," I said. "My mother is calling."

(I didn't lose the client.)

Although the clients took my mistakes with good humor, I suffered for them because no matter how far from Petain Street I went, I didn't outrun the fear that my mistakes would make people reject me.

I saw too clearly all of my flaws and weaknesses and my judgment of them was harsh. But I found there was a market for my quirks. My insecurity and knack for social blundering, for example, would work for me. They would make me seem real and approachable. They would also give me empathy and a better understanding of people. I knew people built false fronts to hide behind, and I also knew the secret to getting past them.

I was meant to make people laugh and I did. My mistakes are funny—at least in retrospect. Business peers, clients, job candidates, and I laughed and had fun. When I made some dumb mistake, why did my clients laugh with me? It could be that they just liked to take the focus off themselves and laugh at me. But I think it was more than that. When they saw me admit mistakes and laugh at myself, it made it okay for them to make mistakes too.

I found out people will put up with most mistakes if you make them with sincere, childlike good intentions. Through experience, I learned that my flaws could be appealing. My assets made me strong, resilient, and convincing. My flaws made me accessible. When I'd come bounding in, exuberant and enthusiastic about some idea, but miss a few details or fall (figuratively) on my face, they would laugh. Is it odd I ended up with clients who had great senses of humor? Sometimes I would get so excited about why I was calling a client that I'd forget all about "hello." When the client answered, I'd launch right into whatever I was calling about, without introduction, and in the middle of a sentence, "And the Wang word processing experience you wanted—I didn't think I'd ever find it, but she has it! She could be the one you want."

When I finally paused, I'd hear, "Hello, Ruthi."

One by one, I gathered dozens of clients who "loved" and trusted me, but I never got enough. I didn't forget what I had learned about love as a child— even people who love you could go away. That fear was one of the reasons I became so successful in business. I had an insatiable drive to get more and more clients, as security, because you never knew who might leave you. It's actually a business truth. Most client relationships end at some point, and it happens for purely business reasons—changes in management or business needs; but I took them as personal losses and drove myself to gather more and more as buffers against the loss.

I climbed steadily up until I was the "number two" person in the company. I still remember exactly how that felt—there is no place better in all of business than being "number two." It's heady. It's invigorating. You're on your way up—nipping at the heels of "number one." Your future is ahead of you. Work is fun.

For me, there was no place better than being number two, until I was "number one"! Being at the top meant more than money. It meant recognition, respect, and love. It meant awards. It also meant constant pressure. It meant fear. But it was still "number one" and I *had* to be there.

Why did it matter so much to me? I worked with people who I believed had the talent to compete for the top spot, and I wondered why they didn't try as hard as I did. The answer is that our pasts dictate our needs. I have two friends who are the top income earners in their fields, both wealthy, yet driven to succeed even more. What they have in common is that their fathers went bankrupt when they were in college. As one explained to me, once you've been through that, once you've seen your dad struggling and embarrassed because he can't be the provider that had defined him, you will do whatever it takes to never be in that position.

Now, after watching two generations come into the workplace, I realize we are shaped by our time in history as well as our place in our families. I was the child of working-class people who were achievers held back and frustrated by the education they felt had been denied them, and I was a baby boomer, the generation born after a great war (WWII) had come on top of the Great Depression—the generation that became hippies and then yuppies who marked success in BMWs. Readers from more recent generations grew up with other experiences, and have their own motivations—thus competition has a different meaning for them.

3

THE ROAD *to* MY FUTURE DIDN'T HAVE ANY MARKERS

Wrong Roads Led Me to Recognize the Right One

It was nine o'clock on a September evening, yet not quite dark. I was eight years old and lying flat on my back on the sidewalk in front of Mrs. Bailey's house. The walk was still hot from the day, and I liked how the air felt cool on my face with the cement hot on my back. The air smelled of wisteria and mimosa trees and the two paper mills a half mile away. I looked up at the thousands of stars, so close I thought I could touch them, and I pictured some other girl looking at those same stars right at that same moment—a girl in a big city, far away, where I was going to live someday. I knew that when I grew up, I'd go to all kinds of places and see amazing sights.

The city is where I made-believe I was when I played alone in my back-yard. My best toys were two sawhorses. Daddy had built them out of two-by-fours when he was building on Grandmama's room. When I played cowboys, they were my horses. Sometimes I turned them over and leaned them against each other, and they became a big Cadillac car, like the ones in the old mov-ies, with seats as big and deep as Grandmama's bed and a gold lady on the hood. I put on Mama's earbobs and beads and the yellow skirt Sister left in the closet—it was long and swung around when I walked. I looked as elegant as a movie star. I brought out ginger ale in the fancy glass goblet Daddy won at the fair, and played like I was in New York City, in a limousine, going to see a real live play, in a theater, with a man who was handsome and rich and so smart he could talk all day and never get boring. He poured champagne and kissed my hand and told me I was beautiful.

Playing grown-up was one thing, but when I thought about the lives of grown-ups I knew, I wasn't at all sure I wanted be one. And I was absolutely sure I didn't want to be the kind of grown-up my friends wanted to be. My best friends were Betty and Sandra. They wanted to be grown already. They talked about it all the time, growing up and dating boys and getting married and having babies. But they didn't understand what happened to you when you grew up. I did.

I had a brother and a sister who were grown and had babies. Sister was there visiting. She had a little boy. He bothered my things. I told her about Betty and Sandra, and that I thought being grown would be awful. But Sister said she liked being grown. She said twenty-eight was the best age because car insurance goes down when you're twenty-eight. I didn't think so. I thought twenty-eight was awful. It was old. You couldn't play with dolls or tightrope-walk brick walls or watch cartoons on TV anymore. And you had to have babies. Betty and Sandra could grow up if they wanted to, but I never would. I never wanted to date boys or get married. I didn't want any children to tear up my paper dolls. And I didn't want car insurance.

What I did want was to see new things and learn about new people. There were things in the world I'd never, ever have imagined. I'd already seen enough to know that, and without even having to leave the Deep South. For instance, my Uncle Van lived on a farm, and he had an outdoor toilet. I'd seen outdoor toilets, but this one had three seats made of smooth wood that my aunt kept clean as any indoor toilet I'd ever seen—and a rack for magazines and newspapers! I not only got to see it, I got to use it.

Grandmama's sister, Aunt Lizzie, lived in DeFuniak Springs, Florida, about halfway between Prichard and Quincy, Florida, where Mama's daddy lived. We dropped Grandmama at Aunt Lizzie's for a visit on our way to see Granddaddy.

Aunt Lizzie was sweet to everybody, but she was dirty and Mama did not like to be in her house. But she had to go in to carry Grandmama's suitcase. She tried to make me stay in the car, but I wanted to see Aunt Lizzie and I whined till she gave in. I'm glad I did, because I walked into the kind of scene most people don't get to see outside of books of art photography or movies. I saw a big black woodstove that spit sparks. Aunt Lizzie and my uncle (I don't remember his name) sat in front of it.

Newspapers were spread out on the floor between them, and an old Folger's coffee "spit can" sat smack in the middle of them. The old people chewed their snuff till their mouths were full, then spit at the can until the newspaper was stained brown with the snuff and spit that missed. Uncle peeled an apple, round and round till he had a ribbon of peel hanging from it—then, almost to the end, the ribbon tore off, and flop, fell into the can, and splashed more brown liquid onto the newspaper. I've never seen anything like it again, and I might have missed it if I'd stayed in the car.

I went into the kitchen and saw pies and cakes on the sideboard. I came out and said, "Aunt Lizzie sure has a lot of pies and cakes in there."

Aunt Lizzie said, "Come on. I'll cut you a piece." But Mama stood up, said we had to be on the road, and dragged me out, gripping my arm so tight I knew I'd better keep quiet.

I loved stories that were about places I'd never been, and stories filled with dramatic images and color. Daddy had been lots of places and seen lots of things. Sundays after church, when I was just a baby, I'd pull Daddy to his chair and climb up on his lap. "Come on with the stories, Daddy." And he came on with them.

My daddy was a tugboat captain, the best one there ever was. He ran tugs and tows on the rivers and all around the Intracoastal Waterway, even all the way to New York City! He had a tugboat named after him, the *Norvelle*. Years later, he took me to see it, where it sat aground on the bank of Chattahoochee River in Phoenix City, Alabama. It was rotted and all that was left of his name was "Norve." I thought of all the people in the world compared to how few tugboats there were to name for them, and I knew my daddy was special.

Way back Daddy had been a prizefighter—when he wasn't so old. His kind of prizefight wasn't like the ones on television. At the port towns, promoters would hire a barn or someplace to hold a fight. Anybody could sign up. When Daddy was in port, if he needed extra money, he'd sign up, and he mostly won the prize. He told me how they paid the prize money. After the fight, the people would throw money into the boxing ring. The money that landed outside of the ring went to the promoter, and what landed inside went to Daddy.

My favorite stories were the ones about what it was like when he was a little boy. His papa, Willie Avant Simmons, was a tall, handsome rogue who chased women. He never had to chase very hard to get them, either (which seems true of this line of Simmons men at least as far back as the Civil War). Papa never took care of his family the way my daddy did. When Daddy was a little boy, he had to go to work and do hard "men's work." He carried food pails and water to the men who worked cutting down the hardwood trees along the Alabama-Florida Panhandle. When he told me that, we were driving through miles of pines. I couldn't imagine what it would have been like with oaks. He also worked for the men in the sawmills, and the men working on railroads that carried the trees north. They were rough men. When Mama wasn't around, Daddy sang some of the songs he had learned from them. I still remember part of one song. It was more chant than song. "Birmingham's no ham a'tall. You ought to see the ham in Liza's drawers."

Papa wouldn't let Daddy go to school after the fifth grade, but made him work every day. Daddy never got over being mad at Papa about that, even though Papa had been dead since I was three. Daddy told me again and again, "I was good in school. Papa didn't care. If he'd given me a chance to get my education, I could have amounted to something." I think he could have, too. Daddy was smart—he read and he could teach himself to do whatever he wanted.

Daddy said that same thing wouldn't happen to me. He'd see to it I'd read and get educated. Once he gave me a magazine with an article about the Seminole Indians. It was a month later and I still hadn't gotten around to reading it. That was it! He had a big temper. He yelled and cussed and said I couldn't leave the chair till I'd read it. I couldn't stand being yelled at, and I cried, but he didn't let up. "You'll sit in that chair till you read every word. I'm going to see that you learn something." I spent more time crying than it took to read the article, which really was interesting—but I never told Daddy that.

One Saturday, Daddy and I were in the car going up to Chickasabogue Creek to see Uncle Stanley's new boat. I started a sentence, "When I get out of high school—"

"No!" Daddy cut me off and pulled the car over. He didn't yell. He talked slowly, and that sounded scarier than a yell. "Nothing happens when you graduate high school. It's when you graduate from college. You're going to college. Don't you forget that. You'll have an education!"

I didn't forget. I knew I'd never again question whether I would go to college and make something out of myself. I never asked what that "something" was, but whatever it was, I was determined it would give me fine dresses and crystal glasses of champagne that would taste like ginger ale. College was to be my first step. Earning grades, class by class, was the goal—and graduating, of course.

Eleven years later, in Athens, Georgia, I was there. I had finished my last final exam and, in a few days, I would be graduating from the University of Georgia. Everybody else seemed to be excited about college graduation. I wasn't. After three and a half years of college, the unthinkable was happening to me. The bottom was about to fall out of my world. I was to achieve my goal of a degree, and with that achievement, lose the only reason I knew for being because I still didn't know what that "something" was that I would make of myself. After three and a half years of the competition for grades, of mentally calculating my GPA, sometimes daily, it was over, and I didn't know the next step. I woke up nights desperate for ideas. I had to figure out what to do. I just knew I couldn't go back to Petain Street.

In the beginning of my last semester, I got an invitation to join the other top graduates at a special awards ceremony. I was excited, but not as much as Mama. She was more than excited. She was vindicated! When the announcement appeared in the paper, she cut it out and mailed it to my high school principal. Years later I learned he had died of Alzheimer's disease. I don't know when he got sick, but if it was before the announcement, I'm glad Mama didn't know it.

I remember what I felt as I sat in the auditorium the day of the ceremony. It was in good part satisfaction. I had done all I set out to do, and more. Here I was, in a small, select group, for the whole university to see. I had my name in the paper. I was a winner. But I had other feelings too: self-doubt and uneasiness. What would be next? I'd won recognition in college, but the questions kept creeping into my head, "Is this it? Will I find other awards to win?"

As the weeks passed moving toward graduation, the uneasiness grew into the same fear I had in high school. Maybe I wouldn't get out of the South. Maybe I would be a failure for the rest of my life.

But I had a more pressing issue to confront as well, and it wasn't just a fear. It was reality. The grant money that had supported me while I was in college was about to end. I was going to have to support myself. I had to do something, but I didn't know what I could do with a degree in history, and I certainly didn't know anything I could do that would get me to New York City. Faced with reality, I decided to do the thing I said I'd never do. I got married. The man I married was Johnny Holliman. He had been one of the first people I met when I moved to Athens, and he had been my best friend ever since.

I met Johnny through Sammy, one of several guys who were what I called "first/last" dates (where the first date was also the last). Sammy decided he liked me, even though we weren't meant to have a second date. He didn't say it in so many words, but I got the impression he felt sorry for me, and was afraid I wasn't going to get too many chances for a relationship that would last more than one date. He thought his friend Johnny might just be one of those good chances. I told him no. I didn't need his help in meeting boys, but he insisted.

That first meeting with Johnny took place at the radio station where he was on the air from eight to midnight. Sammy and I waited as Johnny finished reading the news from copy torn from the Associated Press wire, punched in a tape with an ad for a car dealership, queued up the next record, and finally told the audience to sit back and enjoy "A Whiter Shade of Pale." I didn't know it yet, but he chose that one because it was four minutes long and gave him time to talk. Those were the days of real records and disc jockeys actually got to choose the music they wanted to play. They saved the longer records for times when they needed a break. I'll bet it never occurred to most people that "Hey Jude," which ran seven minutes, usually meant the disc jockey was in the bathroom.

The minute I met Johnny I knew Sammy had me all wrong. I would never date this guy! His radio voice was tall and handsome. But he was short, with thinning hair and a round face, and his rumpled clothes lacked any style—this was not the boy in any dream I'd ever had. I decided then and there this was a one-time meeting and I'd leave as soon as I could politely do so. But as we talked, I realized he wasn't like anyone else I'd ever met. He was funny and totally unselfconscious. He clearly didn't care if I liked him or not—he liked me and he'd win me over. I stayed and we talked. I saw him again the next day, and we talked, and again the day after that.

Johnny had a lot to say. At seventeen, he had already achieved more than many people five years older than we were. I was captivated by what I can only describe as his happy-go-lucky, fearless drive to get what he wanted. It became clear that what he wanted was me, and he got me. I didn't mystically have scales fall from my eyes to see him as a beautiful knight, and I didn't fall in love with him, but I stayed. Whatever I thought of him took a backseat to how he saw me. He elevated me. He saw me as everything I wanted to be but didn't believe I was. How could I walk away from a man who served as the mirror that always reflected me as beautiful, funny, smart, and clever?

Johnny was a first-time experience for me in so many ways. He loved me, so I tormented him to test his love—breaking up with him, coming back again and again, making him fix me up with dates with other boys, even talking him through every twist and turn in my relationships with other boys. He put up with it for a couple of years. Later, I asked him why, and he said, "Because I knew I'd win in the end."

My friendship with Johnny grew into one of the few deep relationships I've had in my life. With most people I never let down my guard. I kept others out, so why did I let him in? There was a screwy logic to it. When I was with a person I was attracted to, I pulled back because I didn't trust people to love me. I was afraid of the pain of losing them, and the shame. I could trust my feelings with Johnny. I wasn't crazy in love with him, so I could trust him because I wasn't afraid of losing him.

It was how I felt when I was with Johnny that kept me coming back to him. With him, I could relax. The world I lived in was exhausting. It was filled with people for whom I spent so much energy being on guard.

Johnny gave me a place where I could rest. I didn't have to measure up. I was already just fine.

We had fun. I found adventures everywhere and Johnny was always ready to get up and go into whatever adventure I dreamed up. He enjoyed my gee-whiz excitement about things. One Saturday I heard on the radio that it was snowing in northern Georgia, maybe forty miles from Athens. Growing up snow deprived, that's all I needed. I woke Johnny at the crack of dawn and we raced to find the snow. I jumped up and down on the seat as the first few flakes fell on the windshield, and opened the windows to catch them in my hands. Actually, the snow was sparse and short-lived, but that didn't diminish our excitement. It doesn't matter how many snowflakes there were, the first one was exciting enough all by itself.

Johnny didn't have dreams. He had reality. He was so certain about where he was going, it was his reality. I felt it too. He was going to surprise a lot of people. WDOL was full of handsome, talented men who seemed marked for success, while Johnny was not. When this happy-go-lucky fellow said, "I'm gonna be a Top 40 disc jockey at WDOL," which was Athens's top-rated radio station, I bet some people thought, "Yeah, sure." When he said, "I'm going to replace Walter Cronkite someday," I can imagine what they thought. But anybody betting against Johnny lost. Of all the talented people at WDOL, Johnny was the one who would go the farthest, even winning the prestigious Peabody Award before he was twenty-five years old.

But I already knew. He would do whatever he set out to do. He always had, starting when he was just a kid in middle school. He talked the owner of the FM station in Thomaston, Georgia, into running the little league games—with him as announcer. He just refused to hear "no," or to quit because someone else said he couldn't have what he wanted, and that was something else to love about him.

More and more of the guys I met didn't measure up to Johnny. The other guys had looks and muscles. He had strength. In the end he didn't replace Mr. Cronkite, but he came close enough.

When Johnny started talking about marriage, I was not ready. I wouldn't even think about it. By this time, I wasn't as adamant about not marrying as I had been when I was eight years old, but I wasn't excited about it either, and certainly not to Johnny. I still had dreams of meeting a man I would think was the most handsome on earth and having a real-life "falling in love" experience. But there was always the question, "What if that kind of love didn't exist?"

Johnny went about marrying me as he did everything else he wanted to do. He ignored my refusals and asked again, and again. There were reasons to reconsider. He loved me unconditionally, and that was addictive. I believed he really did love me and would keep loving me no matter what. I couldn't walk away from that.

I loved him too, in a way, and played at acting out the romance stuff. But it wasn't real. I loved Johnny the same way I loved the old people on Petain Street. I didn't know any other way. There were no love affairs on Petain Street. Maybe that was just the way it was, and love affairs existed only in the movies. For years I held on to the hope that it wasn't true, but that hope had dimmed every time I left him to look for it, only to get scared before I found it, and came back. I finally decided this was the way it was. I wasn't missing out on anything, because there was no such thing as being "in love" anyway. Maybe just caring about him was enough.

When in a brash mood, I sometimes said I married Johnny as a career move. It was a lie, but the truth was too complicated, and it sounded too awful to say I was afraid nobody else would ever love me as he did. Still, if it had been just a career move, it wouldn't have been a bad one. It made leaving college a little less terrifying since I didn't have to worry that I had yet to find a job or to know what to look for. Johnny already had a job with a sure income, and he had a career. Already I was a little jealous that Johnny had a future, while I faced a blank wall.

So, for many and complex reasons, in my senior year I was married and my future was taken care of for the time being. The next hurdle was the graduation ceremony. I dreaded it. When I like a book, I devour it, then pull back as I approach the last page to put off the inevitable ending. I hate last pages. I've been known to return books to the library with one page unread (I wonder what a psychiatrist would say about that and my habit of skipping out on relationships before they have a chance to end). The last page means the fun is over and usually doesn't live up to the book.

The graduation ceremony is the last page of college, and I tried to skip it, but the university system wouldn't let me. I must not have been the only graduate who would skip the ceremony if allowed, because the University of Georgia had a policy of holding your diploma hostage to make sure you showed up. So I went, and this last page definitely did not live up to the book!

The memory is vivid and terrible. I can see myself sitting there, stuck, imprisoned for hours, in the heat of a Georgia August. If you can picture yourself draped in a wool cloak and held captive in an equatorial rain forest, you may have some idea of how it felt to be one of the several hundred graduates wearing heavy black robes over new suits or dresses, sitting on folding chairs in the un-air-conditioned UGA Coliseum that day.

"Most things aren't as bad as we imagine them," a psychologist friend told me. She was wrong about this one. It was worse. If being bored was painful for me, this was agony. The president of Brandeis University spoke for what felt like hours. He, without inflection, dramatic effect, or a hint of humor, told this Kent State generation what *we* thought about the world. "You have seen. . . . You believe. . . . You feel. . . . " He didn't have a clue what I was thinking. I was thinking I wished there was some way to get even with him for this.

I showed him! I staged my own mini-rebellion. I unzipped my robe, pulled it off my shoulders, and let it fall in a lava flow around my chair. I let it stay there until my row was called to retrieve our diplomas. I hoped he had seen my act of defiance.

While he droned on, I heard a train whistling by on the tracks just behind the Coliseum. I smiled as I pictured it suddenly become a cartoon engine, jump the tracks, and crash through the stadium wall and across the stage to lift Mr. President of Brandeis onto the cow catcher and carry him off in a dust cloud. My reverie ended, but he still talked.

Now that I've been to several graduations, I've decided there is a purpose to those speeches. They're supposed to be awful—the last college lesson to prepare us for the times in our lives when we must endure boredom and pain: teachers' meetings, committee meetings, mandatory office dinners. If it was meant to show me life's sometimes hot and boring, and I would have to learn to put up with it, it didn't work. I knew I'd take off my robe every time!

Ceremony over, college done, I was cut adrift with nothing but a degree in history and education and nothing on my agenda except worry. I tried to look into my future, but no other picture came up, nothing even to aim for. My solution was to keep going to school. I enrolled in grad school.

My graduate school career lasted exactly half a semester. I went from the excitement that I was a *grad student* to gloom in six weeks. First, the professors I'd thought were fascinating as an undergrad seemed stale and dusty up close, and I hated the smell of a pipe. Also, I was studying history. Why? I didn't want to teach. I didn't want to spend hours in a library doing research. So one fall day I walked out of my graduate class and never went back. The last time I checked a few years ago, the university still carried my graduate courses as incomplete. I wonder what they'd say if I showed up one day and said, "Okay. Here I am, ready to finish up."

It seemed everybody except me had moved on to something. I thought I was the only person on earth who felt lost and terrified at college's end. I was ashamed to talk about it. Now I know I wasn't alone. I had what might today be labeled "post-college depression." Before the '90s, we didn't have post-event depression, just embarrassing secrets. I was supposed to be excited about jumping into my future—everybody else was, or so it seemed to me. So I kept secret the anxiety I'd felt as far back as the awards day, and which degenerated into crushing hopelessness.

The day I left graduate school for the last time, I took my embarrassing secret and went home, got into bed, and slept—and kept on sleeping nearly twenty-three hours a day for the next three weeks. Few people know it, but sleep can be as addictive as heroin. Johnny was worried and tried to talk to me, but I wouldn't let him. How could he understand? He had a career and a future as bright as mine was bleak. I turned him off and went on sleeping.

Who knows how long I'd have slept if Johnny hadn't gotten my parents to come to our apartment and do an intervention, which they did in their typical, straightforward manner. They woke me up, and told me to get a job.

Okay, but the only job I was qualified to do was teach, and Athens, Georgia, had an overabundance of education graduates to fill the available teaching jobs. I heard of a school about thirty miles away that needed teachers. Begrudgingly, I made an appointment. From there things moved quickly. I arrived at the principal's office, and the next thing I knew I was sitting at a gunmetal-gray desk staring across an island of desks and moss-green cinder-block walls that were mostly covered by chalkboards and corkboards. It was dusty, it was hot, and it didn't look at all like a dream come true. But in that room, in Braselton, Georgia, I would teach Georgia History and World History to middle school students for the next two years.

When I tell people I taught middle school, they tend to smile meaningfully, and say they understand why I didn't like it—because of the kids. No. That wasn't true at all. The kids were the best part. We had fun. They kept me laughing. The kids taught me.

I had things to learn as a teacher if I was to move on to the career I wanted, and Braselton was the place to learn them. There were things in that town that I'd never seen before, and people whose lives were unlike any I'd ever known. I learned there were people who lived without all the advantages I'd had on Petain Street.

Everybody I'd ever known could read. Certainly all the grown-ups read. They read the Bible. They read the newspaper. There were two kinds of people in Prichard, the ones who took *The Mobile Press*, the afternoon paper, and those who took *The Mobile Register*, the morning paper. They argued over which gave the better news.

I assumed it was like that everywhere. Then, in my seventh grade World History class we came to a section on different religions around the world. I thought I had a great idea—we would read from the actual writings of the different religions. I found passages from the Koran, and information on Buddhism, Hinduism, and Confucianism. I told the kids to bring in their Bibles from home so we could compare the teachings. (I know I couldn't do this today but this was Georgia in the '70s.) Only seven kids brought Bibles. I was frustrated and irritated, and I reacted. I turned on one of the empty-handed students. "This was a simple assignment. Why didn't you just do it?" I sounded like my image of a schoolteacher.

"We don't have a Bible."

I thought that was ridiculous. Everybody had a Bible—most people I knew had two or three of them. Even the poor people on the other end of Petain Street had Bibles.

"You must have a Bible," I said. "Did you ask your mother? She has to have one."

"No. She don't have a Bible 'cause she can't read."

I felt my face turn hot. I felt terrible about how I must have made that little girl feel. But somehow I pulled myself up and finished the lesson with the materials at hand. I don't know how much the class learned, but I learned there were people in the world who were nothing like me, and I didn't have the right to expect them to be.

For weeks, the memory of that lesson came back to torment me. I felt sick that I'd hurt the child, but it wasn't just that. Something else gnawed at me too, something about me and what I might become. I'd worked in the school all these weeks and didn't know a thing about the people there. That wasn't me. From the time I was a child, I'd always been curious about other people, and not just open to but excited to see the different ways they lived, and I liked that about myself. I thought back to Uncle Van's outhouse and wondered, "If I saw it for the first time today, would I stick up my nose at it rather than think it was terrific?" I didn't want to lose the wonderment and excitement with which I approached the world when I was a child and replace them with criticism and judgment.

That was one of many lessons I learned in Braselton, a place I'd never wanted to be and where I was afraid I'd be stuck. As my second year moved on, I became more and more afraid I'd never get to leave. The voices in my head at three o'clock in the morning were there again, whispering, "Is this it? Have you peaked out?" And I'd wake up frantic. No! I'm on my way to somewhere else. This was a detour!

Frantic to find a new direction, I decided on art. I had always been good at drawing, and I'd taken up painting a few years before. I'd even sold a painting, a red lion in black grass, and made $35, a third of my weekly teaching salary. Maybe I could become an artist. Three things had to happen to get me there. I had to quit my teaching job and go back to school, and that meant I had to cut back on my lifestyle. I talked with Johnny and decided I'd do it. I gave my resignation and enrolled in the art department of Georgia State University.

Johnny was no longer a disc jockey, but a newsman at WSB Radio, "The Voice of the South." Unfortunately, he didn't make any more than he had playing records. The joke in the newsroom was, "WSB pays in prestige instead of dollars." It was true. With the $125 he made a week, we couldn't afford to keep our townhouse. But artists lived in garrets, didn't they?

We looked for our "garret" and that's just about what we found. It was south of Atlanta, miles from anything. Our apartment was on the second floor of a family-owned apartment building that sat between the parking lot of a Holiness church on one side and an auto mechanic's garage on the other. It was far away. It was ugly. It was way down from the townhouse. But the apartment actually had nice-sized rooms and it was comfortable enough, until the cockroaches came out. I had never seen so many roaches in my life. They weren't just big tree roaches like the ones that would occasionally sneak into our house in Prichard, but full cockroach families with litters of baby roaches, in every cabinet and drawer, and marching across the table. When I complained, the landlords sent a man to spray something I was certain was going to kill me, but on which the roaches thrived. The only place they didn't invade, the refrigerator, was where I kept all the necessities for life: food, cups, plates, flatware, salt, toothbrushes, and toothpaste.

Then every Saturday night pickup trucks wound up the street and around the garage, each blaring country music from their radios, until all hours.

Johnny and I were both suffering for my art, so I figured I'd better be good at it. For that reason—and to stay away from the apartment as much as I could—I threw myself into my drawing classes at Georgia State in downtown Atlanta. I filled books with drawings of vases, buildings, hands, feet, and eyes. I studied and copied drawings by Picasso, Dubuffet, and Rembrandt.

My drawing teacher, Mr. Mafong, gave dramatic and animated appraisals of our work. When I brought him a double page I'd filled with a dozen different sketchy views of trees, he looked at it for a second, then put up his hands to block out the thing lest it be stamped permanently on his brain. "No. No. This is chaos!"

I enjoyed the flair with which Mr. Mafong gave his opinions, even when I was the one being embarrassed in front of the whole class. One day we were outside drawing cityscapes. He came to me, peered at my drawing, and said, "No." He drew his hand, posed almost in salute form, to his eyes, then out, to point two fingers at some place on the horizon. "You have to see—see—see with your eyes to draw." The drama was fantastic, more fantastic than my talent.

I did have some talent for drawing, but I came to realize I didn't have enough to support myself as an artist. I thought, "Here I go again, off to get a degree I can't use once I finish." The class that finished my art school career was three-dimensional art. My first two projects were fun. One was a free-form sculpture made of colored wires stripped out of telephone cables, wrapped around ropes, and joined to look something like two spiders with their feet glued together—although that wasn't my intent. The other was a glass sculpture made by melting glass tubes with the Bunsen burner to form shapes that I then mounted in a block of Plexiglas. That's when I learned melting the glass was no problem, but 90 percent of the tubes shattered when they cooled.

Then came the assignment that did me in. "An award was established in 1960 for the first person to build a man-powered airplane that can actually fly. No one has done it yet. That's your assignment. Design a plane powered by human effort. It doesn't need to fly, although that would be nice. Be as creative and fanciful as you like in your design, and execute it."

I wasn't really interested in airplanes, but I came up with an idea—I don't remember what it looked like, but building it involved two checkers, wire, balsa wood, a mat knife, and a power drill. Drawing it was one thing. Making it into a three-dimensional object was a different story. I worked on it for three weeks, struggling with wire that refused to stick to wood or allow the checker-wheels to turn. The thing was a frustrating mess and so was I. My hands that I'd always thought were pretty were scarred from cuts and scratches made by balsa wood splinters, mat knife, drills, and wire, and covered with black dust from the charcoal crayons that had stuck to the glue and wouldn't wash off.

The day the assignment was due I set my creation in its place along with all the others for the teacher's inspection. He went down the row and gave the artists feedback, one by one. This or that could be better. This one was interesting. That one was creative. Then he came to mine and paused. I waited. Finally he said, "You could make up for poor design and lack of originality with good craftsmanship."

I was done with art school and the way I was living. I was sick of fighting roaches, sick of listening to the good ole boys play country music till dawn every weekend, and I couldn't build an airplane.

Here I was, out of college more than two years already, and I had no idea what I was going to do. I sat in that awful apartment and stared at nothing, sick with fear that I'd be a failure for the rest of my life.

I was sure of one thing: I wasn't going to find what I was looking for in Atlanta. I had to get to the North, to a city where I'd find opportunities. Johnny was ready to move on as well. Both of us dreamed of New York, but instead of New York, Johnny was offered a news spot on WASH, the Metro Media (now Fox) station in Washington, DC. It wasn't exactly what we wanted. It wasn't television and it wasn't New York, but it was out of Atlanta. We thought about it. Washington was a step closer to New York, and it was a city, and it was the capital, and it wasn't the South.

There would have to be a future for me in Washington! Anyway, I already had connections to a senator. Johnny's father knew Senator Talmadge. That gave me an in, I thought. I called the senator's office, spoke with a person I supposed was the head of the office, and explained my connection to the senator. It was a short conversation. She said, "How fast do you type?" I said, "I don't." She said, "Thank you for calling. Goodbye."

If I'd taken that high school typing course Daddy wouldn't let me take, I'd probably have been a clerk typist in Senator Talmadge's office.

I didn't know where to begin my search. Then I learned there was something called a personnel agency where they got jobs for people. It sounded great. They would find the right job for me!

I made an appointment with Snelling and Snelling in downtown Washington, excited, believing I was a short step away from my career. I put on my best Sunday dress and went forward to meet my future. I didn't have an exact picture of what I expected, but whatever I thought it would be was certainly not what I found.

I walked into a small office, empty except for a couple of chairs, a file cabinet, and a table where I was told to fill out the very first job application of my life, and a desk where a pleasant middle-aged woman interviewed me.

She read my application and asked questions, trying her best to pull together some kind of usable experience, although I didn't realize it.

"I see here you were a teacher for two years. How fast do you type?"

"Yes. I don't type."

"Didn't you have to type your papers in college?"

"No. I paid another student's wife to type them."

"Did you ever work in an office at all? What were your jobs during school?"

"My first semester, I worked in the audio-visual department of the school of education, teaching students to use the film projector, change film, splice film. Then I changed to the dean's office where I just filed forms."

"The A-V department sounds more interesting than filing."

"I wasn't very good with the mechanics of the projectors, and the films we used were World War II training films for paraplegics, quadriplegics, and amputees. They were made to teach them to use prosthetic arms and legs and to encourage new victims with the progress of the more advanced ones. After watching them for a few weeks, I preferred filing."

"Did you answer phones?"

"Once I think I did."

"Numbers?"

"No."

"Okay, then. Let's see what we have for you."

She opened her five-by-eight file box and thumbed through it. In spite of my lack of qualifications, she had three interviews for me.

"First, you need to sign this agreement to pay the fee if I place you in a job."

"But," I said, "on the phone I told you I only wanted a job if the employers paid the fees." I'm sure she was thinking I'd be lucky if someone allowed me to buy a job.

"Many of them do, but you can't type and there aren't as many jobs for you. Go ahead and go on the interviews. Just sign this, in case you decide you want to take one of the jobs where they won't pay the fee for you."

My first interview was at the old Lane Bryant store near 14th and F

Streets. The agency lady wrote the address and other information on her business card and told me to go to the third floor at 10:00 a.m. and ask for Mrs. Jones.

Today, 14th Street is lined with glass and brick office buildings. But in the '70s, the area was mostly boarded-up retail businesses, wig shops, bars, and strip clubs. My interview was in one of the few stores left. It was scary but I was always pretty brave. I parked and went in. Mrs. Jones's office was the whole third floor, but not the kind of floor one generally imagines. It was one cavernous room. Its unfinished wood floors were dusty, and it was lit by a single bulb hanging from the ceiling; the three dormer windows were brown with dirt possibly as old as the building itself. In the middle of the room, and looking very small, sat Mrs. Jones at a metal table, one pencil over her ear and one in her teeth, clanking away at a calculator, its tape flowing into a paper pool on the floor.

She saw me and took the pencil out of her mouth.

"You're from the agency for the interview? This is a record-keeping job."

"Yes, ma'am."

"This would be your desk. Do you have any experience?"

I looked down at the desk and said, "I don't. They said you would train."

Mrs. Jones looked at me as if she was trying to find the right words. She must have been one of the most intuitive people on the planet.

"Honey, I'm going to do you a favor. I'm going to let you leave now."

The next interview was on Massachusetts Avenue. Johnny and I were being housed by Metro Media at the Holiday Inn in Silver Spring, Maryland, until we could find an apartment. I knew how to find Massachusetts Avenue. Drive down 16th Street to K Street in Washington, turn up Connecticut Avenue to DuPont Circle, go around it, and get off at Massachusetts. It was only about five miles. No problem. What I didn't know was that Massachusetts runs all the way back to Maryland where the job was located, twelve miles away through rush hour traffic. It would have been only six miles if I'd driven directly to Silver Spring. The drive into the city and back out took an hour and a half, but I got there. Obviously I was willing to do whatever it took.

After my long trip, I found myself in a room that looked prison-like—no windows, gray walls, and fluorescent lights. Crammed into the space were ten or so women, all wearing pants, and several were even in t-shirts. I'm not sure if they had packs of Camels rolled up in their sleeves, biker style, or if I had imagined it.

The boss came out of a door in the back of the room, handed me a booklet, and pointed at a desk. "Here's a test. When you finish it, leave it on the desk and you can go. I'll look at it and call the agency."

I looked at the test cover, a Kuder Preference test. I'd taken these before. My brother went on to become a psychologist. He was working on his PhD when I was in junior high school, and he practiced his tests on me. I wasn't afraid of it.

I opened the booklet, filled in the answers, put it on the table, and left without having a single person in the office so much as speak to me.

The next morning the woman from the agency called.

"You failed the test."

"It was a preference test."

"Well, you failed it."

"It said I didn't prefer anything?"

"It doesn't matter. You failed it. But don't worry about it. I've got another interview lined up for you."

This interview seemed a little more promising, a manager trainee job with Ginns, a chain of office supply stores that also carried business gifts. That afternoon, I met with the man who would be my boss. He was nice and he wore a business suit. We talked, and he said he thought I could do the job just fine. We talked about my experience and what he would train me to do. Then he offered me the job at a salary of $135.00.

He gave back the application I'd completed, told me to take it to the director of human resources, and sent me to the main office to "finalize things" and "do the paperwork" so I could start Monday.

Okay, I didn't have a passion for retail, but I'd already been rejected by the two worst jobs in the city, and $135 per week was good money, even if I did have to pay the agency a fee. After my other experiences, I felt a huge relief that this nice man wanted me to work in his clean, well-lit store with big windows. I also thought it might be fun to help choose the gifts.

The human resources office was nothing like the store. Dark and damp, it had a basement feel, because it was a basement in their main store, and the woman I met there was not the cordial store manager but a large woman with a coarse face and clipped way of speaking—an HR Nazi. She glared at me as if she wanted to eat me alive, then she took the application and tossed it aside without looking at it.

"Mr. Adams said he wants to hire you. Have you ever before worked in an office supply store?"

"No."

"Have you even worked in retail?"

"No, ma'am." (I decided she didn't mean the two Saturdays while I was in high school that I worked in a grocery store and had lines backed up to the meat department because I couldn't catch on to the cash register.)

"Well," she said, "why do you think I should hire you?"

"I thought Mr. Adams already hired me. He told me to start Monday."

"Then I suppose there's nothing for me to do, is there? So you start Monday. You'll make $100 a week."

"I thought it was $135."

"If you were a man, it would pay $135."

"Is this the same job? The manager trainee?"

"It's the same one."

"May I ask you a question? Why won't I make $135 per week?"

She enunciated her words as though explaining a problem to a child, a dumb child. "Because you are a woman!"

"Why does a woman make less?"

"Because a woman has other issues to consider. Look at it this way. What if you are in the storeroom and a box falls off and hits you in the chest?"

I left without a job, still considering if my chest was more valuable than my head, and wondering if boxes didn't fall on men, and if stock people routinely stacked boxes so they would fall—maybe as some kind of joke to break the monotony of retail.

Rejected, dejected, and full of self-pity, I went to the WASH studio to meet Johnny for lunch. Luckily, I was early and Sharon, the receptionist, wasn't busy—because I needed to pour my heart out. She listened as I went through every humiliating detail of my job search.

I told Sharon I didn't see much of a future for myself. I didn't have any-thing companies looked for. Even the education I'd thought was going to be the secret of my success was, according to the woman at the agency, a detri-ment. The only jobs I qualified for were depressing. I'd had bad interviews followed by worse interviews, and no one wanted me. And to top it off, I had to sign a paper promising I'd *pay* to get one of those jobs. I didn't care if Sha-ron had to lie. I wanted to hear her say she was shocked that I hadn't imme-diately been grabbed up by some lucky company. But she offered something better than sympathy; she had a solution.

"I used to work for an agency. You should go to them. I know they can match you with a job, and I'm sure they can find you something better than the ones you've seen. My friend just took over the office right here in Chevy Chase. You should call Karen—and you don't have to pay a fee. They have the employers pay the fee, or at least advance it and take it back from your salary."

"I can't type. Do they have jobs if you can't type?"

"Of course. You have a college degree, and you're smart and you look great. Talk to her. She'll find out what you like and what you're good at and match you to the right job. Take her number and call her. I'll call her and tell her about you." (I found out later Sharon was naïve about the agency's opportunities for me.) She gave me a paper from her telephone message pad. It had the name, Karen Towers, and number to call.

For now, it gave me some speck of hope that this agency could hold my answer. Sharon told me what to expect. Someone would interview me, ask what I was interested in doing, and match me with jobs that fit me. I thought about what she was saying. The people who worked in that agency inter-viewed people? And asked them about their skills and interests? Matched them with jobs? Why couldn't I do that? I left for lunch with Johnny, clutch-ing the paper that contained a new spark of hope.

But Johnny had come to lunch with an even better possibility. Chan-nel 5 television was looking for a courtroom artist. He had already told the manager about my art, and the manager wanted to see some of my drawings.

That afternoon I bought a *Washington Post* and started making sketches of the leading political figures in the nation—Richard Nixon, John Ehrlich-man, H. R. Haldeman, John Mitchell (the men responsible for the Watergate break-in), and others. Unfortunately, when I laid them out side by side, I discovered a problem. In my drawings, every major political figure in the country looked just like John Ehrlichman—including Martha Mitchell.

I held on to Sharon's slip of paper with the agency's phone number. I thought about calling it, but I didn't call. The paper was hope. As long as I had the paper, I had hope. As long as I didn't call, they couldn't reject me. I was not ready for more disappointment. As long as I didn't call, I couldn't fail.

Evidently, Sharon had called Karen to tell her to expect my call. After a week, Karen took charge and called me. We set up an interview. But, wanting to keep hope alive as long as possible, I scheduled it for a week away.

When the day finally came for the interview, the confidence I'd felt after talking with Sharon was gone. This time I walked in knowing from experience what I might expect, but what I saw was different.

The office of this personnel agency was different from the first one. There was a reception room and a receptionist to greet me. I filled out another job application, and the receptionist buzzed the manager. I was ready.

I thought the manager couldn't be more than a couple of years older than I, but she seemed a lot older. Maybe it was her tailored brown suit, or her hair that was pulled severely back into a ponytail. Ponytail sounds cute and perky, but this woman was not that. She was brisk, confident, and all business—just in miniature. Karen was tiny—several inches shorter than I was, and one of the most intimidating people I'd ever met in my life.

She led me from the reception room, walking quickly. I sensed she was setting the pace for a quick interview with minimal small talk. I was ready for her to say, "I'm glad we finally get to meet. What brought you to Washington? That's interesting. What's your typing speed?"

But she asked me about my interests in art and history. As I answered her, I glanced around the office. There were two rows of four desks, lined up like seats on a train. Each desk had a chair for the "account executive" and one for an applicant. Three or four girls about my age were there working, talking on the phone or interviewing other applicants. They looked like they were busy and liked what they were doing. I figured I could do what they were doing.

It took about seven minutes to cover my education and experience and the kinds of things I liked to do. Then my interviewer went on to the kind of job I might like.

"With your background, you might like working in a museum." What I didn't know till later was they didn't work with any museums, and she was trying to end the interview by suggesting I apply at museums.

But I knew what I wanted. I blurted out my request. "I need a job, and I'll do whatever you think fits. If I don't get my first choice, I want to work here."

She didn't speak for what seemed forever. As hard as it was, I managed to keep quiet and wait.

Then she said, "Working in a personnel agency isn't like teaching. You're not here to help people. This is sales. Do you have any sales experience?"

"I sold Avon while I was in college and again when I was teaching."

"Okay. You can start tomorrow."

That was it. I had a job in the nation's capital, the city of equal opportunity for all (or so I thought). I had no idea what the job actually was, but I didn't let that bother me. I was sure it would be something great.

But, wait. Having a job wasn't the best part. I would not be making a salary! I know for a fact this is not what most people consider the "best thing" or even an acceptable thing, but I thought it was my dream opportunity. I'd be paid strictly on commission. I couldn't believe it! I'd found a job that didn't put limits on me. I could soar.

The company would give me a draw (which meant an advance on commissions) of $100 a week, and I would earn commissions after that was paid back. She told me if I did what was expected of me, I was projected to make $12,000 my first year. Wow! Teachers didn't make half of that—I'd made $5,400 as a teacher.

Now I was in a business I didn't even know how to do, and I'd be advanced a loan that almost covered what I made as a teacher, and that was just a start. Karen handed me a paper with projections for what I would make the first two years—$12,000 the first year, but I'd make $18,000 in the second. By my second year, I'd almost double Johnny's salary.

I earned almost exactly what had been projected for me. When I made the $18,000 in my second year, it was like making close to a hundred thousand today, and I was just twenty-three years old. Johnny told his grandmother, a retired teacher in Georgia, about my success. She thought he was joking. When he convinced her he was telling the truth, she didn't like it. "If she is making that kind of money, she can't be doing anything honest."

Before I left the last job interview I'd ever have, with a job and a paper that promised I'd make twice or three times the money I ever had before, Karen surprised me with one final detail. "Have you thought about what name you want to use?"

"No. I never thought about it." That was true. I'd never considered the possibility of anyone except movie stars using made-up names.

She said, "A lot of people take business names, especially if your name is hard to pronounce. Your name is easy. But if you want to keep your identity private, you can pick a different name."

"Do people usually change their names?"

"Everybody used to, but it's not necessary anymore. They changed their names in the past because agencies didn't have the best reputations and they didn't want their friends to know what they did. There were a lot of bad ones that took advantage of people."

I didn't know what the agencies of old might have done to earn their reputations. All the people I saw working in agencies were women. I wondered if any business run by women who weren't teachers or secretaries would have been suspect to some people. I can imagine what they thought, "All those women working in an office—it can't be decent." The District of Columbia must have thought that because they actually had a law on the books preventing personnel agencies from having beds in their offices, and they enforced it. Every year a dapper little man would come by for his bed inspection, looking in every corner lest he miss one. He continued to come at least until the mid-1980s. When he stopped coming, he wasn't replaced and the inspections ended. I like to think the city government, in recognition of his years of service, and the fact they'd never cross-trained him for any other job, kept the law on the books until he died or retired so he could complete his life's work.

Anyway, I kept my own name. I never thought of using a different name and I expected it would be hard to get used to, plus, I have a terrible memory for names and I was afraid I'd get confused. So Ruthi it stayed.

I also learned a fun piece of history from the personnel business. There had been a time when agencies required their newly hired employees to take the name of the person they replaced so clients wouldn't notice the high turnover. When Mary left, they replaced her with "Mary." (As the new "Emily" replaced the original Emily in *The Devil Wears Prada*.) There was even one agency in Virginia, or so I was told, that employed only famous American women—Martha Washington, Dolly Madison, Betsy Ross, Abigail Adams.

Now I had a job, a title (I was an account executive), and my own name. But could I keep the job? I had no idea because I had not yet learned what the job actually was. Still, I sensed it was my one big chance though, and I needed to make it a success. I wasn't at all confident about that. And I wasn't the only one. It was obvious the manager didn't think much of my potential. If they lined up all of the account executives in the office by "most likely to survive six months," I would have been sent to the end of the line—past the rancher with a bigger than Texas personality; past the ex-secretary who complained daily that she was the only person who kept her job orders in alphabetical order and it wasn't fair that we lost ours, took hers, and never put them back correctly; even past the bouncy brunette who soon left to make real money in a massage parlor.

I couldn't blame the manager for her lack of enthusiasm. I was still awkward when I met new people, and I'm sure I was nothing like the people where she came from or, for that matter, like any successful person she could imagine. Karen was buttoned-down, tailored suits, severe hairstyle, New York. I can imagine what she thought of the outfit I wore to our interview. I remember exactly what it was—a red and white flower-print dress with a ruffle around the bottom, white pumps, and white bag. She probably saw fluffy blonde hair, dressed in fluffy clothes, totally down-south style which, to her taste, meant no style. She was New York. I was south Alabama. She was numbers. I was words. She was no nonsense and no time to waste. Sometimes I had to say a paragraph before I found the sentence I was trying to get out. It was one of the effects of attention deficit disorder that some people found entertaining, even charming. She didn't.

Over the next twenty-five years, we were to prove opposites may not attract, but they make extraordinary partners. We were the best team in the industry. She knew the business and the details, and I brought the sales ability. She turned out to be one of the four or five smartest people I ever met, and although it's been years since I worked with her, to this day, when I have a tough decision to make, she is the person in my head I go to for answers.

But all that partner stuff was in the future. Right then I didn't know how long I'd have a job. I decided on a back-up plan. I bought a typewriter and started teaching myself to type. QWERTY—I memorized that far but it was multiplication tables all over again, and it was established I had no manual dexterity, and my Kuder Preference test said I wouldn't like it. There went my back-up plan.

With no other options except failure—unless I found a market for drawings of John Ehrlichman—I had to make this career work. To do that, I had to keep from getting fired. That was simple once I learned the job was to make phone calls. If I stayed on the phone continuously she couldn't get to me to fire me. I did, and she didn't.

4

MAMA'S MARBLES

Play the Game to Win

When I was a child, I loved to play, but not sports. My game was "play like," and I played it with the ferocity and drive of an athlete. Specifically, a quarterback. I had to be the one to make up the game, to drive it forward, and decide how it would end. When it was cowboys, I determined I would be the one who got shot in the heart, fell off the couch, and lay there, dead—till I was bored. Then I'd say, "Okay. I'm alive again." And I'd be back in the play, shooting and riding. I wasn't trying to be bossy. It just never occurred to me that I shouldn't win.

When Mama's brother, Uncle Ervin, came to visit from California, he told me about Mama when she was a little girl. He said she was a tomboy. It was hard to imagine Mama could ever have been a tomboy, but Uncle Ervin said, "She climbed trees and played whatever games the boys played. Sometimes she played them better than the boys. She came out in the school yard when some boys were playing marbles. They told her to go play with dolls. Marbles was for boys and girls couldn't play." I knew my mama wouldn't have settled for that. Uncle Ervin said she didn't. "She showed them. She stayed right there till they let her play, and she won all their marbles. After that, they never would let her play with them again."

Mama listened to him without saying anything. Then she got up, told us she would be right back, and went to her bedroom. When she came out, she had that crooked little smile she put on when she had a secret, and a cloth bag in her hand. She sat down, untied the string around the top of the bag, and put it on the table in front of Uncle Ervin. It was the boys' marbles.

I wasn't surprised that Mama didn't let any boys tell her what games she could play, and certainly not surprised that she beat them. Mama never paid attention to anybody who told her what to do. If she wanted to do it, she did. If not, she didn't. But if they said she couldn't do something because she was a woman, stand out of the way and watch.

J. C. Penney's tried to tell Mama a woman couldn't have a credit card. This was in the 1950s before the credit card explosion. Nobody we knew had credit cards. Visa and American Express didn't exist yet, and department store charge cards were just becoming popular. Mama decided she wanted one and filled out the credit forms in her own name, writing Daddy's name in the blank for "spouse." When her Penney's card came, the name on it was Mr. N. G. Simmons. She took it right to the manager of the store in Prichard. Back then managers were almost always men. "This is my credit card and that is not my name." He argued in that manager-talking-to-a-woman tone. It might have seemed polite if it weren't also snooty. "But Mrs. Simmons, that is how it's supposed to be done. All cards have to be in the husband's name."

She didn't let the man upset her and she didn't back down. She was the one in control and she knew it. "Well, my card certainly does not have to be in any other name, and it will not. I have a job, I earn my own money, and I pay my own bills. My husband did not apply for your card. I did. My name will be the one on it, or you can take it right back. I can shop here, or I can drive right past your store and go to Sears and Roebuck in Mobile. So you can either keep your credit or give me a card with my name on it."

I suppose Penney's had to have a new card press made that let them stamp "Mrs." But Mama got her card.

I wasn't going to let anyone tell me what I couldn't do either—not even if we were just playing. Kenny was my best friend. He came over all the time and we would "play like" we were cowboys or explorers. One day I told him, "I have an idea. Let's 'play like' we live up in a penthouse in New York City and we're having champagne out on the balcony. You put that board on the saw horses, and I'll get the chairs and ginger ale and glasses."

Kenny said he wasn't about to play like he was anything as sissy as that. It was one of the few times I couldn't win Kenny over to my way of thinking. "Okay," I said, "Let's make the sawhorses into the 'Rescue 8' car [from our favorite television show]. You'll be Skip and I'll be Patty, and we will go out and rescue people." We turned the sawhorses around. Then Kenny said he would go out and save the people, but I had to be the wife, and stay home and cook. I told him I most certainly would not be a wife who stayed home and cooked. I'd be one who rode out to save people, or I'd make my sawhorses back into a penthouse balcony. We got in our car and saved people all afternoon.

I didn't have any experience with real competitions until I got to junior high school. At K. J. Clark Junior High I learned I liked to compete and win. There were lots of things to try out for. The school had a football team, so there were tryouts for cheerleader and there were contests for beauty queens. I secretly wished I could be one, but I was still the chubby, bad-hair kid and didn't even consider trying out. Then I heard about a competition I could enter. It was one of the announcements Mr. Gilmore made over the intercom every morning during homeroom. He said tryouts would be held to select a school chorus. I didn't know why, but I knew I just had to go to the music room at the start of our lunch period and sing for the teacher. I was already in the junior choir at the First Methodist Church, but this was different. It was special. Not everybody could get in. I had to try.

I didn't tell a soul I was trying out, not even my best friend, Delilah, until the list was posted. I thought it would be best to surprise people if I won. That created the model for how I would do things the rest of my life. I would never challenge, never let them know I was in the race, till I won. It wasn't just about what other people would think—I didn't allow any thought of winning or losing into my consciousness either. Those thoughts weren't the next right step—they would come at the end. I put them away somewhere and sealed the door. My only focus was on singing the song.

When the list was posted on the music room door, my name was there. I was in! Being in the choir was as good as I thought it would be. I felt special. I never had a featured role, and I might have been there for volume; but most of the kids weren't there at all. I did chorus all three years, and can still sing most of the Rodgers and Hammerstein show songs.

When I went to Fairhope High in the tenth grade, I found it didn't have a select chorus so I didn't do it. If anybody could get in, I wasn't interested. Most of my time in high school, I was just competing to survive high school, until I decided to enter a beauty pageant.

One of the big events in Fairhope was the Dogwood Trail Pageant, a beauty contest for high school seniors, and the first step toward the Junior Miss Pageant. I don't know what compelled me to enter that one. I watched beauty pageants on TV for years and dreamed of being up on the stage. Actually, I didn't think about what entering would mean. I just did it. I had to get on that stage. Everybody knew Amanda Sawyer was going to win. Beautiful, in the band, majorette, and already the winner of one pageant, she was going to be Miss Dogwood Trail. But I didn't let that thought stop me. I added my name to the list.

I didn't know what I was in for. As I would do all my life, I had thrown myself headlong into a project without any idea of what all was involved. As far as I was concerned, my walk across the stage in the most beautiful yellow gown I'd ever seen *was* the pageant. But that wasn't true. I was in for a painful month-long series of events before the pageant ever happened. I'd be using skills I didn't have and meeting people who scared me and whom I was supposed to try to impress.

It started with a lunch at the Parker House, the restaurant for ladies' lunches in Fairhope. I was the only girl who ate. The pageant head, a society matron, whose name I don't remember, greeted us and outlined our activities for the next few weeks. When she said, "I'm happy to greet such a lovely group of young ladies, and I'm honored to be able to guide you through the next few weeks," I heard, "I'm honored to work with some of you. The rest of you should be honored to be here at all, and certainly to be here with me." My attention was so focused on her tone, I missed much of what she said until she got to the part about going to a dance class. I suspected most of the other girls had taken dancing lessons before or been cheerleaders, and I felt a little embarrassed that I hadn't. At the dance studio on Pecan Street, they would find out. She told us we would "learn a dance that will display your talent and athletic ability." I was in trouble. I took a deep breath and steeled myself. I'd be okay, I told myself.

When I got to the studio, it was even worse than I'd expected. The dance had steps! Did I already say I had, and still have, no eye-hand or eye-foot coordination? I would never have survived the sock hops at the American Legion if the dances had steps to follow rather than the freestyle moves of the '60s, like those in the Swim, the Frug, the Watusi. (Look them up on YouTube!)

The lesson started with the simplest step—walk with both arms stretched in front of me, front toe pointed down, then walk one step forward switching toes. I almost got it, but that was the last easy part, and it was only easy if I started on the same foot as all the other girls. Walk, kick, kick, turn—the problem was I was supposed to do them all in the same order, every time.

But then there was the big step—I watched, wide-eyed, as the teacher demonstrated the step. She dipped nearly to the floor, balanced on a bent right knee, while she slid her left leg out to the side, toes pointed, left hand on her waist and right hand pointing skyward. It was a physical impossibility. But I made up my mind—I would get it if it killed me.

With the pageant just a week away, I still hadn't mastered that drop-slide-point dance step. Plus, I had to face the talent contest in three days and I had yet to come up with a talent. What could I do? Clearly dancing was out. I couldn't sing without a choir or twirl a baton either. I had always loved poetry and I remembered poems almost without trying. Memorization! That was a talent, wasn't it? I would recite a poem.

I thought about it. I knew some Robert Frost poems, including "Death of the Hired Man," but that might be too long. The poem should be dramatic. It should have irony. I picked what I thought was an interesting poem by Kenneth Fearing, "Thirteen O'clock."

Not once in all these years did it occur to me that my choice might have been odd, until I was talking with a friend about this chapter and my talent contest.

Recently my husband asked me to read the poem to him. I read it, with the appropriate drama in my voice. "Why do they whistle so loud when they walk past the graveyard late at night? Why do they look behind them when they reach the gates? Why do they have any gates?"

I finished my recitation: "Stay away, live people, stay away. You mean no harm, and we aren't afraid of you, and we don't believe such people exist, but what are you looking for? Who do you want?

"WHO? WHO? WHO? O WHO?"

I looked at Ron for his reaction. All he said was, "And you lost? With *that* poem? Amazing! It never occurred to you that the judges may have been looking for something less . . . Halloween? Had you never seen a Miss America pageant?"

I knew the judges weren't excited by my performance. They didn't say it was bad. Actually, I think they were speechless. But they didn't ask me to perform on pageant night. I assumed they preferred girls who could sing or twirl. I didn't win talent.

I still had one last chance to impress them—the interview. I went into it with my great asset—failure-amnesia—it's a blessing. It's the ability to forget, I mean completely block out, past failures. That's what kept me from quitting in the face of overwhelming odds, time and again. It never crossed my mind that my history of meeting new people had been unsuccessful overall, especially when I felt the people were judging me. The more I felt scrutinized, the more uncomfortable and unnatural I became. I would talk faster and faster, louder and louder, to the point of babbling. But with my failure-amnesia going for me, I was able to walk into that room with optimism. I truly expected to win the interview phase—until I saw the panel and heard the first question and realized: These people were there for just one specific purpose—to judge me.

I didn't put it together yet that an interview was like a first date, and I had never had a good first date. No, the interview was worse than any date I'd ever had. At least my dates didn't have clipboards. They didn't take notes on the things I said. When I went on dates, I could only blow it with one person at a time.

This was a "first date" with five people. Two were men with smiles that just missed having warmth. They had the superior and judgmental demeanors I would encounter again in the future when I met with bankers to borrow money to set up my business. The women were what I thought of as society matrons. As I write this, I think about what society matrons meant to me— married ladies, but certainly not working women like my mama, and not housewives. I pictured them with maids, with copies of *Southern Living* on their tea tables, and enough money and time on their hands to give back to their small town and the "little people" in it. I suspected they had personal copies of *Emily Post's Book of Etiquette* in their purses and judged the quality of a person on proper table setting. I know that characterization was totally unfair, but it didn't matter. That was my perception, and it really wasn't about the women. It was about how I felt about me.

The interview started, and I tried to concentrate on their faces instead of the clipboards (especially the one gripped in the chubby hands of the heavy man in the brown suit who kept making exaggeratedly large checkmarks) as I answered the questions they read from prepared lists.

The first question, as I remember it, was "What is your goal for your life?" I didn't know. I was seventeen, for goodness' sake! My dream was to be in a penthouse in New York City, with a man pouring ginger ale (pretend) wine, and to have an as-yet-undefined career, maybe on Broadway. I decided to hold some details back. "I'm going to move to New York City, and find a career." They scribbled notes on the forms.

If I were to win, how would I use my pageant title to better society? I couldn't think of a single way my being a beauty pageant winner could help society. With nothing to say, I talked for a good five minutes. I have no idea what I said, but I remember feeling my face grow hot and searching for a good exit line. More scratching on clipboards.

Finally, they asked, if I had the power to be remembered by all the world as one word, what would that word be? "Star."

All right. I still had the beauty part. Surprise! I'd gotten pretty—really pretty—since junior high. Even I could tell. It's funny . . . On one level, people kept telling me I was the prettiest girl in the pageant. But I couldn't accept it. I did know that no one could have had a more beautiful gown.

Pageant night counted for at least a third of the contest, with points for beauty, poise, and the dance. I'd been working every day on the dance routine, so maybe, just maybe, I could pull it out. With failure-amnesia again, I believed I could do it, so I redoubled my efforts to master the dance until the muscles in my legs locked up. Practice was my downfall.

You've heard people say how they had a dream in which they fell on their face. I didn't dream it. I did it. But I got back up, smiling, and carried on like a trouper. Later I was told that got me points for poise, teaching me, for the first time, how failing could be turned into an asset. Of course, Amanda won the crown.

After the pageant, I met up with some friends at the A&W Root Beer stand on Greeno Road. I must have heard ten times the last thing I wanted to hear, "I think it was rigged. You should have won." Almost as bad was, "Ruthi, you were a winner just for being up on that stage." No. It wasn't rigged. And I was pretty sure I wasn't a winner just for being up there. I didn't have a bag of marbles and I didn't have a crown.

The next important competition of my life was college, and it was the one I had to win. Fortunately, I didn't have to have talent or coordination. But the truth is, with stakes this high, if I had to twirl to win, I would have twirled if it killed me. Other kids may have had excuses to fail, but I didn't.

I loved competing, and college was all about it. There were five contests every semester for grades and GPA ranking. It wasn't unlike the chorus try-outs. To win, I had to perform and convince the professors I was the best, not by singing, not through an interview, but with my written words and my mind—even my personality. I loved it.

From my first college class, I always chose a seat in the front row—even after I heard some professor comment that coeds who sat up front were just hoping to trade peeks for grades. That had never occurred to me, and I was embarrassed that they might think it of me; but I didn't think for a minute about moving. I didn't care what he thought. It made me mad, and the anger worked to motivate me all the more. I'd show him! That was another new strength I'd found, the "I'll-show-him/her" attitude. It would serve me well.

I wouldn't have recognized most of the teachers if I walked past them on campus. I was interested in one thing—getting all the notes to make the grades—and sitting in the front row to ensure I wouldn't miss anything. I would show anybody who thought differently. I didn't need to show cleavage to win. In college and ever since, I've continued to choose the front row of every class, church service, or meeting.

A few years ago, a friend suggested another reason for my seating choice. "When you're on the front row, you're alone." Interesting, I thought, and a good possibility. I remained afraid of groups, and all those people behind me were a group. But maybe if I couldn't see them, I could make them disappear.

Whatever my reason, I started each class in my front seat, focused on figuring out how to win with the new teacher. My favorites were those who demanded the most or were the hardest to impress or surprise. Number one of all was Mr. Kimball, a New Yorker who had come down to Georgia to teach us Southerners a thing or two. Specifically, he came to bring us the truth about the "Myths and Realities of Reconstruction in the Old South."

Mr. Kimball clearly enjoyed the idea of popping Southern balloons. He started off, more or less, with this: "You've been told things about the South after the Civil War. They are not true. Never were true. Here's what really happened."

He was tough. He was demanding. And I wanted desperately to show him, to impress him. He warned us about his final exam. It would be hard, it would be an essay, and it would count for a large part of the final grade. That exam was my tour de force performance. I got to show off my creativity, my intellect, and my humor.

It had only one question, and there were a few groans when Mr. Kimball wrote it on the board: "Compare and contrast the myths and facts of reconstruction." I opened my test book and began my first paragraph with, "My Daddy always told me . . . " My second paragraph began, "Mr. Kimball told me . . . " I filled three blue books with the alternating views. Afterwards, I was happy enough just to know I'd blown the curve. But even better was to come when, ten years later, I ran into Mr. Kimball in Washington. It was a happy coincidence. We were standing in the same line for a movie. He recognized me and called my name. I said I was surprised to see him and that he remembered me after all those years. He said, "Of course I do. You were one of the few students who surprised me. At the beginning of the course, when you sat in the front row, I assumed you were another coed sitting up front to win grades by showing your legs [that front row thing must have been a problem for more than one male professor]; but I found out you weren't even aware of how you looked. You just wanted the grade. Your final exam blew me away. We have to read the same exam papers again and again. Yours was original. I still use it in teaching the courses." I felt great! I'd blown the curve again.

College was my first taste of success. I wasn't the number one graduate (that went to a first-string football player who was also a Fulbright Scholar—some people just have it all), but I was in the top 20 percent. I wrote on the margin of my program at the awards ceremony, "Out of every ten people in this room, eight are dumber than I am."

After so many heady experiences in college, I wanted more of the things I had learned I loved: intellectual competition, winning grades, setting myself apart by my achievements, and winning the respect of professors. I certainly didn't expect to find those things in my first job as a teacher. That wasn't right, of course. There would be opportunities to be creative, to compete, and to win, and there would be many of those exhilarating experiences I longed for. Still, education was the wrong profession for me.

I didn't have the temperament or the personality to exist in a public school system. High school had already proved that. The bureaucracy strangled me. Whether I was there as a student or as a teacher, public school felt like a prison. It acknowledged only one way to do or be. That wasn't me. Whatever I was meant to be, standardized was not it.

Even worse, I rebelled against the stratification. It was wrong that it didn't matter who was the better teacher. It was wrong that, excellent or evil, we were all paid the same! No. Some made more. It was based on tenure. Where was the competition in that? I needed the award to prove I was a success—the grade, the commission, the marbles. I could live with trying and not winning, but I couldn't handle being forcibly equal. Maybe I would have liked teaching if we had worked on commission.

Only with the kids did I find some of the things that made college fun. I liked coming up with creative things to do with them. I didn't have a professor to give me a top grade for the things I created, or money or recognition, but I knew I was achieving things.

I discovered a new passion—creating change by fighting for something I believed in, and winning, even though it would be one tiny step at a time. On Petain Street, I knew I made a difference in the lives of the lonely old people there. It felt good, but I didn't really change anything. I'd been successful in college, but hadn't made a difference. Now I had the opportunity to see wrongs and change them, and here I learned something else. Whether it was a single school policy or an unfair practice I would find later in business, the dragons I'd get to battle would always be the little ones. But the little ones matter.

My first dragon was a school policy, and what was at stake? Field trips. Before my first term began, all of the teachers went to a meeting led by Mr. Holliman, the county school superintendent, where he announced plans and changes for the year. For once, I was sorry I sat up front. I hoped I looked as though I was taking notes as I doodled on my notebook, really not paying much attention, until Mr. Holliman announced he was banning school field trips. That got my attention. I had never given much thought to field trips before. I had never been on a field trip through all my school years. I didn't even know Jackson County had them. But I was outraged to lose them. This was wrong. That was my first reaction—this man was taking something away from me.

The more I thought about it, the angrier I became. Field trips were a rare opportunity for most of these kids, who were the children of sharecroppers, lived in poverty, and had little hope for anything better. I walked around fuming to myself all day. How could Mr. Holliman justify doing that to these kids? I heard the other teachers grumbling too, but they were accepting it. I wouldn't! I'd show them!

I had never shown much talent for diplomacy. When I was confronted, I got tongue-tied and hurt, and when I got hurt, I threw a fit and cried. Only Child Syndrome? The one time I had a conflict with a professor over a grade, I got so mad I cried until my two sets of false eyelashes fell off. (It was the style—remember Twiggy?)

But this time I wouldn't throw a fit or cry. I planned my approach just like a grown-up, and went in to win. As was my habit since seventh grade chorus tryouts, I didn't tell anyone what I was doing. I just prepared my case and worked up my courage. Then I went to Mr. Holliman.

My speech reflected all of the melodrama that came from being twenty-two years old and having a full two weeks of professional teaching experience. "I know you and I are both concerned about the welfare of these students. That's why I want to talk with you about the field trips. I remember the times my parents took me places like Appomattox and Washington, DC, way more than any classroom work I ever did. Those trips gave me things to dream about. I look at my class and see kids who've never had the chances I had to know so many things that are good and interesting in the world, kids who don't have anything to dream about other than leading the same lives their parents led. The kids whose parents don't have the money to take them places don't have a hope if we don't give it to them. Don't you think we should give them exposure to all we can? Don't you think we should give them dreams? I was lucky because my daddy took me to see different parts of the country. He let me have dreams. You know they're studying Georgia history and they live so close to Atlanta, but most of them have never even seen the gold dome of the capitol. We're all they've got. If we don't give them that gold dome, they don't have anybody else who can."

It was wordy. It was melodramatic, but I won. I won, and I learned a lesson. If you don't define clearly what you ask for, you can sometimes lose by winning. Mr. Holliman gave me exactly what I asked for. Without telling me first, he approved field trips—but only for me. My classes could go, but not any of the others. It was awful. The other teachers were up in arms. It was unfair, they said out loud. Exactly what had I done to get extra privileges? they asked in whispers. It only ended when I went back to Mr. Holliman and said, "You know, I think it would be a good thing to let the other grades learn about the world too."

Jackson County Public School in Braselton/Hoschton got its field trips back and I took full advantage of them. We went to the zoo, planetarium, and parks, and to the Georgia State Capitol, where I met a great man and got a sad surprise. The man was Ben Fortson, Georgia's secretary of state for thirty-three years. I was surprised because I didn't expect our group to be met by the secretary of state. I also didn't expect him to be in a wheelchair, which he had been bound to since an automobile accident when he was twenty-four.

Mr. Ben, the master storyteller, gathered the kids around and pointed out a few details of the capitol building. Then he asked, "Did you know that there was a time when Georgia had three governors?" We didn't, so Mr. Ben spun out the story. It happened after the election of 1946. Mr. Eugene Talmadge was elected governor of Georgia, but he died in

December, before he could take office. Mr. Melvin Thompson was elected lieutenant governor, and he claimed he was to be the governor, but so did Eugene Talmadge's son, Senator Herman Talmadge. So there were two. But then the sitting governor, Ellis Arnall, announced he would not give up the office until a decision was made.

That decision was left up to the Georgia Supreme Court, but Senator Talmadge wasn't waiting for them. In the dead of night, he moved into the governor's office and had the locks changed. Then he had himself sworn in. But there was one more thing the new "governor" needed if he was going to run the state. He needed the state seal. Mr. Ben pointed to a copy of the seal. Without that seal, he said, no official documents could be issued, so no state business could be done.

Mr. Ben said, "The seal is kept in a safe, in my office, and brought out only when the governor needs it to make something official. 'Governor' Talmadge's aides went to the safe, but the seal was gone. They looked everywhere and didn't find it. Finally the Supreme Court made its decision. Mr. Thompson would be governor until a special election could be held. As soon as that decision was made, guess what? The seal came back as mysteriously as it had disappeared." Mr. Ben's eyes twinkled. "Do you know where it was the whole time?" No, we said, we didn't. He grinned and he pointed at his lap. "A place nobody ever thought to look. I was sitting on it." (And I thought Mama could win an argument!)

He had finished the story and was answering the kids' questions, when I noticed we were losing some of our group, as one after another, the kids turned away from him to inch closer to a far wall. I looked to see what was drawing their attention. But all I saw was a wall, with a couple of elevator doors in it. I couldn't imagine what was so fascinating about that. Then I saw. It was the elevator!

This was the 1970s. We'd gone to the moon, and these thirteen- and fourteen-year-olds, who lived twenty-five miles from both the University of Georgia and the State Capitol, had never seen an elevator. It humbled me. These kids had lived their whole lives in Braselton, a family-owned town that had only a small post office and one large, dusty building that was the only store they knew—feed store, grocery store, dry goods store, clothing store, and farm store, all in one. Just across the line was Hoschton, and all it had was a gas station that carried sodas and a few groceries. That was their world.

Mr. Ben understood. He rolled over to the elevator wall and sat there while the elevator operator rode groups of kids up and down to their heart's content. In the battle for the field trips, this is what I'd won. It made a difference.

I love being right. Don't we all? But more than that, I loved convincing everybody else I was right. That's what winning meant. I knew how Mama must have felt when she won the fight to unionize the retail clerks in Mobile. She stood up and argued for what she believed was right, and she won. I could spend a lifetime arguing for what I believed and winning. Wouldn't that be a great job!

Winning arguments and getting paid for it? If that was the criteria for a career that would work for me, I could think of two careers that fit: law and sales. Law wasn't one that would have occurred to most women in the South, even ambitious women, in that era, and it certainly didn't occur to me. I met two girls who were going to law school around the time I started teaching. I remember my reaction very clearly. I was astonished—practically incredulous. It's not that I doubted women could or should go to law school; I had just never met one who did.

I never gave a thought to sales as a career. What I knew of it I didn't want to do. I knew about department store clerks, the Fuller Brush man who used to come to Grandmama's door, and the Avon lady. I sold Avon part-time while I was in college and while teaching, but that didn't hold my attention. I had never heard of sales that didn't involve a product, and certainly not one in which I would sell my own judgment and ideas. But that's what I found in the personnel agency. Finally, a job in which I'd get to do all the things I loved to do—have fun with people, listen to them, figure out what they should do, and convince them to do it. That did it—a career spent convincing people was what I was meant to have.

I found that career in the personnel agency, where the job was actually telephone sales. Perfect. I was the kid who spent Friday nights, when other kids were at parties, making prank phone calls. That was experience I never thought to put on my resume. I may have been awkward and shy in person, but calling people on the phone didn't scare me at all. In those days before caller ID, no one knew I was the kid calling to say, "Is your refrigerator running?" I thought I was hysterical, and made another call and another. But I went a step further. I kept the people I called on the phone. A lot of them joked around with me. They had fun on the calls too.

That was the experience that carried directly into my new job. I got to spend my days making calls to employers in Washington. Instead of asking if they had "Prince Albert [tobacco] in a can," I asked about job opportunities for my applicants. And I kept these people on the phone too, talking, joking, and building relationships.

How many people can say, "Prank phone calling made me what I am today"? It really was the best experience I could have had. I have considered making it a requirement for people who want to work for me. I could run an ad for "Sales position: If you spent your adolescence making prank phone calls, please apply." In all those hours I spent dreaming about a career, I never thought to look for a job that would make use of prank phone calling. And I never dreamed work would be so much fun.

But having found the job I wanted and being happy didn't make me any more secure. I was still afraid, maybe even more so because I was happy. The threat of failure was still there, always there, just behind me. Most of the time I was able to force it away. Somewhere along the way I developed an ability to keep myself from looking at things that bothered me. I put them in my brain's compartments, where I could seal away fears and sad thoughts. I might hide them, but they were there and they drove me. I had to win. I had no excuses. That was the other ghost that haunted me, pushed me, and motivated me. "Other children have excuses," Mama had said. She was right. I had no excuse not to do whatever it took to be a success. Just as in college, if I had to twirl, I would twirl.

It didn't make it any easier that I knew my manager was sure I'd fail. I was under pressure to do something right and do it quickly, just to keep my job. As the Dogwood Trail pageant had taught me, it wasn't enough to merely show up. I had to show up and get the dance steps right. Without knowing how to make persuasive sales calls, I dove into the phone, trying, one call after another, every day. Statistically, I thought, it had to work. If

I made enough calls and asked enough people to work with me, someone would say yes.

Statistics must have been what worked, because it wasn't skill that brought my first result, a placement, in my second week. That was an exciting event and a coup for someone so new, but I secretly felt a little bit guilty that I really didn't earn it. It was just luck that I called the office manager of an insurance company, trying to find a job for my accounting candidate: "I'm working to locate a job for a young man with a degree in accounting." My presentation was just about that lame.

The office manager said, "We don't have any accounting jobs available."

Here's where I displayed my raw sales talent: "Okay. Thank you anyway. Goodbye."

She stopped me before I could hang up. "Just a second. Do you have jobs for secretaries?"

"Yes," I said, persuasively.

"Do you think you could help my daughter? She's been in the same job five years, and she needs to make a change. She is a smart girl, if I do say so. Is it okay if I have her call you?"

It was okay with me. Shirley came in and was the model of the perfect applicant of that day—no college degree ("Why would she want to be a secretary?"), but a year of secretarial school and five years' experience, and she typed 60 words per minute and took shorthand at 80. I had the poster child of candidates, and I'd almost hung up the phone. From there, it all happened so fast I don't remember any of the details. She was hired by the first employer who met her—at the astonishing salary of $8,500 per year (the average salary in the '70s was $6,000!). The fee was $680 at a time when most fees ranged from $187.20 to $490.

I'd won! I could do this! At least I hoped I could. With this placement, and with every placement I'd make for the next couple of years, came the voice of fear, telling me this was only one placement. What if it was a fluke? What if I couldn't do it again? One placement didn't prove anything. I pushed the thoughts down, took a breath, and said to myself, "Okay. Just keep going. Keep making those calls." I hoped, with enough calls, I could win again, and if I won enough times, I might feel secure.

As much as I loved the race, I found something else I liked about my new office. I was enjoying a kind of social life. I liked the people I worked with. This was so different from high school and college social life. We had things to talk about, we had our work in common, and we laughed all the time because we were in a business that had a million funny stories. I went to parties and liked them. We told funny work stories until husbands rebelled, then we played charades. But the big company meetings, dinners, and happy hours were still torture. People were different. We had fun at work but at company events my coworkers seemed to compete to be close to the manager who still didn't like me, and made it obvious. When the vice president was there, it was worse. Some people drink to get through such events. I didn't drink. I talked—and talked, and talked, and felt miserable afterwards. I'd wake up in the middle of the night going over and over every stupid thing I'd said. I wished I could call Mama so she could tell me I couldn't go, but I couldn't do that. So I ended up, again, sitting in places I didn't want to be, with nothing to say to a group of people who I was pretty sure didn't like poetry.

Still, the camaraderie in the office proved once again that Daddy was right. Before I started, I told him I was scared and worried that I might not fit in. He told me to forget about fitting in and forget about the other people and just think about the job. "You've got a job to do, and you can't spend your time worrying about the other people, or about whether you like them or they like you. Just do your job right, and the other things will get sorted out."

If, as I feared, my success was just luck, at least I kept having luck. After Shirley, I placed Ravinder at Perpetual Savings and Loan, then Theresa with National Bank of Washington. Every month I made more matches until the month came when my name went on the board as the top producer. I was cautiously happy. I just hoped I could do it again. The next month my name went up again. Then I skipped a month, and sank into fear again. But the following month I was back on top. I finally knew I had the profession I wanted, and it seemed I was good at it! So far, anyway.

I loved being number one. Once I'd proved I could win my office's contests, I started to look at the world outside of my office. What was next? The company had three locations with two divisions. I could be number one in my division, SOC.

The SOC (secretarial/office/clerical) division was the place for the "girls." The other division, the professional division, was for the men. Everybody knew it was the place for the big hitters, the real top producers. The men were expected to produce revenues (and earn) two or three times more than the "girls." After a while, that didn't sit well with me. I was sure I had never been second best to any man, and I wasn't going to start now. Even if there were "better classes" based on some social ideas, they were not based on sex. I knew one thing for certain—winning was the only measure in a contest.

So, the company executives didn't expect me, or any woman, to be one of their top producers. I decided they would find out they were wrong. I knew women who were leaders. I went to the union meetings with Mama and saw her speak up, right along with the men, about things like right-to-work laws and equal pay. And they listened to her. And Mama made more money than a lot of the men she worked with at the grocery store.

I remember some poor man who had the bad judgment to tell me men should make more money because they had the responsibility for supporting families. Right! I thought that was one of the stupidest things I had ever heard, and I most likely said so. Maybe one of the benefits of being poor is there is a certain equality in poverty. Everybody's paycheck mattered equally. For us to live as we did, both Mama and Daddy had to bring home a paycheck, and the more money in it the better. They never told me men were supposed to be superior or make more money just because they were men, so the situation I was in now didn't make sense. I could just imagine what Mama would have said to the man who told her he was worth more than she was.

But I didn't have to deal with just one man who thought he was supposed to be better, I had to deal with a whole division of them—although in fact, I didn't deal with these men at all. They ignored me. I was invisible. Unless I tripped over a chair and fell on my face, they didn't see me. I was in high school again, but without the stuffed bra. Everybody else was in the A-group, and I was the new kid in school, the one who wasn't good at sports and had bad hair. I wanted them to see me as their equal when they didn't even see me at all.

I made up my mind. No man was going to tell me I couldn't do something as well as he could without letting me try. I would make them sit up and take notice. I wouldn't tell them but I would get into the game! Once I got in, I'd play to win.

The thing that first got me noticed in the company, that set me apart and created my special identity, was the very same thing I used to keep myself from being fired—cold-calling. It happened at a company meeting for all of the offices. I stood alone at the coffee table, although I was beside a group of men from the Virginia office who were talking about sailing and base-ball scores. They didn't see me. When the conversation turned to business I hoped I might join in, but they were talking about a record fee Joe had earned for placing an engineer. Then I had my chance. Cold-calling came up as the one thing they all hated and complained about. "With my production, I can't believe Jim still hassles me about cold-calling. I have to report my calls every week like some schoolgirl. What does he care how many calls I make as long as the production is there?"

The other men nodded and agreed. They all hated cold-calling. "If I could make my production without cold calls, this would be the best business on earth."

I was scared, but I'd had it with being invisible! I said the most shocking thing I could think of: "Actually, I like cold-calling." The truth was, I didn't mind it, but I didn't exactly like it.

They turned and looked at me for the first time. I felt relief that no one said, "Do you work here?"

Instead, Joe said, "You're kidding! Nobody likes to cold-call."

"I do." As I write this, I can see myself standing there, feet planted and chin stuck out in Mama's I-dare-you pose. "It's my favorite part of the job."

If it started out as a brag, by the end of that day, I did love cold-calling! Suddenly people were looking at me. They knew I was there. I was some-body. "Hey, Ben, this is Ruthi. She says she likes cold-calling." I had a name and they knew what it was (not that they could spell it—even today I fight to get rid of that "e" on the end).

By the time the meeting started, I felt two inches taller.

The meeting went on and the vice president continued his "rah-rah" with announcements, plans for expansion, and congratulations for Ben's record month. Then he teased the guys about competing with Ben for the year's top producer award. No mention of the "girls" competing. That award wasn't even a consideration for women. So it was the award I wanted.

I recently read that the Washington, DC, region has more women CEOs than any other place in the country. Just thirty years ago that picture would have been almost impossible to imagine. I came along when it was okay to ask women job applicants about their marriage and baby plans. Women weren't considered for key jobs or promotions because, "after we invest in her, she will get married and leave, or she will get pregnant." Of course it was tough for young women to get secretarial jobs if even Justice Ruth Bader Ginsberg, after graduating at the top of her class from Columbia Law School, was turned down by major New York Wall Street law firms for the same reason.

We were the generation of girls who fought to become women. We were the women who demanded our right to decide for ourselves such personal things as if or when we would have children and how they would fit into, rather than end, our professional lives. Back then, when the first baby was born, we were supposed to stop working. (There's another one of those *supposed to*s.) And not just stop; we were supposed to *want* to stop, and that meant stopping just as we'd started to become productive at work. I rejected that rule way back on Petain Street. There was no way I was going to end my career just because somebody else said twenty-four or twenty-five was the age to marry and have a family, or believe that once I had a family I was done.

I made up my mind. I would beat the "professional" division's top man, but I didn't tell a soul. Daddy had told me, "Don't go bragging about what you're going to do. Why would you want to give them a warning? Go do it, then tell them you did it."

I won the trip to the Canary Islands that year, but it took one more year to take the top-producer position away from Ben and all the other guys in the professional division. Knowing I had won was fantastic. I was giddy with anticipation about the actual award ceremony. But when it got there, it was just okay. It was fun to be called to the stage one time after another to receive awards—monthly production awards, quarterly awards, office awards, division awards, and finally, AE (account executive) of the year award. The company president presented me with a real leather briefcase (my first) and a plaque. But it wasn't as exciting as I'd thought it would be. The only really memorable part of the day came afterwards, when Johnny came to pick me up. He took one look at me, my arms full of trophies, plaques, and briefcase, and said, "Ah, yes. Best-in-Show!" That was another reason I'd married him.

It had taken two years, but a *girl* finally beat their top producer, and they never beat me again. I would never be done building. I would never get to good enough, but I would get to better, then I'd get there again, and again!

It would have been nice if winning had relieved some of my anxiety, but it didn't. Once I won, I had to keep on winning. "You can't be number one once," was how my manager put it, and I didn't need to ask what she meant. I still lived with failure's threat every day. It hung over my head like a knife. Once I was up there, I had to stay there, or I would know I had never really been there at all.

When I let myself look at the big picture, or think about the perpetual battle to stay on top or the complexity of a job that had two clients to please, applicant and employer, with so many things outside my control, and all the things that could go wrong in any placement, it was overwhelming. Candidates and employers alike found more bizarre ways to blow deals every day, and I couldn't stop them.

There had to be a simple answer. There was always a simple answer. The answer was I could only control the actions I took. I looked at all of the things I did in my day and started at the most basic level, with cold calls. I had total control over how many calls I made. If I called enough employers, one would eventually hire from me. If I multiplied that number, I would find enough jobs to be successful. It was easy. Just decide how many calls I needed to make, then make them every day.

That was the beginning of my take-control-by-doing-the-basics philosophy for success. I set my minimum number of sales telephone presentations at thirty, and I made that number or more every day for the rest of my career. I never outgrew it. Every plan I made, even the plan for starting my own business, started with the numbers. It was all so simple. After all, it was just arithmetic. There was a number that equaled a success. Control the numbers and whatever happened in the market, my production was always going to be there.

The numbers became my goals and my benchmarks. I looked to them to know if I was on target for whatever production I wanted to hit, and they never missed by much. I tracked them, every afternoon, writing the day's calls on a chart I made on a gas station promotional calendar. Some days writing down the number of calls I made was the most satisfying thing I did. As time went by, I could see weeks of thirties, months of thirties, years of thirties! Such gratification! I'm sure I sound like a commercial for some hair-growing ointment—the one with the uptight little man claiming the benefit of the product in a nasal voice: "Cold-calling changed my life!" But it was true. It did. It gave me something I could control in a business where the unexpected often happened.

The 1970s and the '80s were fine times for cold-calling—no voicemails, no answering machines, not even faxes during much of that time. It was easier to reach the employer to make a presentation, and then go beyond that to get a job order or just make a connection and have fun talking with them.

I proclaimed myself the "Cold-Caller" just to get attention, but I really did like making the calls. It was a lot easier talking to strangers on the phone than to acquaintances face-to-face. They couldn't see me. Better yet, I couldn't see them. That made it fun because my imagination could take over. They could be anybody. I could pretend I was talking to Kenny, my childhood best friend—and I could talk him into almost anything. And I could talk. I could be funny. I could get *them* to talk. I could come out as myself on the phone, grab people, and make them like me.

This was what I felt when I was in high school plays. Of course, I was only in two of them because I froze at auditions. But once I was in character (one time as the grandmother and the other as a dotty aunt), I felt a rush that was better than anything. The phone became my stage, my Broadway, and I was the star. Every day I had at least a few calls that gave me that same rush I had when I connected with those audiences. It didn't matter to me one bit that some of the people I called weren't nice or that they hung up on me, because they hadn't seen me perform yet. I'd give them other chances to let me win them over.

In those days before automatic phone attendants, I had to get past a receptionist to get to the main event. The receptionists could be the toughest part, like the audition. Their job was to screen—to keep me off the stage.

One particularly tough receptionist took months to get past. I tried again and again and always got the same answer. No, I couldn't speak with the personnel manager. When she finally let me past, it had nothing to do with my talent. One day, in a hurry to get my calls made and get rid of a headache at the same time, I took an aspirin without taking two minutes to get water. My throat was scratched and by the afternoon my voice was a raspy whisper. I had to finish my calls so I charged on down my list until I came to the number for the receptionist-who-only-says-no. She answered the phone and I rasped out, "May I speak with Mrs. Thomas please?" A miracle happened. She didn't say no. She laughed and said, "Sure, honey, if you think you can." And she put me right through. Working in pain paid off in another of those little victories. I was in love with my career.

I was part of a generation of women who believed we could "have it all"—have a family and a professional career. I grew up with a woman who "had it all." Mama did. She had me, a career in the grocery store, she was a union leader, and a Sunday school teacher. She didn't make cakes for school bake sales, but she made my birthday cakes.

When I got sick at school and had to be picked up, mine was the only daddy who ever came. Half the time he took me to the doctor, because Mama couldn't always take time off work. Her job was important. She was head cashier at Devan's, and she cashed everybody's checks and counted all the money for the store until it balanced "to the penny."

I wouldn't find out what having it all meant for a few years. After the move to Washington and my new job, Johnny and I were happy for a while, until my career took off and I fell in love with my job as I never had with him. I had no interest in having children. I had what I wanted. Johnny deserved more. Finally, he left to find it.

I couldn't blame him. I didn't know how to be in love. Mama and Daddy didn't live as a married couple. They slept in different bedrooms and never, ever visited each other in the night. I grew up thinking it was normal that only on special occasions did my parents so much as peck each other on the lips.

I had great parents who raised me, not together, but separately. They worked different schedules, so they were really only together on Saturday nights and Sundays, and then Mama and I spent half the day in church. I did things with Mama and I did things with Daddy. The only things we all did together were Sunday dinners, trips to see family, and watching Richard Boone as Paladin on the "Have Gun—Will Travel" TV series and Marshal Dillon on "Gunsmoke" on Saturday nights. I don't think the two of them ever did anything alone together until I went to college.

When Johnny and I divorced, I was in my late twenties. I thought I would probably want to get married again, and maybe even have a family, but not yet. I had one more milestone to hit first. I wanted to earn $100,000 before I was thirty. It doesn't seem as huge a milestone today, but when the average salary for a teacher was $12,524, US Senators earned $42,600, and the president of the United States made only twice that, it was a huge victory, probably the greatest earnings victory of my career—to make more than the president when I was only twenty-nine years old!

I did it, and I was ready to think about getting married again. Actually, that's not true. I was scared of being by myself no matter how much money I had. I needed to be married for reasons I still held on to from another world. Marriage meant I was safe from dating and from being alone.

But I didn't want a marriage like Mama and Daddy's. I wanted a marriage like the ones I saw on TV, in shows such as "Father Knows Best." I had two notions of marriage, one from my life and one from TV. They jumped from nonmarriage to idealized marriage, but they did have one thing in common: no sex. I hoped there was something in between. Early on I'd decided the idea of being "in love" was just something poets and moviemakers made up. Sex was the only real part, and I guessed I wanted to keep doing it, but not if I wasn't married. That was something only bad women and rock stars did. It was a sin.

Sin was an important part of my life—not doing it, but worrying about it and trying to keep from doing it. Sex was one important reason to get married in the South in 1970, and it was one of the reasons I married Johnny.

But marrying him, for whatever reason, wasn't a mistake. Our marriage worked for nine years. Then it was over.

For years I'd had someone to hold me every night, and now I was single again, although this time I was single with money and security. I owned a house in one of the wealthiest suburbs in the area, and was earning twice what the president earned. You'd think I had the world by the tail, and would be in a place to have my pick of men. No. I was still the girl who didn't know what to do on a date if I couldn't quote poetry.

That's when I met Stuart. He was as handsome as I'd never thought Johnny to be. He was funny, he was a lawyer, and he was an easy conversationalist. He was also smart, well read, and amusing. Finally, he didn't move too fast and scare me away. We decided to get married.

It couldn't have been easy for Stuart to be married to me. In my mind, I had a fully drawn image of the man I wanted to be married to and I compared Stuart to him at every turn. Stuart couldn't win. Even his looks were a disadvantage. Because he was so handsome, I expected him to live up to my Cary Grant and Clark Gable (or Brad Pitt and Hugh Jackman) image. How many men can do that? He also didn't have Johnny's advantages of being my best friend and a rising star in television. Being an attorney for a government agency didn't come close.

We had several happy years. They were the acquiring years. With my personal life under control, I was free to focus on my career, and my income soared beyond anything I had ever dreamed. It enabled Stuart to leave the government to build his own successful law practice, but I was there for the years when he made next to no money. I didn't stay long enough to see him become successful.

Who made the money didn't matter, I thought. We had plenty of it and we used it to acquire things we thought mattered, the Tudor house on a hill, furs, jewelry, Persian rugs, and antiques. We had a lot of fun building the picture-perfect home where we "played life."

Stuart and I did one good and lasting thing together. We had babies. I'm not sure what I expected children to be, but they were better. I loved everything about being their mother. Sometimes I thought about how I'd said, "I never want to have babies." I pictured my eight-year-old self looking at me and thinking I was crazy to say I like my babies so much I wouldn't even care if they tore up my paper dolls.

Finally, I was really, truly movie-magic in love. My children enchanted me, grabbed me, wowed me every day as no other person ever came close to doing. No man ever said I was beautiful and made me feel as I did when two-year-old Eric held his hands apart to show me how much he meant it when he said, "Mommy, you are so, so, so beautiful," his emphasis growing with every "so."

Nobody was ever so deep as Alex, my philosophical three-year-old. "Mommy, how do I know I'm really here right now? Maybe I'm already grown-up and this is just a memory." And nobody surprised me as Joey did when I found him sitting alone, reading a very clever children's book aloud, when I was sure he couldn't read yet. I looked at the book. It was upside down. He came up with a pretty good story for a four-year-old. I can't wait to read the book he's writing now.

The birth of my children began the happiest time of my life, and the saddest. For the first time in my career, choices weren't easy. It took more than forty hours per week to earn what I needed to maintain our lives, but I resented any extra minute away from my babies.

This life cost money and I had to earn enough to pay for it. I alone had to pay for it all. I had to worry about money for the first time in years, and that worry changed how I felt about my job. For years it had been success, respect, or the fun of my job that drove me, not the money. Now that changed. Instead of doing my job for the thrill of it, I had to bring in money.

Instead of getting up and going to work excited, I started going in feeling trapped and deprived. It wasn't that I didn't want to work. I loved my job. I had to have that spark that work gave me. I had to have the challenge, the race. It was what made me feel alive, and I wanted to feel it again. I wanted to love my job again, and I wanted time for my boys. I wanted to have it all.

I didn't understand why I couldn't make it work out. I had always made things work out. I figured all I had to do was plan better and I could still produce, even if I didn't work seventy hours a week anymore. Pressure mounted from three sides. The first was from me and my own desperate need for time with my boys. Then there was the company that expected me to continue to build production as I had in the past. Finally, there was the pile of bills growing on the foyer table.

The house on the hill lost its charm as I struggled to pay for it. I didn't like the horsey country anyway. I hated being stuck miles from the city in a place where all there was to see was nature. The house and its sweeping lawns were more like a photo-op than an authentic home. I wasn't meant to be a suburbanite. I detested dealing with the problems of a house in the suburbs—lawn companies, septic systems, landscape that didn't weed itself, and carpenter ants.

Very little about that picture-book life worked for me. We met some people and had a social life with splashy Potomac parties we were obligated to attend, but after the first few, I hated them. I would rather have been home. All they did was talk and eat. I still wasn't comfortable with small talk, and they never played charades.

Stuart and I were still having fun going out, antiquing, and raising our children. But I started to resent him for not making more money. I didn't want him to support me. I'd have been insulted at the suggestion. I wasn't raised to depend on a man to support me, but I'd have liked it to be a little more equal. I don't know where I got such false expectations, but I had no idea it would take so long to build up to the practice he has today. I somehow thought he would—poof!—be a moneymaking lawyer in a day.

I didn't know how to give myself a break. When someone noticed me with the boys and tried to give me a pat on the back for how hard I worked, they heard back, "I'm not the one who has it hard. There are working mothers out there who have it ten times harder."

It was true. I did have it easier than most working mothers. Having a live-in nanny gave me freedom and time, but I quickly learned the danger there. Joe was only a few months old when I saw the first problem. Gloria was as sweet a girl as I could have wanted, and she clearly cared about my baby. She cuddled him, played with him, held him when he was sick, fed him, and sang to him all day while I worked. That was all wonderful—until the day he cried when I came home to take him. It broke my heart, and I wasn't going to stand for it. I made up my mind it wouldn't happen again. I would not have my babies think the nanny was their mother! I could do it. I could work, support us, stay number one, and still make sure my babies would know I was Mama. I just needed a plan.

My plan meant putting my life on a schedule. I assigned times to the key parts—work, children, husband. By getting creative, I made room for everything that mattered. I made a few decisions other people might have considered strange. For example, I planned to have more babies, but maternity leave had to go. I couldn't determine when my babies would be born, but maternity leave was another story. I could take it when I pleased. December was my least productive month, so that's when I'd have leave for maternity. I was healthy. I didn't need more than three or four days to recover enough after giving birth to get back to work. Alex and Eric were born in March and April. By Christmas, they were more fun to play with anyway.

I got creative with my work schedule too. Planning and thinking took at least two or three hours each day, and I traditionally did that after four o'clock in the afternoon. But my planning and thinking didn't have to be done then, exactly. With a little shift, I could give everybody the maximum attention. I would focus on my clients between 8:00 a.m. and 5:00 p.m. when they were available. Then, I would focus all of my energies on my children after five and on weekends. Planning and thinking could be done before the rest of the world woke up. I started coming into work at five o'clock in the mornings, when the boys were still asleep. It would work. I wouldn't miss a thing.

I must have been good at sales because I actually convinced other people to adjust to my schedule. "You're interested in the position with my client? Great. I can see you at five thirty tomorrow—that's a.m." There were plenty of people willing to drag themselves out of bed before the crack of dawn for our meetings. It worked.

My days, weeks, and year were scheduled to the minute. Every day, I left my office at the stroke of five—ten minutes earlier if I could manage it. I timed how long it took to get out to Potomac where I would grab my boys from the nanny. That schedule gave me nearly two hours to play with the boys before Stuart came home to join us.

The minute I came in, we ate whatever dinner the nanny had cooked, then we left her behind and went to my bedroom where they loved to jump on my bed. That's why I say I raised my children in my king-size bed. It was our playground where we played games, read Dr. Seuss, sang songs, and made up stories. With that huge house and grounds around me, much of our lives took place in that one room.

Whether through heredity or exposure, Joey, Eric, and Alex shared my sense of humor and taste for funny, quirky books and songs. We sang, "There was an old lady who swallowed a fly . . ." and "Bill Grogan's goat was doing fine, ate ten red shirts right off the line . . . " And, of course, we read poems, lots of poems, not just E. E. Cummings, but Emily Dickinson, Lawrence Ferlinghetti, Shel Silverstein, and Japanese haiku. They didn't run away, but stayed and listened. But then, they were just babies. They couldn't leave really.

That was my nightlife in the '80s. Whatever happened on TV from 1981 to sometime in the '90s was lost to me. We never turned it on. I also never used a stroller if I could avoid it. With too many hours away from them, I wanted to take advantage of every opportunity to hold the babies in my arms. It all worked—for a while.

My business soared for the next few years. A serious recession started in 1991, but I didn't know it; 1991 was the best year I'd ever had. For the seventeenth year, I got the award for being the top producer, but I got another award too, the best one I ever had. It was based on popularity! The newly created "Account Executive of the Year" award was not for production at all, but voted on by the staff, based on contributions to the office spirit and success of the team. I never even considered that one for me. Everybody knows the same person does not win Miss America and Miss Congeniality.

I was sitting in the awards ceremony and wondering what it would be like if they did call my name when it happened. The president called my name. I'm sure there was no one there who was as surprised as I was, just as I'm sure no one had any idea how much that award meant to me. It was just a silly foot-high cardboard star, painted silver, with my picture in the middle, and it was the best award I ever got—until 2010, that is. That's the year another staff award was voted. My company's staff nominated and voted RuthiPostowStaffing, Inc. into the *Washington Business Journal*'s "Best Places to Work."

My schedule worked, and worked, and worked, but not painlessly. As my kids got older, they needed more of me. At the same time, the market was tightening and pressures increased at work. Sometimes I felt I was living in a vise and the rigid schedule I created was tightening around me until I thought I wouldn't be able to breathe.

Thoughts were the enemy, thoughts and fears of what might happen, of where I might fail. One day stands out in my memory because my thoughts beat me. It was Saturday and the nanny was off. Alex, my third son, was three months old, and we had just moved to "the big house on the hill." I was standing in my perfect kitchen, surrounded by my little boys and my beautiful things. It was like a movie. I should have been so happy. But as I scanned the room, looked at the boys playing, then at Alex, gurgling and happy in his bouncy bed, a wave of panic came over me. I've heard people say a "wave came over them," and this really did feel like a wave overtaking and threatening to drown me.

The thought that brought on my panic was, "This is a house of cards, and I am the only thing holding it up. One little slip and it could come crashing down around me." The weight of just that thought was awful, but it got worse: "What if something happened to me? What would happen to my babies?" I leaned on the counter, feeling sick. I tried to bury scary thoughts as I did so many times in my career by telling myself, "Stop it! It doesn't help me to think about this." It was good advice, but that day it didn't do a thing for me. I leaned on the counter, cold, too scared to cry, frozen in fear and helplessness—and guilt. I felt guilty for things I didn't do and guilty for allowing myself to let the feelings take over, for feeling sorry for myself. There was no excuse! Other working mothers had it so much harder. It was a fact. They did. They might have excuses for letting the pressure get to them. I didn't. I had it easy.

When I was able to hold the bad thoughts at bay, and that was most of the time, I was happy. It was easiest when I was busy, whether I was at work or playing with the boys. With my mind engaged there was little room for the enemy thoughts to creep in. The dangerous times were when I was alone, and I faced alone time five days a week on my drive home from work—I don't know why the drive in wasn't so bad. Some afternoons, the minute I drove out of the office garage, sadness would surge over me and it felt so heavy I didn't think I could stand it. It took my breath away. There were times when I pulled the car off the street, lay my head on the steering wheel, and sobbed. I let my boys down; I let my business down. I let everything and everyone down. I cried because there just wasn't enough of me to go around. "I can't do this."

When I finally pulled myself together, guilt came, guilt from breaking down emotionally. I didn't have the right to have a breakdown, either. I had three boys to support and a job to do. I got myself under control, drove on home, and took the boys to my room to sing and laugh and revel in them. I buried those bad thoughts, until the next time.

I often thought about Mama. I wondered if she had felt the same things. Mama never seemed to think she missed anything, but she had to, I thought. Mama was a realist. She had to know she was paying a price. Every commitment to one thing takes its toll on others. She must have felt it too. She must have felt the pressure to be in two places at once.

The job that applied so much pressure also provided the big rewards. I was able to do special things with my children, take trips, horseback riding lessons, and put on spectacular parties with clowns and games. Even our simplest rituals cost money that wouldn't have been there without my job. One of my favorites was our birthday ritual. For each boy's birthday, I left the other two at home with their dad and took him on a special outing to a hotel where we ordered room service, used the spa, or went sightseeing. Then we ordered movies on TV and opened gifts, one of which was always a special book with a note from me. I pictured them saving both the book and note to rediscover and read again when they were grown. But I couldn't be sure.

My most vivid memories are of two kinds. They are divided between the special times with the boys and the times when I let them down. Whatever I did, they all grew up to be all I could have wanted them to be. They went to college and started their own careers. They are independent and interesting men. And, whatever I did or didn't do, they love me. They come home for Christmas. They argue with me, and try to straighten out my thinking. They use bad grammar just so I'll correct them.

Since graduating from college, Joe has dedicated his life to serving others. In his role supporting adults with developmental disabilities, he has earned a reputation for being a dedicated advocate who empowers people to achieve independence as well as professional success.

Alex is doing what he has wanted to do since he was little more than a baby. As Senior Recruiter at Ruthi Postow Staffing, he has established his name in the business community as the expert at managing complex searches for c-suite executive assistants in the most competitive markets in the region.

Eric is married to the beautiful and accomplished Katia, who speaks three languages and also manages to "have it all" by working fulltime, studying for her master's degree in finance and accounting, and being the mother of baby Maxim Nikolai Postow—all at the same time. After serving as a Marine Corps officer, Eric went on to law school where he was elected president of the Student Bar Association. He also found time to start a nonprofit organization dedicated to serving the community through benefit concerts. Eric continues to be a businessman, musician, philanthropist, philosopher, and poet. He sent me his journal—half prose, half poetry—of impressions of the heat in Iraq, his job, and his life.

When I read his journal, I thought about my life. I mentally listed the ways I had let my children down. I hadn't been as good a mother as I could have been. I could always have done more and done it better.

Then I read one sentence that said I didn't mess up too much. It said I had made a difference in his life. Eric wrote:

> I remember a trip for my birthday
> To a hotel downtown somewhere
> I received a book—
> And it is my favorite present ever—
> *Oh the Places You'll Go.*

That was the whole bag of marbles. I stopped and wrote to him.

Dear Eric,

I read your journal and I can't tell you how good it is. It's interesting, it's funny, it's dramatic, and it makes me cry. You'll see for yourself someday. You go along through life and sometimes you feel pretty good about yourself, and sometimes you feel guilty for all of the things you didn't do— although rarely for those you did do. Sometimes you get

awards and cheers. They're nice. But you question your decisions and worry that you let down your children and other
people you loved. Then, you hear (or read) something your
child wrote, something wonderful, just a sentence—thirty-
two words—and they matter more to you than all the honors
in the world because they were written by one of the three
most important people on earth, and they say you didn't
mess up too much, that you made a difference."

5

HIGH SCHOOL WAS
SUPPOSED *to* BE FUN

And a Job Interview Is a Lot Like a First Date

Aunt Pauline said high school was supposed to be the happiest time of my life. I hadn't been in high school a week when I was hoping she was wrong. I didn't want this to be my happiest time, because life ought to be better than this. And even if I'd liked high school, I would hate to think of myself peaking out at age eighteen.

I learned along the way that life was full of supposed-to-bes. High school was just one of them. People were always telling me how things were supposed to be, and most of the time they weren't that way at all. I was supposed to be happy and popular when I lost thirty pounds. I spent my junior high school years as the chubby kid; not the chubby life-of-the-party girl who compensated, but the chubby, insecure girl. It didn't make it any easier that my best friend, Delilah, was popular with everybody and looked like a Bobbie Brooks (the teen designer of the day) model.

As I was becoming interested in boys, I found out boys were not interested in me. I had crushes on a couple of boys in school and one in church, but they never looked at me. Actually, most of the boys never seemed to see me at all, and the few who did made me wish I were invisible. Those boys made me wonder how people learned to be mean on purpose. They knew just the names to call and words to use to hurt the most, and send me crying to the girls' room. The worst of them was a boy named Bubba. He tortured me throughout the ninth grade. What does a mean boy with a ridiculous name grow up to be? I can't be sure it's true, but I heard he became a psychiatrist.

Mama tried to convince me I was never ugly, but I knew. But then, the summer between junior high and high school something happened. I lost thirty pounds. I gave away my chubby juniors. Mama bought me sweater sets, cute skirts, and dresses with tight waists and full skirts. When I walked down the street, people looked at me in a different way. Boys in cars whistled. I loved it, but not as much as I loved looking at myself reflected in store windows as I walked past.

I couldn't wait for school to start so everybody could see me. But something happened between the last day of junior high and the first of high school that kept my great unveiling from happening. We moved away from Prichard. It was only thirty minutes away, just across Mobile Bay to Fairhope, but it may as well have been across the state. Fairhope was a much better neighborhood than the one we left on Petain Street. It was a lovely resort town on the bay, and much of its population was wealthy.

Aunt Pauline said I should be excited. It was my chance to meet new people, "better" people. I was excited about the beach and the town at first, but not so excited as I set out to find my place there. I left behind the neighborhood I grew up in. I left behind the kids I had known all my life and who were no better than I was. I knew how to talk with them. I knew who I was with them.

I also left behind the boys in junior high who were mean to me, and that was actually an awful consequence of the move. I never got to go back to see those boys, and show them. It's what I thought about every day as I saw my body changing and the fat melting away. Every time I looked in the mirror, I fanaticized about what I would do when I encountered those boys who never noticed me before.

They would see me and come over to me, with big smiles, "Hi, Ruthi." Then I would smile impassively at them, and say, "Do I know you? What's your name? You were in Mrs. Miller's class with me? I'm sorry, but I just don't remember you. Did you change something?" And for Bubba, I came up with meaner things to say every day, but never mean enough. Sadly, I never got to do any of it.

So the move brought one of my great disappointments. Instead of getting to stun the Prichard kids, instead of hearing those boys who ignored me say, "Wow! Hey, good looking!" and being able to dismiss them, I was beautiful for a bunch of kids who didn't know the difference, and didn't care, and whom I couldn't talk to anyway. I missed out on what I knew had to be one of life's greatest rewards, the chance to "show 'em" I wasn't ugly anymore; and I'm still not sure I'm over it.

In Fairhope, beautiful as I might have become, I still had worries—new worries. I had to meet all new people, and teenagers at that, most of whom it seemed to me were rich, or at least from that "better class." The whole idea was scary. I had enough trouble with regular people. What could I expect to happen with "better" people?

With every year, I became more self-conscious. As I met new people in Fairhope, that self-consciousness grew into something else—a feeling of separateness, in addition to that of being watched. For as long as I could remember, I felt as if other people were watching me. Now I started to have the sense I was watching myself. I would be in a group of kids, but somehow apart from them. It was strange. I knew I was there. I might even be talking, but at the same time, I had the strong sense of standing back, watching. I wasn't watching anyone but me, and I was judging me, measuring every word and gesture. "No. No," I'd tell myself. "That was stupid. She must think you're boring."

I didn't make it easy for the kids I met to embrace me. I was one of those people you meet and don't enjoy because they try too hard. It was uncomfortable. I didn't think I was trying to be someone I wasn't. But I suppose I was. It might have worked except I didn't know who that "someone I wasn't" was supposed to be.

Slowly, I made a few friends, but I was never comfortable in Fairhope or high school in general. But one thing I did develop after junior high was a sense of pride. No more crying in the girls' room. I wouldn't let them know I was afraid and miserable. I'd make them think I didn't care about them at all. I did the only things I could do. I stuffed my bra and walked down the halls, almost prancing, smile glued on my face, pretending I didn't notice anyone and I didn't care if I had friends or not. Using a smile as my armor must have worked even better than I realized at the time. A couple of years ago I ran into a woman from high school. I didn't remember her at all, but she remembered me. "I always noticed you walking between classes. You were just always so happy and friendly."

In high school, being one of the popular kids was about the most important thing there was. I hung around with popular kids, but I wasn't "in." Being popular meant more than the definition suggests. More than being "widely accepted and liked," it meant being "in" with the other popular kids. Unless they had really great personalities, the "in" group consisted of all cute people. I had lost weight and was cute. But that wasn't enough. You had to be cute plus something more. Maybe you were a cheerleader or majorette or member of the yearbook committee. I couldn't jump or twirl, and being on a committee meant going to meetings, and for me, even popularity wasn't worth that.

I'd gone to a meeting once and I didn't like it. It was a Brownie meeting when I was in the third grade. I went with my best friend, Sue. The girls wore brown dresses and hats; they drank orange Kool-Aid, and talked about projects to do, like building birdhouses out of Popsicle sticks. The next week Sue asked me to go again, but I told her my mother didn't want me to be a Brownie.

Not knowing anything about football didn't help when I lived in the middle of the high school football belt. I didn't know how to sail or surf either, and I was (deservedly) the last kid picked for a volleyball game.

Dating! It was supposed to be fun. To have a boyfriend who was a football player or basketball player or any boy from the popular crowd was supposed to be the best thing that could happen. Maybe it was. So far I didn't have a way of knowing. I was wondering if that would ever happen when, amazingly, Robbie, one of the most popular boys in school, asked me to go to a movie. I couldn't believe it. I called my girlfriends. All day we gossiped and giggled, we did our hair and our nails. I tried on everything I owned to pick the perfect outfit that would make me look thin and popular. The girls went home and I was on my own to wait for my date to start, and to get more uneasy by the minute.

What had I gotten myself into? What did I even know about this boy? He was in my French class. He was really funny. That's all I knew. Other girls were jealous that I was going out with him, which was reason enough to be excited. But I increasingly wasn't. What would we talk about? Would he like me? Would the movie be boring? Would he be boring? Would he talk too much? Not enough? Would I talk too much? (Probably.)

Nothing good could come of this. I was sure of it. Either he wouldn't like me or I wouldn't like him. When we went to the movie, I'd probably hate it. Whatever the case, I was going to have a miserable time. He was going to have a miserable time. The whole school would know what a bad dater I was, and they would all laugh at me.

About thirty minutes before he was supposed to pick me up, I begged Mama to tell him I was sick and couldn't go. She wouldn't, so I was forced to go out with this relative stranger who might either hate me or bore me to death. I decided this boy-girl thing would be better if we could start out married, find the relationship more and more fun, then finish with the first date when we could part and forget it all.

I went on the date and I had been right to dread it. The movie was *Village of the Damned*, a science fiction movie about scary, staring blond children taking over the world. It crawled by in black and white. It finally ended, and Robbie and I went for hamburgers. That was worse than the show. I felt a little sorry for him. We didn't have anything to talk about. He was into baseball, football, deer hunting, and beer. Sex was another of his interests, but that was totally against the rules unless you were really in love and had been going steady for at least a year, and that wouldn't happen unless I somehow got past date number one. This was the late '60s and the sexual revolution hadn't come yet even to big northern places like New York City, and it was decades away from the parking lot where we sat overlooking the big pier on Mobile Bay.

It's really sad that I remember most of my high school dates so clearly, not because they were exciting, but because they weren't. Boys asked me out because I looked like a thin, beautiful blonde, but what they got was a scared, fat kid in a pretty girl's body. I had a crush on a boy who was not only one of the most handsome, but one of the nicest boys in Fairhope. On our one date, I couldn't string three words together. He was polite. I was polite. It was awful. Today he lives in my memory only as Greg, the handsome boy who taught me how to inhale a cigarette.

But a lot of my dates were not even that good! My most memorable first-last date ended poetically. That is, I started talking about poetry. Did the guy have any interest in poetry? Please! This was south Alabama! He couldn't admit it if he did.

I knew I was doing the wrong thing, but I couldn't stop myself. I talked away at that poor captive date about my passion for E. E. Cummings. Then I quoted several poems to him. ("The little lame balloon man whistles low and wee and eddie and bill come running from marbles and . . . ") He must have been an exceptionally kind person. He said, "Ruthi, I don't think reciting poems is something you should do on a first date."

Poetry wasn't the only topic I could speak on. On other dates, I talked about my plans for my future. I found there was little that was more romantic to a sixteen- or seventeen-year-old boy than talking about career choices.

With my talent for making sure a first date would be a last date, I worried. What was going to happen to me? The time was going to come when I was "supposed to" get married. Maybe I wouldn't. I didn't necessarily want to go through my life alone, but I was afraid I would end up spending my life with some person with whom I couldn't have an interesting conversation—or worse, one with whom I couldn't even stand to sit through a movie.

By senior year, everybody who was at all cool was going steady, and maybe for the second or third time. I wasn't and it didn't look likely. To go steady, I would somehow have to manage to get a boy to date me more than twice. Finally, in the spring of my senior year, I did it! I met Jimmy and managed not to alienate him for long enough to be called his girlfriend. He gave me his high school ring to wear on a chain. I was actually going steady—for about three weeks.

Our break-up was caused by racial differences. I was excited about integration, and he wasn't. There were times, I'd been told all my life, to "keep your mouth shut and your opinions to yourself." I couldn't. I had a childlike belief that we were on the verge of a utopian world—one in which all races and cultures would live together in peace. My vision wasn't shared by a lot of people I knew. A couple of years before, my best friend, when she found me reading a book about Hinduism, snuck it from my bag and returned it to the library, lest my soul be lost.

Growing up, I had heard people use the "n" word, although not as often as you might think. Most of the Southern people I met didn't want to be cruel or crude, and my close friends were more curious about what having black friends would be like than they were bigoted. We were the generation who watched *I Spy* and were caught up in the Bill Cosby/Robert Culp relationship. The "n" word was already becoming uncool, and the person most likely to use it was a good ol' boy wanna-be with a cowboy hat and a six-pack. Anytime I heard the word, I would rage—inside. I wish I could say I always stood up to the people who said it, but I didn't. I was afraid. But that changed one Saturday night on a date with Jimmy.

The whole scene is as clear to me as if it happened last night. We sat in his car, on the bluff above the White Avenue Pier looking at the lights from Mobile reflected on the water. It was a Saturday night, a couple of weeks before senior prom, which made this one of my more significant *last* dates.

Jimmy said something about black people. I don't remember what, but it was mean, and he used *that* word. This time I told him what I thought in a way that was more sermon than sentence. I went on and on about how we *should* live. All people were created equal.

My lecture didn't move Jimmy to feel anything except disbelief and scorn. "You think 'they' should be forced on us? We have the right to choose the people we want to live around. The man who owns a business has the right to say who comes in and who doesn't. 'They' have their places and we have ours. What if I owned a restaurant and the government decided I had to allow dogs and cats in? I'd have to let them?"

I finally found the voice that would end more than one conversation and carry me away from more than one relationship. It conveyed an incredulous disdain and ended with dismissal. I rolled my eyes and said, "That is the dumbest thing I've ever heard. Are you trying to sound like an idiot on purpose? [I stopped myself before I said, "Please tell me you didn't think that up all by yourself, but borrowed it from a moron."] We aren't talking about animals. We're talking about people, dressed appropriately, polite, and with money to pay for their meals."

"Right! And that man would lose his white business because we wouldn't eat there."

"I would."

"I suppose you wouldn't mind having 'one' move in next door to you!"

The look on my face took over where my voice left off as I just stared at him for several seconds. "Of course I wouldn't. If we like the same neighborhood and can both afford to live there, then we have something in common. Actually, I hope I do have black neighbors."

"I just want you to know I'd never marry someone who thinks the way you do!"

"Are you crazy? I'm seventeen. I'm going to college next month. I'm going to have a career. I'm going to live in New York City. There's no way I'd marry you!"

I went to the prom with yet another first date—and a stranger—a friend's cousin who was home from college. I don't know what I did to him, but he never asked me out again either.

So I failed "first-date dating," but when I went looking for my first job, I learned that job interviews are a lot like first dates—but without the specter of "to kiss or not to kiss." (It's best if you don't.) I had my first interview when I was sixteen. That's when I found out I was just as bad at interviewing as at dating. I wanted to put my best foot forward, but I didn't know which foot that was.

I walked into the five & dime in Fairhope and asked to see the manager, Mr. Walker. On the application I wrote down my experience from the summer before when I worked for two Saturdays as a cashier in a grocery store. (My mother had gotten the job for me without an interview.)

Mr. Walker read the application and looked up. "Is this right? You were there only two days?"

I nodded.

"Why did you stop?"

"Because I hated it. It was awful trying to hit the right buttons on the cash register every time and then having to remember the prices for carrots and parsnips all at the same time with the line getting longer and longer. And I didn't even know what a parsnip was."

He was supposed to call me about the job, but he never did.

I got a lot more practice saying the wrong things and doing the wrong things in the six years between that first date and my last interview. When I met with Mr. Abernathy for the teaching job, I may have done a better job, or he may have been desperate to find one more teacher.

My last job search happened in Washington, DC. It was high school all over again—interview after interview, meet new people, try to say the right things, and try to fit in when I didn't know what was what.

Then it happened—my very last interview. I got the job and a career, one for which my past history should have made me totally unsuited. If I was awful at finding my own job, now I was going to help other people find jobs that suited them. To top it off, I would educate them on how to interview so *they* would get hired. At first glance, it didn't seem to fit me, but when you think about it, it was perfect. I already knew most of the wrong things to do. Just eliminating those was a big step!

Once I started, I discovered so many people needed me because they didn't know how to handle themselves on first dates any better than I had. Secretly, it felt good to find people who were even worse at it than I was. The more fantastic their mistakes, the better I felt about myself, and it was even better when they made mistakes I never made.

For example, I never once talked about bodily functions on an interview (or a date, or to anyone else for that matter). I always thought those things were supposed to be kept private. But I met quite a few people out there who were less uptight than I was, and things came out, especially when they got nervous. When I got nervous, I only quoted poetry. In my very first week on the job, bodily functions were an actual interview topic.

Donna, an office veteran having been there for two whole weeks, sent a young man to apply for a teller trainee job at the National Bank of Washington. After his interview, we gathered around to listen to Donna's follow-up call with Helen Dwyer, the bank's venerable director of human resources.

Donna was as smooth as you would expect of a two-week veteran. "Ms. Dwyer, Frank called after his interview. [Long pause met by silence.] You interviewed him?"

We didn't need a speakerphone to hear Ms. Dwyer. Her voice was a bassoon that rose emphatically on key words, or even syllables, then dropped a full octave or more as it advanced steadily onward. It dripped drama as she delivered the verdict.

"Ahhh, Donna . . . Yes. I had a lovely meeting with Mr. Smith. He was so very forthcoming. In fact, he shared with me, in great detail, all about his hemorrhoid*ecto*my." The word came out as music, every syllable distinct, building to a crescendo on the fourth, and the final syllable, a whisper.

Then there was silence—Donna didn't say a word. I don't think she was able to speak.

Mrs. Dwyer went on, "Donna, did you know that, after a hemorrhoid*ec-to*my, with the first bowel movement, the pain is tre*men*dous?"

I knew this was going to be a great job!

I was right. You never knew what would come next. I had an applicant blow her interview and get the job, thanks to her great-grandmother. Kendra had done well enough on her first interview to be asked back for a second meeting with the director of human resources, who was a stiff retired army officer. She really wanted the job, and she sought interview advice from me and from her grandmama.

She went in promptly at 2:00 p.m., ready to win that job! Yet I was surprised and discouraged when the director was already on the phone asking for me at 2:15 p.m.

I answered, "Hello. This is Ruthi. Kendra did come for her interview, didn't she?"

He sounded even more uptight than usual. "Yes. She was here."

"What happened?"

"Wellll," he said, as he drew out the word and then paused to take a deep breath. "She walked into my office and sat down, then she clapped her hand onto my desk and said, 'I claim this job in the name of Jesus!'"

"What did you do?"

"Well, I hired her."

When I spoke with Kendra, she said her grandmama told her, "Honey, if there is something wholesome and fine that you want, you just claim it in the name of Jesus and He'll give it to you if you're meant to have it." She did, and He did.

I threw myself into the work of matching up people and jobs, and fixing up people so they could present themselves well and get hired, but I learned there's God's work and there's my work. Once I thought I could teach anyone to interview. I was young. I learned. Candidates taught me. Jean was one of those candidates. She had excellent skills and experience, having worked ten years for one boss. I had met her boss and knew he was nasty and mean, even to his peers and clients. But he saved his meanest behavior for Jean. Still, she didn't quit. He finally offended the wrong person and was fired. Then Jean's job was eliminated.

Jean was brought to my attention by Jim, the organization's personnel manager, who called and asked me to help her. "I would like to see her get into a good job. She has lived with a nightmare. She's good. She's a little mousy, but she has the fastest typing I've ever seen. I don't know why she put up with him, but I can tell you she must be good. He went through secretaries like water before her."

Today, my alarms would go off at Jim's description of events. I would ask, "Why had she put up with it?" But not then. I brought her in for an interview. "Mousy" was an overstatement of her personality. Jim was right though—her skills were amazing—96 words per minute on my typing test (80 was considered excellent) with no errors. This was the day when typing speed was everything. Her personality didn't matter. I knew I would find an employer who would want her.

That very afternoon a client called us with a job that was perfect for her. They cared about one thing—typing speed. "I don't care what the personality is. I need a whiz typist—90 wpm or better. The salary is $9,000 per year [this was the 1970s], but I'll go up if I have to."

Perfect! I set up the interview and phoned Jean, full of enthusiasm. "Jean, I'm so excited! I have the perfect job for you and you have an interview today at four. It's an engineering company. They asked for the best typist we could find—and that's you. Be here at three and I'll give you all the details. They are so excited about you that you're the only applicant they want to see."

I was making a copy of her typing test to send with her on the interview when Jean called back. I answered the phone to hear her voice, so nasal and tense. I couldn't imagine working with her every day.

"I don't think I want to go to that interview."

"Why? It's perfect. The salary is even more than you were making, and they're so ready to hire you. All you have to do is show up."

I wouldn't have thought she could sound even more nasal and mousy, but she did. "I don't want to work there. If they are excited about me, they can't be a very reputable company."

I left Jean in God's hands and moved on to other candidates, ones who were willing to go on interviews whether the companies were excited about them or not and who didn't have Kendra's "in" with God. Those were the ones who could use my help, advice, and preparation to go meet employers and get the jobs.

I had the life experience to know the mistakes people might make, and I tried to anticipate anything that could go wrong, but just when I thought I was ready for every pitfall, some candidate would come along and create a new one. Even when I correctly anticipated a problem, I couldn't control people once they left my office. My world would have been less interesting if I could have fixed every problem. The most amazing things happened on or around interviews, things I never could have made up—sex, for example.

I never expected to encounter sex in the interview process (outside the books I read about Hollywood). But sex happened—and what shocked me even more was that people talked about it! It didn't happen all that often, but when it did, it was something to remember.

It was an average, everyday Tuesday afternoon. I was sitting at my desk when the phone rang. The caller was a woman I had sent to interview with a law firm early that morning. I was irritated that she hadn't called immediately after the interview, but, she told me, there was a good reason.

"I couldn't call you till I got home because I didn't have money for a pay phone. I was out of the interview and back at the garage before I realized I had left my wallet at home. I didn't have a cent with me to get my car out, and I didn't know what to do. I just stood there talking with the parking lot attendant about my problem. He had a little office in the garage and offered to help me work it out. At first I thought 'no,' but then I thought, 'Oh, what the heck? He's awfully nice.'"

It took me a few minutes to get what she was saying she did to pay her

$3.00 parking lot fee. Then I just sat there stunned. Even if I could have imagined myself doing it, I certainly couldn't imagine telling anyone I did it. Those moments that left me speechless made my days fly by.

I wasn't the only one with interesting applicants. My coworker Pat had Paula, a complex person who was explicit about her job needs, and about her reasons for leaving her current job after only two months. "I hate changing jobs so soon, but this job was a mistake from the beginning. The building is just too small."

This sounded as though it was going to be good, so the rest of the account executives stopped what we were doing to listen. It was one of those times we appreciated working and interviewing in one big bull pen.

Pat asked, "Do you mean you want a larger company?"

"No. I mean a larger building."

"I don't understand."

Paula took a deep breath before she answered. "Okay. You see, I have some needs. When I worked for Mr. Smith, the office was in a five-floor building. There were three partners with Smith and Jones, and three associates. Then there was an investment broker on the third floor and I spent lunchtime with him two or three days a week, and the engineering firm on five was the nicest team you could want. So you can see I had no problem. I was taken care of in the morning, at lunch, and on my three o'clock break. I loved that building. I would never have left that job if Mr. Smith's wife hadn't decided she wanted to come back and run the office."

She continued: "The building I work in now is not only small, just three stories, but it's suburban. There aren't even any other buildings around it. The first floor is a florist owned by a woman. The only other man in the building is sixty-five years old—not that he isn't sweet, but it's just not enough."

I don't remember whether Pat found a building appropriate to Paula's extraordinary needs.

Sex seemed to come to everybody but me. Over years and hundreds of meetings with men, only two ever suggested anything inappropriate. One was a mid-level manager with an insurance company. I called him several times to ask for his business. He was chatty as so many of the people were. On the third or fourth call, he asked, "Do you know how attractive you sound?" I thought it was odd because nothing led up to it, and even more so because of my voice. When I answered the phone at home, telemarketers generally asked if my "mommy or daddy" was home.

I know I laughed and said something goofy like, "I'm seventy-five years old and wear bottle glasses."

"I know that's not true. I'd love to take you away for a weekend. There is a Holiday Inn in Cherry Hill, just outside of Philly."

I didn't skip a beat. "Right. If I would go away with some man I'd never laid eyes on, and if I would go away with a man I met as a potential client, and if I would go to a hotel with that man, trust me, it would not be the Holiday Inn in Cherry Hill, Pennsylvania."

The only other man who suggested something other than business was an octogenarian. I went to meet with him about his need for an executive assistant. He actually chased me around his desk. I was impressed with his speed, but I escaped with whatever virtue might have been at stake, intact.

As I heard other women in staffing say men had hit on them, it kind of hurt my feelings. I was still cute—even better than I was in high school. During all of my years going to networking events and serving on committees for the Greater Washington Board of Trade, no hits. A couple of years ago, a young woman working for me took over the networking events and came back from every gathering with another story of one man or another hitting on her. I tried to reassure myself: "I bet they had hit on me too, but I was just too focused on business to notice." That, or maybe I really wasn't the pretty one.

Sex wasn't the only thing that happened around interviews that made for good stories. No matter how I tried, I could not anticipate all of the odd things candidates might do or say. When the phone rang in my office after an interview, I never knew what was coming. One of *those* calls came from Janice, the human resources director of Bendix Aerospace. This was a plum client and I sent someone who I thought would be a great match. I couldn't wait for the interview to be over. Then the call came. But instead of being thrilled to offer a job to my candidate, Janice was upset.

"I want you to know, I would never hire that woman!"

"I'm so sorry. What happened?"

"I give every person I interview a packet of information on our company. Even if I know I wouldn't hire them, I do it so they leave feeling good. Don't you think it's a nice gesture?"

I agreed. It was a nice gesture.

"Well, your applicant is the first who has ever refused to take the information. When I offered it, she flipped her hand up and said, 'I don't need it. I know Bendix makes refrigerators, and that's all I need to know.'"

Actually, I knew they were aerospace, but thought they still made refrigerators too. I kept my mouth shut—and I like to think I'd have taken the packet.

Remember the TV show, *The Twilight Zone*? People would move from what seemed a normal, even placid world into the surreal. A lot of my job took place there. That was where I thought I was when my client, a real estate developer, called me after he interviewed a potential assistant I had sent. He sounded stunned. "She turned the job down."

I blurted out the obvious question, "Why?" and he said, "We don't know. We thought the interview was going well. We talked about some of the projects we're planning. Then she said she could never accept a job here, and that she would never have even come on the interview if she had known what we do."

"I don't understand. I know the recruiter told her about the job and your company. He gave her your website. Let me call her and ask what happened."

When I reached the candidate, I asked, "Didn't we tell you this was a real estate developer?"

She said, "Yes, but you didn't tell me they cut down trees to do it!"

Some phrases never lead to anything good. Two of the worst are, "Did you know . . . ?" and "I just needed to be honest . . . " In my experience, "Did you know . . . " typically leads to something I should have known before but didn't, and didn't want to learn now. "Did you know he can't work our hours because by the time he drops his child off at daycare, it will be nine fifteen or nine thirty a.m. before he can possibly get to the office?"

"But he told me he worked nine to six at his previous job."

"Yes. But did he tell you he was always late?"—the question I failed to ask.

When a candidate coming out of an interview tells me, "I just needed to be honest . . . " it usually means he told the client something he had failed to tell me, that the something was bad, and it was told to the client I most wanted to impress with my thoroughness. "I needed to be honest with Mr. Jones. My family comes first. I know I'm going to want to take off for my son's soccer games."

"But aren't those games generally on Saturday when they won't affect Mr. Jones?"

"Yes, but I also like to volunteer in his classroom. The truth is I really don't want to go back to work. My husband wants me to go back to work. He says we need the money, but I really like staying home with my kids. Money just doesn't make up for the time with them, or going to their games and school parties. I thought it was only fair to tell Mr. Jones."

Another candidate, Beth, interrupted my client Nancy in the very process of making a job offer with: "Okay . . . I have to start at eight thirty every morning, right? Ummm—that means I need to leave my house at seven thirty and my daughter's bus doesn't get there till seven forty-five. I suppose I could ask my neighbor if Susie could wait the fifteen minutes at her house. She has a son in Susie's class. But if he's sick, I'll need to wait until she's on the bus. Actually, it's no problem. My ex lives a few blocks away and when he's in town, he can take her to school. Of course the parkway is one way that time of the morning—but that's fine. I'll just cut through the Roswell neighborhood. Yes. The commute won't be any problem at all."

Nancy listened. She was warm; she was sympathetic, even helpful. But she didn't finish making the job offer.

Why didn't their need to be honest overcome them when they were with me? I'm an open person. I listen. I can even be sympathetic. After a few experiences with this last-minute honesty, I started begging applicants before their interviews, "Please, if there is anything about you that you haven't told me, either tell me now or don't share it with anyone else."

No matter the level of the job, there seemed to be no end to the ingenious ways people could find to blow their interviews. Even when they managed to present themselves and their experiences well and avoid introducing problems, they could lose the job by involving the interviewers in their personal problems.

My daddy told me when I was just a kid, "Baby, if you don't want your boss minding your personal business for you, keep your mouth shut about it." I passed along Daddy's advice to just about every candidate I met, but not all took it.

When I heard some of the personal things candidates told interviewers, I wondered if they actually wanted the jobs or were simply trying to sabotage themselves. Or maybe they thought of the human resources manager as a counselor who could solve their life's problems, if only they shared.

Sometimes an interviewer can see that a candidate is going down a road that leads to a bad end and will try to take it in a different direction. But some people can't be stopped. Ms. Akins was ready to hire Charlotte halfway through the interview when the conversation took a bad turn. Charlotte volunteered, "My husband turned our divorce into a nightmare—forcing me to come back to Philadelphia every other weekend."

Ms. Akins tried to help her out. "So now that you're through with all that, you're ready to carry on with your career. Let's move on."

But there was no stopping Charlotte. "I hope it's done, but I just know him. He will probably keep on calling me and bothering me at work day after day after day. I dread it."

The unfortunate thing about Charlotte is she would have done a great job for that employer. The man she worked for during the divorce had already told me she never missed a day of work or did anything to disrupt work no matter what she was going through.

Some people can't be let off the hook. Charlotte's story reminded me of a boy I dated in college. Larry was a first-string basketball player at the University of Georgia whom I dated twice, of course, but this time it was my idea. We just didn't have things to talk about and ended on a friendly note.

A couple of years later, I ran into Larry on campus between classes. We sat on the chapel steps and chatted. He said he was doing great. He had a serious girlfriend, and he had just pledged Kappa Rho fraternity. I remembered that one of our dates had been to a fraternity party, but it wasn't Kappa Rho. "Weren't you in Theta Chi?"

"I was," he said, "but Sally Lindstrom—she's my girlfriend I told you about—Sally had slept with most of the guys in Theta Chi and had a bad reputation. She didn't like going to their parties and seeing guys she's had sex with, so I depledged and joined Kappa Rho."

I tried to stop him. "Larry, I didn't need to hear this. If you didn't tell me, I wouldn't know anything about that part of Sally's life. Now one more person knows. Do you get what I'm trying to say? You're making her reputation worse."

"Yeah. But she did sleep with all the guys in Theta Chi!"

There are a lot of good jobs, but few truly exceptional job opportunities. Giving a candidate the chance for a position that could make a difference in his or her life was one of the best things about my job. When they blew one of those interviews, I wanted to say, "How could you have done something so stupid? You just blew your chance to have the best job in town." But that is exactly what *I* had done a few years back.

Before I left Atlanta, I had a chance for a job I believe I would have loved doing in public relations for the state's Department of Transportation. I even had a referral from Bert Lance who was head of the department. I'd get to meet all kinds of people, coordinating meetings for visiting dignitaries, and I would actually get to go with them.

My first interview was with the state's recruiter, and it went well enough to get me a second one with the director. In fact, the recruiter said she thought the job was mine. But my meeting with the director was a different experience. She fired off questions and I was in high school all over again, intimidated, afraid, and without answers.

I can imagine her feedback to the department head. "Why did you think Ruthi could do this job? She is barely articulate, but jabbered on and on in spite of it. And she didn't have a clue about what work would be involved."

That wasn't true. I did know the job. I knew I would be spending 90 percent of my time behind a desk, making calls to schedule appointments, arranging meetings, and creating itineraries. I just couldn't put it together for that woman. With every question, it got worse. Her last question was, "What do you picture as the ideal job for you?"

I masked my fear with bravado. "I think it would be fun to be Miss America and ride around in the parades and wave at people."

Okay. I have to give even me a break. It's easy to falter under the pressure of an interview and to allow the situation and the person to bring out the worst in you.

Taking tests is something that brings out the worst in a lot of people, but it's something that has to be done in administrative staffing, from the typing tests of the 1970s to advanced software tests today. Nobody likes them, but some people self-destruct. Some simply refuse to take them. Others complain about them. Some fight back at technology, and that's harder to beat than city hall.

One young man, angry that he was asked to test, decided to compose his own test rather than follow the script. His test read, "This test is xm2@#% b%&$#. These people are %^&&E idiots who don't know what the @$%^#k they're doing, and . . . " The recruiter was kind of sorry the man had shown himself to be such a—whatever—because he passed the test at 60 wpm with 98 percent accuracy. I assume he didn't realize the recruiter could read every word he typed.

After all these years meeting people, learning about the mistakes people make, teaching them to interview, you would think I finally mastered the art of the first date. But no, I didn't. My last opportunity was fifteen or so years ago. It was a blind date. We went to a café and hadn't been seated long enough to have water on the table when the president (of the United States) appeared on the television over the bar. I didn't even hesitate a second before opening my mouth to express my opinion, and that was the end of that.

6

TIME IS *a* PRECIOUS THING

Waste Some of It!

Summers on Petain Street went on forever, and afternoons were long, and I was free. I had time to waste, time to let my mind soar, time to wonder. I was curious about people, not just what they were like, but about what made them that way and what they did behind the walls of their houses. Houses held all kinds of secrets. I knew it, and I wondered what they were.

Our family vacations meant riding in the backseat of our Plymouth for hours on the long drive from Mobile through Alabama, Texas, Georgia, and Florida to Granddaddy's farm in Quincy, to Aunt Lizzie's house in DeFuniak Springs, sometimes even all the way to where Grandmama lived in California.

We did a lot of our driving at night, and we passed hundreds of windows that glowed yellow in the black night. Mama liked to drive at night because she only had one week of vacation from the grocery store, and she said, "I'm not about to use up a whole day of it driving." Even if we couldn't leave at night, we got up and left two hours before sunrise because our car, a ten-year-old brown Plymouth Savoy, didn't have air conditioning, and wherever we were going, the roads we traveled were hot and steamy.

As soon as Mama got home from work and changed out of her store uniform, we packed the car with cold fried chicken and biscuits and started off, Mama driving. Mama always drove. After two or three hours, we stopped at a gas station for Cokes and ate supper by the side of the road. Later, when she was too sleepy to drive, she would find another gas station and ask the owner if we could park in back, and we would sleep.

On those trips, when it was too dark to read or play with my paper dolls or my Colorforms, all I had to entertain me were the houses we passed—houses with windows lit so they were gold and warm and friendly. I wondered about the people behind the windows. What were their lives like? When we slowed down in towns, I strained to look in, to see if there were books on shelves, whatnots on mantels, or brown photographs in oval frames hung high up on walls. I wondered what the people were doing—if they were watching TV, eating supper, or talking. Did the house smell like the apple tarts they had for dessert? Or were they waiting for relatives to arrive for a visit?

I wondered if we stopped and went in, would it be like going into the houses of Grandmama Simmons, Granddaddy Richards, or Aunt Lizzie? When the door opened between black night and golden light, what would the people be like? Would they tell old stories about the family and laugh? Would they be mad at some uncle and call him a liar? Could I touch their things and ask questions? What smells? What colors? What sounds?

In every house on Petain Street, I learned there were stories and people who wanted to tell them to me. When I was nine years old, I spent my fall and Indian summer afternoons selling birthday cards, Christmas cards, and all-occasion boxed cards for a school fundraiser. We had the freedom of safety then and I went to every one of the shotgun clapboard houses that lined Petain Street, even some of the ones on the really poor end. Most of the houses looked just alike because they'd been built by the paper mill and sold off after the war. (I don't know which war—Grandmama always dated things by "before the war," "after the war," or "after Papa died.")

The neighbors who were home in the afternoons were mostly old people who lived alone and a few women who couldn't work because they had little kids; and they all seemed happy to let me come in. We would sit on chairs that had crocheted doilies on the arms and they would look through the cards, ooh and aah at pictures of Christmas trees in snow, or flowers spread on beds of taffeta and lace. "Doesn't that look just like a Christmas window at Gayfers [the big department store in Mobile]?"

They would look at the cards and launch into stories. "This looks just like the puppy we got for Sam. Sam's daddy put him in the laundry basket and I tied a big red bow around it. Sam was my oldest son. You never met him—he was gone before you were born. Here, look at this card with the tree in the window. It reminds me of the tree we had the Christmas before Sam went away. He loved Christmas trees, and the bigger the better. That year he turned seventeen, he worked all summer to buy an old Ford. He came in with that tree tied to the top and it was so tall we could have made two of it, but he got it in here and put it right there, in front of the picture window. It filled the window so you couldn't see out past it. Every night Sam would stand outside and stare in at the lights that filled up the window. That was the last Christmas he was here." I was dying to ask where Sam had gone, but she was so sad that I was afraid she would cry. But I wasn't always so self-controlled when it came to things I shouldn't ask questions about.

Some people had secret stories they never told me, and you couldn't tell from the outside who had the sad secrets. I never expected anything sad at the Webbs' house. Mrs. Webb was always so sweet and her house was the richest house on the whole street. Mr. Webb had redone the front, adding fancy brick trim, and had planted two real palm trees. He put in a big picture window with shelves where Mrs. Webb displayed a hundred little glass animals and snow globes. One night Mama and I were there for a visit. Mrs. Webb had a fresh apple pie. While I was waiting for the pie and looking at her snow globes, I heard Mrs. Webb say something to Mama about still searching for Buddy and another soldier turning up alive after all these years. We had been neighbors with the Webbs for as long as I'd been alive and I had never known a Buddy. "Who's Buddy?"

Mrs. Webb said, "He's my oldest son."

Mama made a face and shot a look at me, meaning to hush me up. Of course I didn't hush—I was eight years old. I asked where he went and why I'd never seen him. Mama grabbed my arm; it was time to go—no pie. When we got home, she told me I was not to interrupt grown-up conversation ever again. But I had not gotten all my questions out and I was too curious to be stung by her scolding. "Well? Did you know she had a son named Buddy? Why didn't I ever know him? And what's an unknown soldier?"

As I sold my cards up and down Petain Street, it happened the same way pretty much all of the time. People talked and told me all about their lives, and sometimes bought the cards. But my best friend Elizabeth told me I was doing it all wrong and I wasn't going to enough houses. She was in my class and was selling cards too. She said I was wasting time. I was supposed to stay at the door, show the cards, get the two dollars a box, and go to more houses.

I didn't care if she thought I was doing it wrong. Maybe sitting and listening to people and asking questions wasn't her kind of selling. But I liked going in their houses, and I liked listening to the stories, from where their children lived to how they made doll bridal bouquets from the little white flowers growing along the fence when they were little girls. So what if she thought I wasted time? So what if I didn't sell right? Not everybody bought, but all my cards got sold and I had to get more boxes! Elizabeth didn't have to get more boxes.

I kept right on listening. Some people told me funny stories about when they were young. Some told me stories about things that made them sad. Sometimes they told me secret things, things I thought they were ashamed of. One lady told me how her son had gone off and got a girl "in trouble." (I wasn't sure what "in trouble" meant. It was a different time.) And she never even got to see the baby now that her son was in jail.

I knew we had some secrets in my family, but I didn't know so many other people had secrets too. And I kept their secrets. Except for the few things I had to ask Mama, I never told anybody the things they told me, not even Grandmama.

That fall, selling cards was giving me the best experience I could have for the career I would find in staffing more than a decade later. I was learning that the greatest part of selling is listening. In staffing, people were going to be my job. I would talk with them all day. It was just like Petain Street! People wanted to talk to me, wanted to tell me stories, and secrets. I listened. If my Christmas card selling was wrong, I'd be "selling" wrong for the rest of my career and being successful at it. Imagine what Elizabeth would say to that! I got everything I wanted as career waster-of-time on people.

As I went through my career there were some people with whom I "wasted time" for selfish reasons, because they couldn't pay me, only enrich me. It didn't seem to hurt me because the money flowed in from other people.

Leon was one of my favorite people. He walked into the office one day without an appointment when I was next in line for a "walk-in." The receptionist came into the back to tell me the guy I had to interview was scary. Leon, even sitting down, looked seven feet tall. He had huge hands and arms, but his face had an earnest, innocent look about it. I walked him back to my desk, and the other girls in the bull pen looked uncomfortable. But Leon didn't scare me.

I saw that he was having trouble filling out the application, so I told him we could do it together. He could tell me what he had done before and I would write notes. He had played football, but he couldn't play anymore because he had been hurt. "I went to the UDC [University of the District of Columbia], but it didn't work out."

What had he been doing since? "I've just done a few jobs here and there. I live with my mother, and I help her around the house. I cook dinner and sweep. I keep it real clean. But I need to find steady work because she's getting older, and I want to take care of her." He beamed when he told me how he helped her around their house.

I had to help him—but I couldn't place him in an office job if he couldn't write the answers to questions on an application. We needed to build on something else. What had he done around the house to help his mother? "I sweep. I keep the floors real clean. And I cook. I can make stew, and chicken and dumplings, collards, whatever we want to eat."

"Leon, you can get a job that will pay you to cook and clean. I don't have that kind of job, but I'll tell you how to get it. Let's make a list of places you should apply."

"I already went to a lot of places, but they didn't hire me."

"Don't worry. We'll go over what you need to do. You will probably have to write an application." I took a new application and had him write UDC for education, write his mother's name for last job, and for "duties," write "cook, wash dishes, clean."

I thought about the local restaurants. Hot Shoppe was a chain of family diners. They served pretty basic foods; I thought he could help cook, and there was one nearby. They would be likely to need kitchen help. We came up with a list of other places he could apply, if the Hot Shoppe didn't hire him. Finally, we practiced how to ask for a job, and he went on his way. I never expected to hear from him again, but Leon's mother raised him to be polite. Two days later, he called. "I got the job! I'll work in the kitchen and clean up and the boss said if I do a good job, he'll let me cook." He called again when he started cooking.

I didn't hear from Leon again for a couple of months. Then one day the receptionist buzzed me. She was new and hadn't met Leon. With a quavering voice she said, "There's a man out here who doesn't have an appointment but says he has to see you. His name is Leon. Please come out." I came right out to get him, and he grabbed my hand. The receptionist looked pale.

"Leon, it's good to see you. How are you doing?"

He sagged and hung his head, "I'm not doing so good. Will you help me get a new job?"

"Why? What happened to your job at Hot Shoppe?"

"I don't work there anymore."

"What happened? You were so happy there."

"My boss was mean to me."

"And you quit? You go right back there and tell him you were wrong to quit."

"I can't. He was mean to me and I had to hurt him."

"Leon! You can't do that. You're too big. You could kill someone, and then you'd go to jail and who would take care of your mother? Have you told her?"

"I called her. That's what she said, too—not about taking care of her, but she said it would break her heart. She said to ask you to help me and tell you I'll never do it again, no matter how mean anybody treats me."

"Okay. Let's list some places you can go to find a new job. Before you do that, I want you to call your old boss and tell him you're sorry. Tell him you don't expect him to give you your job back, but you know you were wrong. Maybe if anyone calls him, he won't say too much."

"I can go back there right now and tell him."

"No! Don't do that." I could just imagine how much he would scare the man if he showed up. "Just call him."

After we went over interviewing tips again, I walked him to the elevator.

On the way, I told him, "Leon, I'm really sorry, but you can't come here anymore. I can help you twice, but I can't do it again. It's a rule and I'll get in trouble. But I'll be rooting for you."

When the elevator, full of people, opened, I was saying, "Leon, I want you to promise me you won't hurt anyone ever again." I led him in by the hand, and watched as the doors closed.

I lied to Leon about getting in trouble if he came back again. My manager agreed with Elizabeth about my tendency to waste too much time on people, but by the time I met Leon, however much time I was talking to people, something was working. I was breaking production records.

That was the secret. Have enough success and I could waste all the time I wanted. I remember reading a quote somewhere (I think it was Otto Preminger), "Success is what you have to have so they will keep letting you do what you love to do." I had success so I could talk with more people, which meant more success so I could talk with more people and . . .

There were plenty of people who just seemed to be waiting to talk to me. Some wanted to ask me for advice, even if they wouldn't take it. Some needed a laugh, and I could provide that if only by the mistakes I made. But most just needed me to shut up and listen.

If I was surprised at the things neighbors told a nine-year-old, I was amazed at the things these people—often strangers—told me as an adult. Whether on cold calls or after we'd developed a telephone relationship, people told me without reservation or excuse the most private details of their lives. Vice presidents, human resources managers, executives, office managers—most of them twenty years older than I—confided in me. It was a sort of confession for business people. They told me about fights with wives, husbands, children, about abusive brothers-in-law and sisters who wouldn't get out. I heard the gory details of divorces, stories of horrible stepchildren or in-laws, and their desires and regrets. I didn't know how to respond—which was a good thing because they weren't looking for my ideas. It occurred to me that the only words I needed to be successful in this business were "Really?" "Wow!" and "You're kidding."

I never knew when a conversation with a client would turn into a great story. One ordinary day I was sitting at my desk, hardly aware of the smoke that filled the bull pen from the cigarettes that burned in ashtrays on eight out of the ten desks (it was the '70s), phone receiver in my hand, listening to the person on the other end tell me about a job we needed to fill. The speaker was the vice president of a prestigious bank and one of my biggest clients. She stopped in the middle of the description and asked, "Oh, did I tell you about the new board member? I've decided I'm going to have an affair with him."

"You're kidding!"

"Absolutely not! I was waiting to talk with the CEO when he came in, and the minute I saw him I was turned on."

"Really?"

"It may take a bit of doing—he's married. But it will happen."

"Wow."

I thought I was pretty sophisticated—after all, I'd read *Playboy*. I really had no idea how naive I actually was. Some of these revelations left me feeling more like the cartoon character Little Annie Fannie in *Playboy*. She went from one outrageous sexual situation to another with absolute gee-whiz surprise. This bank vice president was planning to seduce a married board member? "Wow!" Married people were having sex with people they weren't married to? "Really?" And talking about it to a relative stranger, someone she was doing business with and would have to face again? "You're kidding!" Maybe this kind of thing happened in Washington, but I was pretty sure it didn't happen on Petain Street.

I wondered, "Why did they tell me all of these things?" Maybe it was because they thought I had a sympathetic voice, but I didn't think it was all that sympathetic—I sounded like a five-year-old. I thought it was more likely because the phone provided a kind of anonymity. But their revelations didn't stop after meeting me face-to-face. Maybe it was just because I listened, with my only occasional comment being, "Really?" Or because I didn't know them well enough to tell anyone, or that I heard them out and didn't add a one-up story of my own, saying, "You think that's a good story? I have one that beats that."

Not all of my conversations were about sex, thankfully. I had people talk to me about serious problems. There were some who told me stories so painful I wondered if they didn't have friends who would be better confidants. I'm sure they did. But I realized there are some things we can only tell strangers because we don't want our friends to know.

Mr. Singleton was a new vice president of human resources with one of my largest clients. I had only been working with him a month or so when we got into a conversation about a headline in the morning paper, the legalization of marijuana. I don't know how or when it went from one of those innocuous discussions about a headline to an emotional story. I don't even remember what I said, but it must have been something about the article indicating that pot was harmless. I didn't know enough about it to have an opinion.

He snapped, "There is nothing harmless about it! I hope you've never tried it." The truth was I never had. In my first couple of years of college at Georgia, we were behind the times and I didn't even know anyone doing drugs, so it wasn't an issue. When it started popping up, I was too afraid of getting "in trouble" to go near it. ("In trouble" was a threat that always kept me straight. Thinking back, I wasn't even clear what it meant, but it sure sounded ominous.)

"Good. You stayed away from it. Just you don't let anyone tell you marijuana isn't addictive. It is, and in some people, it can trigger a psychotic reaction. I know because that's what happened to my son. He got into a group of boys who used it and they talked him into trying it. He was just fourteen when he started. By the time I knew what he was doing, it was too late. He's been in and out of institutions for most of the last two years."

This man was a forty-something vice president of one of the city's most important commercial real estate firms. He was a former Lutheran minister. He had a background in counseling and he was talking to me, a kid. I was twenty-something and single. I didn't have any children. It was a good thing he didn't want answers from me because I didn't have any.

A few weeks later, he talked about his son again. "My son's counselor called. He said he's encouraged by Andy's recent progress and he expects him to be able to come home again in a week."

I said that was wonderful, but he hadn't sounded wonderful.

"I know this is a terrible thing to say, but I don't want him to come home. He made our lives such nightmares. I just wish they would keep him."

In his case, I understood why he would talk to me rather than a friend. I couldn't imagine a father admitting something like that to his family or to a neighbor, even a minister—anyone he would have to face every day.

What could I say? "I know it must be awful to feel that way."

I didn't tell Mr. Singleton, but I knew something about drugs that would keep me away from them. I knew drugs meant you had to take shots. I hated shots. When I was little, my granddaddy had a wooden box on the breakfront with his medicine in it. I wasn't allowed to touch it. Granddaddy took it down every morning, afternoon, and night. It had bottles and cotton and a shot needle. He wiped his arm with cotton, filled the needle from the brown bottle in the box, and gave himself a shot. I heard Daddy tell people it wasn't Granddaddy's fault. "It was that damn doctor's fault." I didn't know what Daddy meant by "fault." Later I found out doctors had, at one time, thought morphine would help heart conditions. They gave the morphine to Granddaddy, and he got addicted to it. Then they decided it wasn't a good thing and wanted to take him off of it, but by then he couldn't stop because his heart wouldn't stand the strain of withdrawal. So Granddaddy's shots were just part of his everyday life, and just another part of my life when we visited him. I knew I would never do anything that made me take a shot three times every day.

Granddaddy lived to be close to ninety. Several times the doctors would say, "This is it. Come say goodbye." But he lived right on through each time. I remember one time we went to Greensboro to find the farmhouse filled with family and friends. I was five and Mama sat me in the parlor and went back to the kitchen to help warm up the food friends had been bringing all day. People from one of the evangelist churches were in Granddaddy's room. I could see them through the open door. Then they started praying and yelling. I had never seen anything like it. I thought they were screaming and raving so because Granddaddy was dead. Then I started my own screaming and crying. One of Mama's cousins, a stout peanut farmer with a lisp, and one of the sweetest people ever, grabbed me up in a strong hug and took me from the room. When she finally got me to Daddy, I calmed down enough to tell them my granddaddy was dead. She hugged me again, and Daddy too. "Honey, don't you be afraid. Your granddaddy's not dead. Those folks are praying for him. That's just how they talk to God because they think God's hard of hearing."

Mr. Singleton was just one of the people I met who had something in common with Granddaddy and with me. To look at them, you would never guess the loads they carried, just as you would never have guessed this old man, a Baptist preacher who read his Bible every day, would be a drug addict, or that the Webbs back on Petain Street, who had the best of everything so far as I could tell, lived every day with great sadness. To look at me, you wouldn't know I was afraid all the time, of everything. I was afraid all I had would go away if I took vacations or slowed down for a minute. I was afraid I was always being judged. I was afraid people wouldn't like me if they really got to know me. Maybe that's one reason I spent time listening to other people's stories, so they wouldn't learn mine.

Sometimes I had serious objectives for a meeting, and listening to personal stories was not what I wanted to be doing. But they came just the same. I had a lunch meeting with the new regional head of my largest client. It was important to impress him because he was in a position to decide whether his company would keep working with me or change to another service. We were in the recession that followed the real estate crash of the '90s, so I needed his business. We went to the restaurant at the Mayflower Hotel, and over Caesar salad, I opened with an innocuous question about his move to Washington. But his answer went in a direction all its own. He said he really hadn't wanted to move. He was sad to leave his home in Rhode Island, an eighteenth-century shingled farmhouse with four fieldstone chimneys, a columned porch, and a view of the Narragansett Bay. It had been in his family for four generations. He clearly loved his home. The only reason he left was because the best school in the country for his son was in this area. His son was autistic.

I had read a little about autism, just enough to know that at that time it was considered quite hopeless. I didn't know where to go with this, but ventured, "So there is a good chance they can help your son?"

"They don't have a cure, but there have been some breakthroughs at this school. It's a terrible disease. My son was perfect when he was born, perfect and beautiful. Then he didn't respond to us as he should have. We took him to doctors who couldn't find anything wrong with him. But we knew something was wrong. Finally they diagnosed him as autistic." He spent the next half hour telling me about his son, about going from doctor to doctor in hopes of a cure.

"It must be hard for you and your wife."

"You can't possibly imagine. My son is a beautiful little boy." He took out a picture. He was right. "I want to hold him or cuddle him and I can't. He won't let us touch him. There is no way you can understand how heartbreaking it is to have this beautiful, perfect boy, who can't say or even understand the words 'I love you.'"

I couldn't wait to get home, hold my boys, and clean up their crayon marks on the walls.

When my boys were eight, ten, and twelve, I had another conversation that sent me running out to Potomac to grab them up again, and hold on for dear life. This one was with a tough union man. I only knew him through the few sales phone calls I had made to him. Actually, he rarely took my calls. But one day he did. I asked if he had a position available for a secretary I was representing. He said gruffly, "We don't need anybody."

Then out of the blue he said, "Do you have children?"

I told him I had three boys.

"Well, then, you tell them to stay away from construction sites."

I didn't think he was making a joke, but I didn't know, so I waited.

"Tell them those places are dangerous. My boy was hanging out with his buddies, around where there were concrete pipes stacked up to go into the new sewer lines. The boys climbed on them and they started to roll. My boy was crushed."

His voice was tearless and flat and horrible. "I should have been watching him. I should have been there. I should have told him to stay off them. They shouldn't have left those pipes stacked that way—they should have put up a fence. My son was fifteen. He was dead before the paramedics got there. You tell your boys." He never took one of my calls again.

I don't know why, but I'm able to listen to people tell me stories that I can't stand to watch on television or read in the paper. I turn the TV off when any mention is made of hurt or abused or sick children. I can't shake the images for days. But when I'm with someone who needs to talk, I'm able to listen, and let it go afterwards.

I never know when a meeting will bring me a personal story, even when that meeting is only supposed to be a handshake and a nice-to-meet-you. Recently, a client came to our office, not to see me, but to see the business developer. As a courtesy, she brought the client to my office to meet me. I expected it to be a couple of minutes for a handshake and thank-you-for-your-business chat. But the client needed to talk. After we shook hands, he didn't leave, but took a chair by my desk. I sat too. The business developer went out to delay their lunch plans.

He asked how long I had been in business and we talked for a few minutes, then without warning he said, "Did you follow the news last year about the fifteen-year-old girl who disappeared from her home in Maryland?" I didn't remember it, but I said I thought I'd heard about it.

"That was my daughter," he said. And then the client—this father—talked to me for a full twenty-five minutes. He talked about his daughter, her straight As in school, her troubles, her disappearance, and the manhunt. It was all over the news, he said again. Then they found her dead. She had killed herself. When the business developer came to my office door to retrieve her client, I held up a finger and she closed the door.

He didn't need me to say much. He had a lot more to say. I just said it must have been so awful for his family. He went on to tell me how it affected his wife and him differently. He wanted to clean out the girl's room, take away the sad memories. She wanted it to stay exactly as it was. Then he talked about his other daughter. The ordeal had been hardest on her. He and his wife worried every day. The girl never cried, not even at the funeral, and she refused to discuss her sister or her death for a whole year.

"Then, yesterday she had a fight with her mom, and broke down in a rage. 'How did you let her get killed? Why didn't you do something?' My wife was devastated, but it was a good thing she finally broke down. It was a breakthrough. She finally let out some of the rage she was carrying. It had to happen. If she didn't talk about it, she'd always carry it around."

I nodded that I agreed with him, but the idea of talking about grief took me someplace else. I'd had sad things happen in my life, but I don't remember ever talking about them to anybody. I experienced my first real tragedy when I was twelve. My three-year-old niece, Charlene, drowned. Charlene was the third of my brother's four children, and my favorite. I loved her so much. It was the most horrible thing that had ever happened to me. But I never talked to anybody about how much it hurt, and I managed to live through it.

Actually, I wasn't even sure what my feelings were. The only time anything seemed to come to the surface was when I got out of the car in Athens, Georgia. My brother saw me, and did something he hardly ever did. He grabbed me in a hug, crying into my hair. He said, "She loved you so much. She loved you so much." I loved her too. In that one second, my brother and I shared something. In another, it was lost again.

Over the next few days, I knew what I needed to do was stay out of the way. Mama and Daddy, my brother, sister-in-law, and all my aunts and uncles had important things to do. Most of the time, I stayed off by myself, and I didn't cry anymore. For some reason, I didn't believe I had the right to cry. Crying belonged to Charlene's mama and daddy. It belonged to Charlene's brothers, and to Mama and Daddy. From that time on, I only felt I had the right to cry at two funerals, Mama's and Grandmama's, and I don't think I cried much at those.

My attention returned to the man sitting across from my desk. He was still talking, saying something about getting help for his family. He didn't seem to notice that my mind had strayed for a second because he didn't need me to relate or even stay focused. He just needed me to be there and listen. When I didn't say anything, he must have thought I was allowing him to continue.

There was one day, many years ago, when I found myself on the other end of the conversation with a stranger. I wasn't the one listening, but the one talking. It happened when I was in the office of a potential client. I was telling him about my company's ability to staff his organization when we were interrupted by a phone call. But the call wasn't for him. His secretary came in and said my manager was on the phone and it was important that she reach me before I left for my next meeting (this was before the day of cell phones). He handed me his phone.

My manager kept her tone calm as she delivered the news. My sister had called. I had to come to North Carolina—it was Mama and there wasn't much time. I had to go now.

Business stopped. The man I'd come to sell to helped me make my airline reservations, supplied tissues, and listened. I told him about Mama, how she looked when she smiled, how funny she was. I told him how I spent hours as a child drawing pictures of the house I would build for her someday. I had never gotten to do it, but last year I bought her an expensive coat—the first big gift I ever gave her. Now I never would have the chance to build her that house with terraces and a swimming pool and fountains. I left his office for the airport to spend my last afternoon with Mama.

After the funeral, I went back to work, and never talked to anyone about the potential client or what happened in his office. I can't remember who the man was, if I ever did business with him, or even talked with him again. He was just the stranger who was there when I needed one.

7

LIFE IS FULL *of* BORING TIMES
MEANT *to* BE FILLED *with* DREAMS

Dreams Create Maps

Third grade was boring.

In first and second grade, school was fun. We colored and played games, and we were always busy and had a lot of different things to do. In second grade, we started reading real books about Dick and Jane, and I liked that. Every day we had reading time when we sat in a circle and took turns reading. I liked reading. Even arithmetic was fun because we did games and puzzles. The only part I really didn't like was nap time. I was supposed to be still and I wasn't ever sleepy. After a time, Mrs. Perry let some of us color as long as we were quiet.

All of that changed in third grade. Mrs. Williams didn't like to play games at all, and she hardly ever read to us. It seemed to me all she ever wanted to do was spelling and multiplication tables. There were long times when I was supposed to sit still—just wait and do nothing—like after I finished taking a test. Tests were what Mrs. Williams seemed to like most of all. They were awful—not taking them, but waiting. If I finished my test first, I couldn't go play or take out books to read, but had to sit there till everybody, even Josetta, finished—and she took forever.

That's when I decided there were two kinds of time. There was doing-things time and there was waiting time (later in school I learned there was you're-speaking-a-foreign-language-and-I'm-lost time too). I hated waiting time and looked for things to fill it. While I waited for everyone to finish their tests, I started filling time by drawing pictures on the bottoms of my test papers, pictures of horses or flowers. Then I started drawing little girls, then little girls carrying umbrellas. Finally I decided to draw the little girls with raindrops coming down through the arithmetic problems and bouncing off their umbrellas. Mrs. Williams didn't like art at all. She just liked multiplication.

In Mrs. Williams's third grade, I learned about waiting time, and that I didn't like it. I learned I wasn't smart in arithmetic. I learned I hated being bored more than just about anything, and I started learning ways to avoid it. I learned one way to avoid being bored was to draw stories.

Sometimes Mrs. Williams caught me drawing stories and told me to stop wasting time and do other work, boring work, like memorizing the multiplication tables. That was the point. While I was drawing, I wasn't doing boring stuff. The most boring stuff I wasn't doing was memorizing multiplication tables.

A multiplication table is a box with rows and rows of numbers. We had one printed on the back page of our arithmetic books, and we were supposed to learn all of them. Daddy said it was the most important thing I had to learn all year. He was mad at me when it was almost Christmas and I still didn't know the seven or eight or nine tables. (I never did learn the eleven or twelve tables.) Daddy said he didn't understand why I didn't just get on with it and learn them. "You walk around here saying those silly riddles and poems all day," he said. "You've got a good mind. If you'd forget about such silliness and concentrate, you'd learn."

But learning poems was different. They were interesting. They told stories. They had a rhythm that made them easy to remember, and once I memorized a poem, I could take it with me and "read" it again anytime I wanted, anytime I was bored.

I didn't see one good thing about multiplication. Learning it meant I had to write or just repeat the numbers over and over till I knew them: 7 times 7 is 49, 7 times 7 is 49, and I tried. But after a few minutes of that, I'd be gone. At least drawing instead of repeating the tables kept me in the room. Otherwise I would have daydreamed all day.

The good thing about Mrs. Williams's class was she didn't have much time to watch me to make sure I was writing multiplication tables, because she had a double class. We had both the third and fourth grade in one big classroom, with about thirty kids in each, and just one teacher.

While she was teaching the fourth graders, and while I wasn't learning what 7 times 9 equaled, I drew my own comic strip stories, and they ended up illustrating my future life. They were all about the Yellow-Haired Girl with blue eyes who looked like me. Day after day, I drew scenes from her future. I had plenty of paper—rolls of it—and it was free because the paper mills gave it to the school. I tore off sheets as long as I needed for my stories.

The Yellow-Haired Girl had her own place to live. At first it was just one room, but it was all hers and she could arrange it any way she wanted. She was born standing in the middle of that room. It was pretty simple . . . just a bed, a television, a picture of a horse on the wall (that was one of the things I did best—draw horses), a chair, and a closed closet door, behind which I knew she had lots of beautiful clothes.

As the year went on, the Yellow-Haired Girl's house was decorated with blue flowered wallpaper and curtains I copied from a magazine I saw at Aunt Pauline's house. We put carpets on the floors instead of flowered linoleum, and real wood furniture, colored brown, not blond laminate like the tables in our living room. And she had real flowers, never fake wax ones. Everything matched. But in all the stories, I drew only the inside of her home, so I had to wait till I grew up to learn what the outside of her house would look like. I certainly wouldn't have drawn it to resemble 13 E. Petain Street, but life takes funny turns sometimes.

As third grade went by, I became more ambitious and gave the Yellow-Haired Girl more style options. In early cartoons, she had only two outfits to choose from, and they hung on the closed closet door. Then she got a coat tree to hold her hats and a red coat. In later scenes, her closet door opened to show a wardrobe that grew with each picture. She added a purple coat and matching dress. For going out to balls and fancy restaurants, she had a yellow evening gown with tiny yellow roses embroidered around the hem. It was astonishingly like the gown I would wear years later in the Dogwood

Trail pageant. Sometimes on her dresser she laid out hats, gloves, even lace handkerchiefs.

By the end of the school year, the Yellow-Haired Girl was going out into the world to carve her own place. She was independent. She had a job, a good job, and it was in a brick office building in a big city that looked a little like Mobile, but I knew it was way away, in a place like New York. Then I drew her going out to work. In the first frame, she stood in front of the brick building, poised to go in. Dressed all in red—coat, hat, and pocket-book—she looked as successful as any career girl on TV or anywhere. Then she walked into a big lobby. You could see she was important by the way everybody smiled, nodded, and talked to her. It's too bad I stopped short of drawing what she did at work. That would have made my life a lot easier when it came to career decisions later.

It's funny. The Yellow-Haired Girl got ready for parties, but never went to any. She got dressed up and went to the building where she worked, but never got past the lobby. There must have been other people working with her, but they weren't visible. She knew they were there, but she couldn't see them, so she was always alone.

I wish I still had some of those drawings, but they are all gone. After all the time I spent drawing and writing, through at least four of my elementary grades, the only thing I have is one poem I wrote in Mrs. Green's sixth grade. She told us to write sentences using our spelling words, but I made mine into a poem. Spelling was another thing I wasn't good at doing. It was just like multiplication tables but with letters. All the letters had to be in exactly the right order, just like the numbers in the table. I thought the poems and stories I wrote were good, but no matter how good they were, Mrs. Green always counted off when a word wasn't spelled right. Even for this poem, I only got a B because I spelled some words wrong. It wasn't fair. Here is the poem—clearly it deserved an A.

I take piano <u>lessons</u>
What about you?
I don't like to <u>practice</u>
What about you?
I'd like to quit finding that old middle C
It's just a lot of <u>extra</u> boring work for me.
I'd much <u>rather</u> play with dolls that smile
And say "Mama" all the while
Or play with <u>miniature</u> paper dolls
Or read a book or make a call
Mama says I'll get <u>success</u> from it
And says she'll listen while she <u>knits</u>
The teacher says I have a terrible <u>touch</u>
And all I do is bang too much
She says I'm in rank zero
But all I do is laugh, "Ho. Ho."
I wish I had to practice never
I guess I'll have to take piano lessons forever.

We had to learn definitions every week too. They were right in our spellers, and all I had to do was study them. I always meant to, but every week testing day would come and I'd never have gotten around to it. There were just so many other things that took my attention—like honeysuckle flowers. One day I had just picked up my speller when I remembered Delilah's mother had said you could taste the sweet nectar in the flowers, and I'd had to stop and go outside to find a honeysuckle vine and suck on the flowers to see if there really was sweet juice in them. There was!

Actually, the definitions weren't so bad, even when I forgot to study them. Words came easy to me, and I could figure out what most of them meant. But I do remember one test where I defined the word "patent" as a kind of shiny material they used to make Sunday shoes. I used it in the sentence "The little girl kicked the mean boy with her new patent leather shoe." I still think my definition was clever—and creative. But it was marked wrong.

School wasn't the only place I had to go that was boring. Every Sunday at 11:00 a.m. and 7:00 p.m., and every Wednesday night, I had to go to the First Methodist Church of Prichard with Mama. The bad thing about church was that I just had to sit there. I couldn't walk around, or kick the pew in front of me, or talk. It was awful. Mama wouldn't let me take in books to read or big sheets of paper and Crayolas, so all I had to draw on were the little offering envelopes, once I carefully peeled the glued tabs open. Sometimes I counted things to help the time go faster. I counted things shaped alike, or yellow dresses, or women with blue hair, or red hats, or the repeated stanzas in the hymnal. Some hymns had two, or three, or even four measures that were exactly alike, note for note and word for word. I thought that was interesting.

When I got tired of counting things and drawing, I learned a new way to escape. I'd "go away." The first time I remember doing this was in the fourth grade. The teacher was going on and on explaining how to do some art project I had already figured out. One minute I was totally in the classroom, then suddenly I was gone. I was outside and I was saving a little boy who had climbed a tree and gotten stuck. Then everybody was clapping for me and saying I was a hero. I didn't hear a word the teacher said while I was "gone," but I knew when she finished talking. I knew then it was time to come back into the room.

Going away was something I would do for the rest of my life when I was bored. I'd stare into space and dream myself into some scene or story I made up. Maybe I'd go to a party. Or I'd meet the president of the United States and give him good advice.

Sometimes I "went away" not because I was bored, but because it was too sad to stay where I was. I would go away to a place where the bad things hadn't happened and stay there as long as I could. I learned to do that when Charlene died.

I was twelve. It was just after supper on a Saturday night when the phone rang. Daddy answered it, and I could tell something was wrong. He said, "Slow down. I can't understand you." Mama was in the kitchen, washing dishes. She came out drying her hands on a dishrag, to stand by the phone stand so she could talk to Buddy too. All of a sudden Daddy's face changed.

"Tell me again," he said. "What happened? Are they sure? Make them try again. I'm coming. We'll leave as soon as we can pack a few things and be there by morning."

When Daddy hung up, his eyes were red and wet. Mama twisted and squeezed the dishrag as though it could hold her up against whatever news there was. Daddy just said, "Charlene is gone. They were at the lake. She got away from them. She drowned." I stood by the door. She wasn't even three years old yet, and she was dead. Then Daddy said we had to leave right then to go to Athens.

For the rest of the night Daddy didn't talk about Charlene at all. All he kept talking about was money. He kept saying, over and over again, the banks were closed already, and he didn't have any money in the house. Nobody we knew had credit cards back then. He went across the street and borrowed money for the trip from Mr. Bailey. Daddy hated borrowing anything. He came back and said he would never be caught like that again. He would make sure he always had money in the house. It was something I heard him say again and again over the next few days.

Mama put my pillow in the car and I took books to color till it got dark. I took my last Christmas doll—the one Charlene loved. She was there the Christmas I got the doll, and that night I didn't want to go to bed, but Charlene cried and wouldn't go to sleep unless I stayed with her. We slept in my bed. I thought about that night as we drove away from Petain Street. I was glad I had gone to bed and hugged her all night, because now she'd never sleep with me again. In the car, I didn't want to color, and I was so quiet Mama and Daddy thought I was asleep. But I didn't sleep. I just looked out the window at nothing—and then I wasn't really there at all, but gone away, and they didn't know I was gone. It was like the times I went away in school, and the teacher didn't know it because I was right there the whole time, in the room, looking out the window—at nothing but the scene I'd created in my mind.

Just like that—I was gone, out of the car, and to the funeral home in Athens. I can still see myself in the scene I'd created. Everyone is there. And my brother is crying, and Mama and Daddy are crying and hugging him, and nobody sees me go over to the casket. They don't see me talk to Charlene.

Then she sits up and hugs me because she loves me and I'm the only one who knows she isn't really dead.

The problem with going away was it took a lot of energy and sometimes I didn't want to come back. I had to be careful with that.

Whether I was drawing them or daydreaming them, I spent a lot of time making up stories. That's what I would do just about any time I wasn't playing games, engaged in a project, or listening to somebody else tell a story.

I've always loved stories and storytellers. I come by it naturally. I'm Southern. The Deep South is known for its characters and the characters are known by their stories—and my family was full of characters and storytellers. They told stories to pass the time, to prove points, to teach us children our lessons.

Mama's daddy, Wylie Booth Richards, was a Baptist lay preacher. He seemed to know something about everything. At least he had something to say on just about any subject. That's what Daddy said. Sometimes Granddaddy was funny, but sometimes he was scary, like when he started listing all of the things you could go to hell for. He said it was a sin for a woman to cut her hair, but Mama cut her hair, so I knew he was wrong about that one.

On Daddy's side, they could keep the stories going all day, and they did when we all got together at the annual homecoming at Providence Church outside of Brewton, Alabama. Once the fried chicken, fried okra, creamed corn, and fruit pies were eaten, the stories began. The good ones were repeated.

I don't remember a single family reunion where Daddy didn't tell the story of how he came to get his tattoo. He got it to ease Grandmama's mind. He was running boats on the Intracoastal Waterway and all the way up as far as New York City. She worried every time he was out on the boats. Something might happen to him. What if the boat sank and he was eaten by sharks? What if they couldn't identify his body so she could bury it? But if he had a tattoo, she reasoned, and his boat sank, and sharks ate him, they would be able to identify him by the tattoo. He told that story every time, and every time we all laughed as though we'd never heard it before.

The great-uncles, George, Rufus, Gus, Bruce, Eb, Tup, and Collis told stories about the old days, and Aunt Ella Belle, my favorite of all the great-aunts, would laugh till she cried her flowered handkerchief wet with tears, even if she'd heard the story a hundred times.

Stories about family and neighbors sometimes took on lives of their own. One person would start, then others would tag on with their own spins or opinions—especially when gossip was the subject. "I told those boys time and again they were going to break their necks diving in that creek. Well, did they listen? No sir, they didn't! And see what happened. Charles went down there with a bunch of boys, showing off, and now he's in a cast up to his ears. I just wish you could see his mama. She must have aged ten years nursing him back, and we still don't know if he'll ever be right again."

An uncle chimed in. "Of course Charles isn't right. He's never been right. That daddy of his isn't right either. You can't tell him a thing, and he is the sorry-laziest man in the county. He asked me to show him how to build a cattle gap, but what he meant was that I should get out there and build it for him. I wasn't about to do his work. I told him what materials he needed and how to build it, but he didn't listen—made such a sorry mess of it that you couldn't drive a car across it. He tore up two tractor wheels on it. Poor old Miz Jane. I don't know how she carries on."

Aunt Sally sniffed at that. "Well, you can't tell Janie anything either. I told her years ago to leave that man. Janie was as pretty a young girl as could be and she could have had her pick of boys. I was sitting right there on her porch when Luke Jordan asked her to go to the church picnic. She acted as if he was nothing more than a bothersome gnat. Now Luke's got a good business in Chattahoochee and his wife has the life of Riley, and not one care in the world. That could have been Janie, but no, and now there she is, with a sorry husband and a mule-headed son in a cast to tend to."

I soaked up the colorful images, and sometimes slightly colorful language. I liked the stories that moved along at a gallop, and most did because a lull would give someone else time to break in with his own story. But there were times somebody would get into a long, dreary story with too many details and too few punch lines. Then I'd get bored and go off to color, dream, or read a book.

I looked for the same things in books that I did in stories. I liked things romantic, or that had a powerful moral. But even more, I liked them to be funny, with humor that was a little outrageous, and they absolutely had to move quickly from event to event. I wanted to see the point fast. I think that's why I liked poetry. The first book I remember owning was a poetry book, *My Little Golden Book of Poems.* I loved that book, and carried it around with me constantly, reading and rereading the poems until I knew them by heart and the book was in tatters. I can quote most of the poems today. There was one that sparked the romantic in me. I would sit in the backyard and say it over and over, savoring the images I thought must be the loveliest ever—and I was only seven or eight!

> I had a little nut tree and
> Nothing would it bear
> But a silver nutmeg
> And a golden pear . . .

I even memorized this poem about love, even though I didn't think the boy sounded appealing:

> Bobby Shafto's gone to sea
> Silver buckles on his knee
> He'll come back and marry me
> Pretty Bobby Shafto.
> Bobby Shafto, fat and fair
> Combing down his yellow hair
> He's my love for evermore
> Pretty Bobby Shafto.

I discovered my next book of poetry on the bookcase alongside Daddy's encyclopedias. It seemed so out of place, and I never found out how it came to be there. The poet was Edgar A. Guest. I wondered why he didn't change his name, or why he used all of it. The poems were really sappy ("It takes a heap o' living to make a house a home, a heap o' sun and shadow, and sometimes you have to roam 'afore you finally realize the joys you left behind"), but I devoured them, and memorized them too.

Before we take an auto ride
Pa says to Ma, My dear
I hope you'll just remember
I don't need
Suggestions from the rear . . .

I grew up thinking of books as rare and precious. A lot of my friends had only a Bible and a few religious tracts. We had the Bible, Compton's Encyclopedias, a set of children's books, a book of funny anecdotes, and the Edgar A. Guest poetry book. They took up two shelves on the metal bookcase, painted to look like wood, that Mama bought with S&H Green Stamps. Until I was in the seventh grade, these made up my only library. It's hard for people to imagine today a school without books, but at Turnerville Elementary School, we didn't have a library at all. In our classrooms, just about the only books were spellers, arithmetic books, history books, and readers, starting with "Dick and Jane," and sometimes there weren't enough of those to go around. In fifth grade, Mrs. Stowell brought in one of her own books and read it to us, *Miss Pickerell Goes to Mars*. I loved the days she read it to us.

Finally, when I was in the sixth grade, they built some bookshelves in what had been a closet. It didn't have a lot of books, but one it did have, *Pippi Longstocking*, was the funniest and most exciting book I'd ever read, and it is still one of my favorites. With so few books, I treasured them, and read and reread the ones I liked until I knew them by heart. They entertained me, stirred me with romantic ideas. They fired my curiosity and a burning desire to see the places they described. I would always look at books as travel guides. They showed me all the remarkable things there were to see. One year our reader had stories about a family that got a trailer and moved all over the country. The part about the rocky coast of Maine was vivid. When I was finally on my way to Maine twenty years later, my feelings of anticipation and excitement were as fresh as the day when I read that story.

When I left Turnerville for K. J. Clark Junior High in the seventh grade, I found a new world. K. J. Clark had a real library, with books about poetry and art and all the places in the world. And our English classes had literature books with plays, stories, and whole sections of poetry. We could read instead of taking spelling tests and diagramming sentences. But we still had science and arithmetic, and we had more things teachers thought I should memorize—periodic tables, formulas, percentages, French. I couldn't get away with spending my days drawing anymore.

The more charts and numbers I had to memorize, the further behind I got and the lower my grades went. They hovered at the B–C level through junior high and most of high school—until I hit algebra and geometry. Then they got worse. My senior year I finished plane geometry with a D minus. I think the teacher gave me that grade just to get rid of me. But I keep making confessions so . . . here is another one. I got the report card before Mama or Daddy saw it, and made a little up-and-down mark to turn the D minus into a D plus. It took all I could do to keep Daddy from calling the teacher to tell him off. "If you worked hard enough to get that close, it wouldn't have killed the son-of-a-bitch to give you a C."

As high school went on, I faced more classes I thought were boring and tedious, but of course I had to take them if I was to have any hope for future success. Sometimes I felt afraid I wouldn't make it. Bad thoughts crept in: "Was this it? Would I be a failure my whole life?" I fought them back. Maybe I wasn't a star in high school but I was going to be one someday. I told myself, "I'll make it. This is not the top for me! I won't end up in Fairhope. I won't peak out in high school." I kept telling myself the thing that mattered was college. Someday high school wouldn't matter anymore. I was going on to college and that's where my life would start.

Then the day came. I was at college and I knew I was going to be okay. I felt such a huge sense of relief. Life did start here and I loved it! From the very first day, college felt right. The freedom of it was as exhilarating as high school had been stifling. I wasn't limited by school bells. There was no more waiting time. When I finished a test, I could close the book and leave, no matter how many people hadn't finished. No more 8:30 a.m. till the 3:00 p.m. bell. After classes, and even between then, I could go anywhere I wanted. I had the freedom I'd given the Yellow-Haired Girl. There was so much to take in, and I was free to explore. I was in charge. I got to pick the classes I wanted, and make my own schedule.

My first semester, I decided I'd better go ahead and sign up for Biology 101 and Math 101. I figured there was a chance I would fail them the first time and have to take them over. This way, I'd get started early. In high school I'd learned I wasn't good at math and science. But I was in for a surprise. In college, I learned I was.

In my last high school math class, plane geometry, I was hopelessly lost by the second week, while other people in my class, even the football players, seemed to get it right away. Remembering that, I walked into Math 101 afraid. I chose a seat on the front row because I couldn't afford to miss one word. I was also nervous about the professor. Would she be like all the other math teachers I'd had? The minute she walked in and introduced herself, I knew she wasn't. Everything about Mrs. Perez was different. She was a tiny, compact woman, barely five feet tall, whose dress was more corporate than academic—tailored tweed suit, smart shoes, and styled hair. She exuded a spark of energy and, I could hardly believe it, fun.

Even the way she spoke was different. Mrs. Perez taught math in a Spanish accent that was musical. I wasn't surprised to learn she had been a concert pianist in Cuba before she came to the United States. She was so exciting. I had never met anyone from Cuba before.

I knew something special was about to happen, and it did. Mrs. Perez loved math. It showed in everything she said. Her teaching style was so far from the dry, sexless Mr. Whatever-His-Name-Was in high school. It had passion. (She was the first math teacher I ever had who I could picture being passionate enough for sex.) She saw beauty in numbers and she made me see the beauty too. It was a joy to watch her when she put some complex calculation on the board. She would get so excited she sometimes lapsed into Spanish, then turned to face us, raised her hands joyfully, and said in English, "Isn't that beautiful?" Yes! I believed! I went from my senior year D minus to a 99.5 average.

If my math class was music, Biology 101 was art. The teacher, Mr. Simpson, was a new experience too. He was the oldest teacher I ever had, probably seventy, with a booming voice in which he repeated every question we asked so all the class could hear it, even when we wanted to ask quietly so as not to sound dumb. He explained what he expected. This was a lab class. We were going to dissect a series of animals, and make illustrations of them, whole and in pieces, in our lab books. Part of our grade would be based on identifying the names of animal parts on the final. The greater part would be based on the accuracy and quality of work in our lab books. I'd grown up a squeamish child who cried because a worm landed on my shoulder, but I didn't have a choice now.

Actually, it wasn't as bad as I thought it would be. The work was creative. I dissected one creature after another, and pinned tiny intestines, hearts, antennae, and esophagi to a board. Then I made precise drawings of them in my book, colored them with colored pencils, and labeled the parts. All that drawing I did in elementary school came in handy. Luckily, Mr. Simpson didn't share Mrs. Williams's attitude about art. He loved my illustrations, and held them up to the class as examples of the kind of work he expected. That recognition was fun.

I got through earthworm, grasshopper, rat, and frog. Then I came to an animal I couldn't stand to touch, let alone cut up. I know how strange it sounds, but I was fine with the rubbery—even the hairy—dead animals. I held them, cut them open, and took out all their little parts. Then I caved on the crayfish. When Mr. Simpson took it dripping from the vat, my stomach turned over. When he gave it to me, I dropped it on my table and left the room gagging. Maybe it was that things that could be food but that reeked of formaldehyde were too much for me. Luckily, Mr. Simpson loved my illustrations so much he let me off the hook. I didn't have to touch the vile creature again, and I walked away with another A and a thrill that I was building a track record of successes.

Class after class, it all just fell into place for me. Next came the classes that were neither "music" nor "art," but were based on text and information. I've heard people say they had to learn how to study. I had to learn how *I* learned. By the time I got out of high school, I knew I didn't learn the way other people did, but I hadn't figured out any other way. So I went into every class wanting to do well and wanting to pay attention. My big problem was I got bored and lost focus, and I just didn't get why some things were worth remembering. I liked learning about President Taft and the corrupt politicians in New York City, but then we got into names and dates. Teachers seemed to love making us learn lists of things. I suspected it was because those tests were easier to grade, but learning the name of every state capital in alphabetical order was multiplication tables all over again. The same was true for tracking Civil War battles. When we got onto those, I would get distracted by—it could be anything. I might see an autumn tree outside and get caught up in how many brilliant colors there were. I could hear the teacher assign questions about the chapter on Abe Lincoln, but would leap from the word "Abe" to his mother, repeating the poem "Nancy Hanks" in my head, while the most important parts of the assignment were explained.

I hated the textbooks not only because they were dry, but because they also held my most dreaded assignments—read the chapter and answer the questions at the end. I never had a textbook that wasn't bone dry, and I never could find all the answers to the questions. Nothing in the chapter ever seemed to correlate to the wording of the questions. And I was never able to guess what was going to be important enough to memorize for tests. I couldn't imagine why anyone could possibly care if I knew the exact date of the Battle of Little Bighorn. But Mr. Wallace did. (It was June 25–26, 1876.)

High school had done nothing to build my confidence. I thought I was as smart as the other kids, but I worried. Something was different and maybe that meant something was wrong with me. When I got to college I learned I was different, but not wrong. I had my own way of learning, and once I knew what it was, I realized I never again had to walk into class and suddenly get that sick feeling that I had no idea what they were talking about. I made the Dean's List, and kept making it, semester after semester, as though piling up trophies. I loved college, almost to the point of euphoria.

Textbooks weren't a problem anymore either. Every professor spent every minute of every class lecturing and they each had an individual style and flair that kept the classes interesting. I figured it stood to reason, if professors went to the trouble to plan all those hours of lectures, the lectures would be what they cared about. I was right. I never had a single question on any test throughout college that didn't come from the lectures.

Even from the lectures, I found it difficult to tell exactly what was most important to remember, so I had to learn it all. I set up my system the first week of college and followed it through to the end. I bought a different spiral notebook for each class, and wrote down every word the professors said in every lecture, in every class. Taking notes did two things for me: It kept me from floating out of the room, and it gave me all the material I needed for tests—without textbooks.

I thought it was curious that other students could make only the simplest outlines of the lectures and still make grades almost identical to mine. I looked at a friend's notes in my sociology class. He had written only a couple of dozen words to my four or five pages. I was stunned that he could take those few words and fill a test booklet. I asked how long it took him to study for a test—a couple of hours. I didn't know how he did it, but it didn't matter. I was different.

As midterms approached, I had at least one book for every class filled with notes written in my tiny handwriting. Then all I had to do was learn them.

A few days before a test, I started. I sat in my bedroom, or somewhere I could be totally alone, and I memorized every word in those books. I learned the text as an actor learns lines, one at a time. I would read a paragraph over and over, then close my eyes and say it out loud. If I didn't have it, I'd keep going. After I could repeat the words, I would add feeling to the words I said aloud, as though I were speaking to an audience. Then I'd go on to the next, and the next, until I could quote the whole notebook. After that I would paraphrase it, repeat it in my own words to make sure I understood not just the words but also the professor's personal opinion about the subject. That could be as important as the text.

One book sometimes took two or three full days to learn. With five or six lecture classes at once, I had a lot of study time. It was time consuming, and laborious, but it worked, and that was all that mattered to me. I knew I had to work harder than other people who made pretty much the same grades as I, but if working harder was all it took, I was set. There was something else I had learned about me. I had a rare gift, and it was one that would make everything I ever wanted possible: I had the ability to work harder.

I was lucky to be born when I was, because I came along before people started labeling things as disorders. It wasn't until I was out of college more than twenty years and already in a successful career that I ever heard there was a label for why I had to learn the way I did: attention deficit disorder

(ADD). I don't know how it would have affected me then to be called anything that had the word "disorder" in it. I would have been embarrassed by it, and I know I would have worried about it, but I don't think I would have let it stop me. I might have worked harder, daring it to beat me. By the time I heard about it, I was glad I had it.

Some of the things I liked best about me and my life were byproducts of a "disorder." The world would have been so much less exciting without the childlike wonder that seems to come with ADD. I've also been told ADD made me a quicker study, which was probably why I faded out on long, repetitive explanations. Once I got the first point, I was ready for the next. If it didn't come, I was gone. Everything I've accomplished from college to teaching to staffing to owning a company has depended on my ability to "get" people quickly, to intuit their needs and their motives. As for my attention, I'm glad it was deficient. I got to see so much more of my world. I didn't just stop to smell the roses, I smelled them, hugged them, told them how beautiful they were, and never slowed down. I'm glad no one was there to give me pills to make me better.

I had the Yellow-Haired Girl's big dreams to make happen. ADD determined how I'd have to make them happen. With nobody to label me and nobody to teach me how to deal with it, I was able to make my own way and build the self-confidence to know I could do whatever I set out to do. I graduated in the top 20 percent of my class.

I came to Athens with fuzzy expectations for the social part of college— sororities, football games, and parties. Once I was there, I learned those things were like dating—more exciting to watch than to take part in. More exciting for me were the new experiences and ideas, competition grades—the "race." Parties were certainly available. The University of Georgia was a party campus. I knew that because *Playboy* magazine said so. They listed it as one of the top five party schools in the country. It had one of the top three football teams, Dooley's Dogs. Football, sororities, and fraternities dominated the social scene. But I ended up standing back, a spectator, watching the partiers whirl around me. Who I was hadn't changed. I was still uncomfortable in a group of people. As a whole, the University of Georgia had way too many people to be called a group.

Sororities were different. They were groups, and therefore intimidating. But I started the sorority rush process without considering what being in a sorority would mean to me. The first step was a round of "ice-water teas." We paid visits to each sorority house all in one afternoon to meet the girls and sip ice water from punch cups. The girls were nice, enthusiastic, and warm. But they were a group. Maybe if I'd drawn the little Yellow-Haired Girl a social life, I'd have had some idea how to go about having one.

As the next round of rush parties approached, someone told me all pledges were required to study at the sorority houses four nights a week. I panicked. I couldn't do that. For one thing, it sounded way too much like prison (or high school) to me, and one of the best things about college was the freedom. But I was also terrified for my grades. I couldn't learn that way. My studying required absolute silence. When I studied at home, Daddy would actually use earphones to watch television, or I would go to the radio station where Johnny was the night rock-and-roll disc jockey. There, I would put on big headphones that deadened all sound, and study till he got off at midnight. I couldn't live up to the plans I'd drawn if I couldn't keep up my grades, and I definitely could not do that in a group.

The next morning, my mind was on the question of whether to drop out of rush as I walked into my US Politics class. Then something happened to make my decision easy. That something was a boy. He sat down in the seat next to me and asked which sorority I planned to pledge. When I told him I probably wasn't going to pledge, he reacted with way more emotion than I thought the situation merited from a virtual stranger. I certainly wouldn't have cared about his fraternal plans. (Is that an ADD thing too, I wonder?) As though warning me about the consequences of doing some disreputable thing, he said, "I guess you know you'll never have another cool date if you don't pledge." I looked at him. I didn't get what he had to qualify him as a judge of cool. I saw a skinny sophomore who had the oily lack of charm I would later associate, unfairly, with used-car salesmen. "Yes," I said, "I do understand, and you're the next cool date I won't have."

I not only didn't join any clubs, but before my first year was out, I moved out of the dorm to live with my parents who had retired and moved to Athens so I could qualify for in-state tuition. I found out I liked being an only child.

So I shunned communal living and passed on the sorority, but I did have a social life, and it was fun. Every experience was new and it all felt so collegiate or intellectual—even going to see a ten-year-old movie, *The Mouse That Roared*. It was the first movie I'd seen outdoors where we sat on blankets on the grass. Clearly I was easy to impress.

I met new people and took part (usually as listener) in deep, intellectual discussions over pizza or Chinese food. One memorable night we watched *The Hunchback of Notre Dame*, the silent version, which someone pointed out was by far the best. Afterwards, meanings and symbolisms were discussed as though they had never been noticed by anybody before. I didn't get half of what they talked about, but it was great. This was what college was supposed to be about!

One of the best times I had in all of my college career happened in Birmingham, Alabama. I was there because I'd been invited to spend the long weekend at the home of a new girlfriend, Laney. I'd only heard about Birmingham being black with dust from the coal mines. I was surprised to see that it was so beautiful. Laney's family wasn't like the families I'd known. It was more like the family of *The Donna Reed Show*, complete with a teasing brother and a German Shepard—the first dog I ever met that I laid on the floor and hugged, totally in love and unafraid.

We spent the day exploring the Japanese gardens and parks, then we went to a party that night. That was the single best party I have ever been to. The host was several years out of college, and he was fascinating. I had never before known a man who wasn't married but owned his own house, and he had a real banana plant in the kitchen. Bill had traveled all over, and he was giving the party to show slides and talk about his most recent trip exploring the Mayan ruins on the Yucatan Peninsula in Mexico. We had beer and I ate my first bratwurst, and we watched his hundreds of slides while he described and explained the wonders of the civilization. I was spellbound by his stories of a civilization that existed so long ago, one that had a calendar. I was mesmerized by Bill's explanation of it. He showed us enormous pyramids and temples, and pointed out the size of the steps, and how they were perfectly proportioned to look the same height all the way to the top. He described how the Mayans did it all without ever inventing the wheel! He said they didn't even use animals to haul the stones. I couldn't wait to go to Mexico and see the wonders for myself. But twenty years later, when I finally got there, the experience was not even close to being as heady as seeing them through his slides that night.

In college, I finally had a dating experience that lasted long enough to be called a romantic relationship. (I didn't count Johnny in that category.) I may have even fallen in love. Henry was handsome, smart, funny, and popular. He was comfortable with everyone. I loved being with him. I loved how he looked, dressed, and how he fit in with every group. He was the coolest boy I had ever been out with. If I ever felt "in," it was with him. But we were doomed from the start by the same insecurities I always had with me. The beginning of the end came the night Henry asked me to go on a fraternity ski trip to Gatlinburg, Tennessee.

At first, I was excited to think I was going on a real college weekend, but then I started thinking, worrying, and imagining. What I knew about these things came from teen beach movies with Annette Funicello, and the girls and boys never shared rooms in Annette's movies. Would it be like that or did Henry expect me to sleep in the same room with him? If that was the case, was he asking me because I wasn't Jewish and it would be an insult to even suggest such a thing to a Jewish girl? Did it mean he liked dating me but he didn't respect me? The next day I broke up with Henry. That's when I agreed to marry Johnny—before I ruined my reputation. I was more afraid of being bad or being seen as bad than I was in love. This has to be mind-boggling to those who grew up later and in a less guilt-intensive place.

Even with my fears and demons, my college experience was exciting. But in the blinking of an eye, or so it seemed, it was over. It was time to leave college and go out into the world. But was there a job out there that would give me the challenge I'd had in school? Was there a job that would be as ever changing, with a surprise around every corner? Considering my degree in history and my skills, was there a job for me at all? As far as I could see, there was only one.

That's when I became a middle school teacher in Jackson County. It was not a one-room schoolhouse, but it was not far from it. It was a school for all, first through twelfth in a two-wing schoolhouse, and it stood squarely on the line dividing the two feuding towns of Hoschton and Braselton. The two towns added together wouldn't have equaled what I considered one small town.

I threw myself into my first career. Even if I didn't want to teach, I was used to success, and I absolutely did not want to be the worst teacher in the school. My experiences with my school teachers had been generally boring and miserable and I couldn't stand that again, so I found other role models. Mrs. Perez had made math fun. I determined I would make Georgia history fun. I spent the planning week before school started thinking of interesting things to do with the year's topics and looking for resources. I found the Coca-Cola Company had teaching games they would give me for free.

I was actually getting excited. Then I was handed a problem I hadn't expected. Teaching wasn't supposed to be my only job. My first day before I even met the kids, I was presented with a stack of forms stapled to make a book. The stack of oversized papers was at least an inch thick. I spent the next hour frozen at my desk, icy cold with dread as I stared at the massive thing spread in front of me. I turned the pages to find spaces for me to post days present, days tardy, quarter-days out, half-days out, excused times out, early dismissals, the reasons for early dismissals, unexcused times out, and spaces for five to ten words as to the reasons for absences. Then there were pages to total up the daily pages, and pages to total up the weekly pages, and pages to total up the monthly pages. Then there were pages to total and average the information from all the other pages.

I was ready for the parts of teaching that meant putting pictures and charts on the walls, making up games to explain population explosion, and writing multiple choice tests. And I had the bell-curve grading system down cold. Planning lessons was fun. I figured if I created lessons to hold my own interest, they would probably keep the kids' interest as well. But not this! Not forms!

I stared at the threatening stack in front of me, and dread turned to a panic that gripped my throat and tightened until I thought I wouldn't be able to breathe. I couldn't do forms. I knew it. All those boxes, like little prisons, overwhelmed me.

This wasn't right. I was supposed to be doing some exciting job in a big brick office building, but here I was, buried under a mountain of forms in a little school in Georgia. Furthermore, the principal had made it clear they had to be 100 percent accurate and turned in on time—no excuses. I was miserable. Teaching and small-town politics had never been in my plan, and forms were beyond me. I had to do something. After lunch I gathered up the thing in both arms and went to see the principal, the long-suffering Mr. Abernathy.

My demeanor was grave. "I'm worried about something, and I need to talk with you. It's about these forms I'm supposed to keep." I looked down at them on my lap. "I'm not good at keeping records."

I was new, and he tried to be encouraging. "I'm sure you'll do fine. If you have questions, I'm here."

"No. You don't understand. I'm really bad with them! I try to do them right. One year I was elected Sunday school treasurer. I was supposed to keep up with money from offerings to buy snacks and make a report on what more we needed to raise for a picnic. I kept the record book straight for a couple of weeks, but then I forgot to take out for Kool-Aid and cookies, and the whole thing was out of whack. Then I thought I didn't need to keep the record book at all because I had all the money in a box, so I could just count it when we needed to know how much there was. But that didn't turn out to be such a good idea, because when I went on vacation with my parents, I put the box in a safe place. I didn't find it again until we moved to a new house two years later."

I got all that out without taking a breath. Mr. Abernathy was staring at me, speechless, so I launched into my hook.

"You have to take these reports from all of us and put them together for your reports to the county? I think those reports you make are probably important."

He nodded. "Uh-huh."

"I know how hard it is to untangle scrambled reports," I said. "So it seems to me you've got two choices. You can fix the reports after I've done them, or I can bring you the daily reports and you can do them clean."

Mr. Abernathy saw my point. He did all of my reports for two years.

With my fear of forms relieved, I went on to teach. I couldn't tolerate boredom any better as a teacher than I had as a student in third grade, so I worked at making it fun. I laughed a lot and I enjoyed the kids. Still, it wasn't a job that got me excited to get out of bed in the mornings. I knew there had to be some job, somewhere, that would do that. But what?

The problem with finding it was I couldn't even imagine what it would be or even what I would want it to be. As I went through my second year, I kept asking myself questions to which I had no answers. "What can I do? What kinds of things are done in companies that I can do and that excite me?" The reality was I carried around the shadow of my childhood fantasy— Broadway. Even if I was too insecure to step out and try, I still ached to be a star. I wanted action. I wanted to make people laugh, to grab them, and motivate them. Was there a job anywhere that would give me an audience to show off how clever and funny I was, and give me applause, but without making me audition first?

Luck had to be with me here, because I did find the rare job that would give me the things I wanted and pay me for it. It didn't give me one big audience, but plenty of single ones. It let me talk to people, show off, be funny, and talk people into doing things my way, one person at a time. It was in a business I had never heard of, a personnel agency. Once I knew it existed, I grabbed it, hoping I was right. I was. I'd found something I could throw myself into for the first time since I left college.

It didn't take long for me to know I was in the right place. It was even better than college had been. There was no chance I would get bored. There were hundreds of people out there, sitting in offices, at desks that held phones, and they were just waiting for me to call them up, learn about them, entertain them, and get them to work with me. They all had different personalities, different experiences, and different stories to tell me. The variety was endless.

Two things I'd developed as a child turned out to be keys to my success in this business. One was how much I loved to win. I loved to convince people my ideas were better and they should play the game my way.

The other was the fact that people would tell me anything, things they might never tell someone else, just as the old people on Petain Street had told me their stories years before. For some reason, people trusted me. Without that I wouldn't have been able to get to know my clients and applicants well enough to match them to each other. I interviewed my clients to learn about more than what skills would be necessary for the job. I had to figure out if the two people were going to be able to stand each other. So I asked them about their personalities, quirks, habits, decisions, and their mistakes. They not only answered my questions, but they went on to answer questions I didn't even ask, and they told me all kinds of personal things, things I thought would be kept secret.

If I was surprised by the secrets people told me, I was more surprised at the subtle changes in our relationships that seemed to come after they shared them. Instead of being embarrassed to face me again, they seemed to feel closer to me. It intrigued me. There were times I'd sit back in my chair and stare into that point in space where we look for answers to our philosophical questions. It wasn't what I told people that won them over, but what I let them tell me. That was fine with me. I could listen to stories all day, and these stories had a greater value. They took me to the goal. So here I was, right back at a family homecoming or sitting on Daddy's lap saying, "Come on with the story!" and getting paid for it.

I rose steadily until I was the top producer in the company. I was happy, going a million miles an hour and in five directions at once. I loved the pace, the variety, and how things changed in a snap.

One of my friends, Bonnie, is a psychologist. I was talking with her one day when I was all excited about the projects I had going, and I was telling her about them all at once, jumping from one thing to the next, probably without taking a breath. When I finally stopped, she asked if I had ever been tested for attention deficit disorder. I didn't try to hide how offended I was. I couldn't have anyway. I remember I felt my eyes widen until I imagined they were as big as half-dollars. I stared at her speechless for a minute while a jumble of reactions went through my mind.

No . . . attention deficit disorder meant something was wrong with a person. What she said was ridiculous. It hurt my feelings. It embarrassed me. How could she suggest it? Of course I didn't have that, or any other kind of disorder. But undermining all of my denials were my old fears of failure and of not being good enough. But, no. I'd proven it. In college I'd competed and come out at the top, and I'd had a history of successes since college, even as a teacher. Now I was one of my industry's top people in the whole United States of America, and one of the most respected in the region. I had a huge base of clients who wouldn't trust anyone else to understand their vision for their companies and fill their positions. Candidates sent me notes thanking me not just for listening, but for hearing and understanding them, and making a difference in their lives.

I was so insistent I did not have ADD, she dropped the subject for a time. I don't know why it mattered to her—maybe I was an interesting specimen for her psych side—but a few weeks later she came back to it from a different angle. "Ruthi, I just want you to consider something. It might make some things make sense to you. Imagine yourself," she said. (Psychologists always want you to imagine yourself somewhere you're not.) "Imagine you're in a car. Your dear friend is driving, and she is telling you about a crisis in her life, something she is heartbroken about. You are taking in every word, you feel for her, and you're thinking of ways you can help her. Then you see a beautiful cherry blossom tree in full bloom, standing against a slate blue sky streaked with flamingo pink clouds. You want to share it with her and so you say, 'Jean, look at that tree. Is it the most beautiful sight?' She reacts hurt that you weren't listening, but you were totally listening, and you feel misunderstood, maybe even falsely accused. Can you see yourself in that situation?"

Okay. I had to admit I could see myself doing that. If that was all there was to ADD, it wasn't so bad, and I supposed it could explain the times I had been hurt and angry because I felt misunderstood or falsely accused. I supposed she might have a point. Okay. I'd listen to her and take it under consideration.

My favorite illustration of the difference between having ADD and not having ADD involved a motorboat. "Picture yourself in a motorboat [again with the "picture yourself"]. You are going to cross this beautiful, calm lake. If you are the person without ADD, you just rev up the engine, hold the rudder in place, and zip straight across. Now you're the person with ADD, and you're going to do the same thing, but with this difference: Your motorboat has a bent rudder. To make it go straight across, you have to turn the wheel first to the left, then to the right, then to the left, then to the right, all across the lake. It takes you five times as long to get across, and that much more energy, but you have seen so much more and have taken in so much more information along the way."

That summed up my life. Suddenly I suspected I might be even more different from other people than I had realized, and that proved to be true. One day I found myself in a conversation with my friend Erin about our morning getting-dressed-for-work routines. This was a few years after Bonnie's proclamation about me having ADD, so I was not so much surprised as amused and curious about how different our routines were. I told her my routine changed every day and from minute to minute. I might start by blow-drying my hair, then stop with one side done to brush my teeth, splash water on my face, and dab on the cleanser, but decide to look for my stockings before I washed it off. Then I'd blow out more hair, rinse my face, remember I hadn't picked out my shoes, but stop on the way to the closet to apply mascara. By the time I got to the part about mascara, I didn't have to tell her about my return to the bathroom for moisturizer. Erin was already staring at me as though I was mad. She said, "I'd have a nervous breakdown if I had to be you."

I thought about the motorboat story and what it said about my life. As a child I was never still. I remembered Grandmama getting exasperated with me and demanding, "Can't you ever sit still and be quiet a few minutes?" But I couldn't.

One day she corralled me, sat me down, and tried to teach me to knit. I was supposed to just sit there and make the same motions over and over again all afternoon. I did it, but after a long fifteen or twenty minutes I had made only two rows. I decided two rows were enough for me. I know there are many people who find knitting or needle work relaxing. But with each minute of looping and pulling, my stress level climbed.

Grandmama tried to teach me to sew on her sewing machine too. Another failure. She couldn't comprehend my inability to grasp sewing. Was her favorite grandchild really incapable of doing something every other woman on earth could do? Yes. I was utterly dumbfounded by the mechanics of the sewing machine. How was it possible that a needle could go into a tiny hole in a metal plate and come back up from the very same hole, and somehow have made a stitch in a piece of cloth? It was one in a long line of mysteries I encountered in my life.

Bonnie was right. Things did make more sense. Of course I had hated high school and its constrictions. I needed space and time and freedom to explore whatever attracted me. Of course I'd loved the freedom of college. ADD meant I needed the space to move and the freedom to do things my own way. The study system I devised made use of another ADD "symptom"—hyper-focus. Going into a hyper-focused place kept out distractions so I could learn. And of course I'd had to find a career that would let me have new experiences every day. And I couldn't imagine wanting to live any other way.

Since that conversation with Bonnie, I've met many business leaders who have ADD, and many of them recognize its value. In a meeting with a new client who was a famous artist and philanthropist, the first thing he said to me was, "You need to understand me to find the right assistant for me. I have ADD." I said, "So do I. Aren't we just so much quicker than other people?"

Even before we knew what it was, my manager learned something about ADD. Give a person with ADD two phones, and before long she will be on both of them. The staff had grown until there weren't enough phone lines. At that time our system couldn't be expanded. The answer was to put a second phone on my desk. Before long I was on both at once! It must have been some show—with me in hyper-drive, both phones at my ears, two conversations going at one time with two clients. I would be talking to one while covering the mouthpiece and "listening" to the other, then switching off. I was exhilarated, getting two deals going at once. Unbelievably, the clients didn't like it.

Dual phones aside, when I look at the aspects of my life that were created by traits that fall under the ADD label, I think it just might be the best thing I've had going for me. I still reject the two Ds, deficit and disorder; but if what I am is disordered, I never want to be cured. And with all the medicating going on in schools today, I hope they don't cure too many other people.

8

QUESTION AUTHORITY

That Rule Can't Mean Me

Southerners question authority more than other people—or so it seems to me. I grew up watching my daddy and mama question things—laws, religion, practices, and ideas. I've not met any other group of people who maintained so strongly their right to evaluate the usefulness of any given rule and decide for themselves whether it was worth arguing against. Sometimes they ran into a rule they didn't even consider worth talking about, so they simply ignored it. That's one of the things that makes Southerners so much fun.

Until the day he died, if Daddy didn't think a rule was worth keeping, he broke it. He was close to ninety when I took Stuart, who was from the North (New York and Washington), down South for a visit. Since I've lived "up north" (anywhere above Birmingham, if you're from Mobile), it has seemed to me Northern people take rules more seriously than we did down South—at least Stuart did. We got in the car, Stuart driving, to take Daddy to dinner at his favorite café where they had "the best fish and grits in the country, but they're nothing compared to the fish you get at that café out past Meat Camp [in Boone, North Carolina]." Daddy directed Stuart through several turns, then told him to take the next right and cross the bridge. But the bridge was blocked by orange traffic cones. Stuart pulled over and turned to look at Daddy for new instructions.

"What are you waiting for, boy? I said turn right here."

"But, Mr. Simmons, the bridge is closed. It's blocked off."

"Hell! Those little yeller things? Just drive on around them. They couldn't hurt your car if you did hit one."

"But the orange cones mean we can't cross the bridge. It may be down."

Daddy cussed. "It's nothing of the sort. Get on over that bridge! They finished building it a week ago. The only reason they're blocking it is to keep folks off of it till some politician can come cut a ribbon. No damn politician's going to tell me I can't drive across a bridge I paid to get built. Now, get on!" Daddy didn't just question authority, he attacked it.

We went over the bridge. He was right—the fish were good, although I'm not sure Stuart would admit they were worth crossing the bridge for. But at that moment, Daddy became his hero, although a scary one.

The only thing Daddy was ever afraid of was Mama. Everything you hear about Southern women is true. They're soft. They're charming. They're defiant. They're scary. There's a quality they have, black or white, rich or poor, that makes people take notice. It's attitude. And a Southern woman who believes in what she is doing not only has attitude, she becomes a force to deal with. She will do what she thinks is right and dare anybody to try to stop her, regardless of the danger. My sister-in-law met such a woman on a train.

When his family was young and growing, Buddy decided to become a preacher. With two babies and another coming, he and his wife, Leona, knew it would be tough for awhile, but they had faith that God would see them through. Mama prayed about it and said she believed God would want her to use her tithe money to pay his tuition. That plus the money Lee could earn with her bookkeeping skills would support them.

By the time Buddy applied and got accepted at Tennessee Temple University, he had only days to move his family from Houston, Texas, and get them settled in Chattanooga. They got packed and ready to go but there was a problem. Charlene decided to be born. Leona couldn't travel for ten days, so Buddy took the two boys as far as Prichard to leave them with us, and Leona stayed on with her folks till she was well enough to take the train to join the boys in Alabama.

That's how Leona ended up sitting in a day coach for three days and nights with a ten-day-old baby. I didn't understand why it was such a big deal, but Mama and Grandmama kept talking on about "that poor girl," and how exhausted she would be taking care of a baby, and with no help. Why should Leona be so tired? It sounded exciting to me. I loved going on the train, and I thought little kids were a nuisance, but playing with babies was fun.

I only half understood when Leona got to Prichard and told us about the three days. "Charlene wouldn't sleep. I tried to keep her quiet but she was fussy. When she cried, people around me were glaring at me and making nasty comments under their breath. Nobody seemed to see how exhausted I was. And nobody offered to help. By the second day, I felt helpless. Charlene cried, and I sat there and cried with her."

"The second night, I couldn't stand it anymore. I took her, went into the women's lounge, laid down on the couch with her on top of me, and tried to sleep." Back then the bathrooms on trains were lounges with sitting areas, couches, and dressing tables.

"I was thinking I didn't know how I would get through the night when the door opened and a black woman walked in." This was a huge thing back then, because the woman wasn't supposed to be there. In those days in the South, black people were supposed to be kept apart from white people on trains, in bathrooms, and in every other public place. I had never thought about it before—it was just the way we lived. Until that day, I didn't know there were actual laws for it. I would be in college before I'd know they had a name, "Jim Crow laws." The penalties for breaking those laws must have been pretty tough, because I didn't see people breaking them very often.

Today it's hard to make people understand how shocking it was for a black woman to walk right into a "white" women's lounge. It was marked plain, on the door, "White Women." But Leona said she came in "as though she belonged there," walked straight to her, reached down, and took Charlene from her. "Young lady, you give me that baby. I saw you in there, sick and weary, with those people acting like you were doing something to them."

"Now hush," she said to Charlene as she rocked her, "You just hush now and let your poor mama get some rest." Leona slept. During the night, white women came in and out. I can imagine their faces, some outraged, some shocked, but there was not one with the courage to challenge that lady. She had God on her side, and she had attitude!

Mama had that same kind of attitude. When she came up against something she thought was wrong or unfair, you saw it on her face. Her whole body had attitude, all intimidating five feet three inches of it, from her chin that stuck out, big as a dare, to her firmly planted, size five-and-a-half shoes. Mama would stand up to anybody and tell them what she thought about it, and I don't remember one person who didn't listen. Family member or preacher, coworker or manager, they took her seriously. She knew right from wrong. She read the newspaper as well as the Bible, so she had the knowledge to back up what she said, whether it was about the Bible, right-to-work laws, or the draft. She didn't talk unless she knew what she was talking about. She spoke her mind, and people still loved her. No matter what Mama said, nobody got mad at her. I would stare, amazed that she would tell somebody he or she was dead wrong, explain how to fix it, or say she wouldn't be a part of it, and the person would walk away loving her, or at least respecting her.

There was one IRS man who was probably an exception, but only because his mama never taught him about respect. Who had ever shown the courage to stand up to an IRS man, no matter how stupid he might be? My mama! The man dared question her integrity.

I don't know why Mama went directly to the IRS office to submit her income tax form, but she did. The man read through it and looked up at her. "These numbers are not true, Mrs. Simmons," he said. "Nobody at your income level could have the charitable or religious deductions [tithe to the church: 10 percent] you claim on your tax form."

The man called Mama a liar?

Daddy got out of the way—he pushed his chair as far from the action as he could, leaned back, and muttered under his breath, "Oh, no. Here we go."

Daddy was right. Mama sat that IRS clerk down, and took out her record. "Young man, you will sit here and add up every receipt, every check, and you will go through this form, line by line. See if you find one mistake." So he sat and did it, because Mama wouldn't let him go till he sounded contrite enough in his apology.

That IRS man clearly didn't know about Southern women. He certainly didn't know what he was dealing with in Mama. And he was small potatoes compared to some of the others Mama had taken on.

When it comes to a showdown, who could be tougher than a Baptist preacher? But Mama didn't even blink. The Preacher at the Shadowlawn Baptist Church was certain of his God-given power until he went up against Mama. She had been a Baptist her whole life and a member of that church for years until we moved to Memphis. She didn't have a car and the Memphis neighborhood where we lived didn't have a Baptist Church near enough to walk (which in and of itself is mind-boggling), so Mama joined a Lutheran Church for the year until we moved back to Prichard and, she assumed, Shadowlawn. But no.

"Mrs. Simmons, you've been outside of the church. Before you can come back as a member, you need to be baptized again."

"I most certainly will not! That is the silliest thing I ever heard in all my life. I know the Bible, and it says nothing of the kind. I have been baptized by water and the love of Christ, and I need never be baptized again." She didn't even give him a chance to surrender. That's the day we became Methodists.

I started questioning authority before my third birthday. One day while out shopping, I got tired of walking between my parents, holding their hands. "Daddy, carry me." He said no, he had packages to carry. "Daddy, my back hurts." I believe I actually remember my outrage that he laughed at me. I wouldn't lose! I held on to their hands and picked up my feet. They carried me. It worked, and thus I started my long career of defying authority.

Sometimes you have to break a rule to make a difference. It wasn't just a right to question authority, it was a duty. Taking those lessons with me, I went into the work world where, if they didn't make a difference or change the world, they at least spiced up my workplaces.

I feel pretty good about most of the rules I've broken. But a rule I should have broken and didn't is the one I feel guilty about to this day—guilty and stupid. It was when I was teaching middle school. In a whole world full of rules aching to be changed or broken, bureaucracies, especially school systems, have more than their fair share. This rule was one I shouldn't have missed.

The new rule was announced at one of those teachers' meetings I hated so much. I was probably thinking of an excuse to leave or something, but couldn't have been paying attention when the policy was announced. If I had been listening, I'm sure I'd have put up a fight. The policy mandated written excuses for student absences. "A written excuse from the parents must be handed in within three days of a child's absence. If the excuse is not brought in by the third day, the student will be kept in the detention room for one hour after school." Mr. Abernathy gave us printed notices to send home with the students. The teachers were to send in the names of excuse-less kids to the principal with our morning attendance reports. Teachers would rotate after-school detention duty.

How obvious could it be? But I missed it. Where was my head? Wherever it was, I didn't use it because I should have seen it was an impossible rule. The kids would miss their busses. Few lived walking distance from the school, and some lived ten miles away. More than that, half or better of their parents were sharecroppers, and I knew several of them couldn't read or write.

I didn't think it through. I didn't fight it. I did try to ignore it, but I got caught. It was a girl in my homeroom who finally brought the policy down. Mattie had been out with the flu. I knew she had the flu. The other kids knew she had the flu. Every teacher in our section knew she had the flu. Mr. Abernathy probably knew it too. Even when Mattie came back to school, you could see she still looked pale. So it was clear—she'd had the flu but she didn't have a written excuse. I told her, "You have to bring in the note from your parents!" Two days passed and no note. I begged the girl to remember the note. "Please get your mother to send a note. Please. You'll have to stay after school if you don't." Another two days went by.

Knowing I tended to ignore what I didn't like, Mr. Abernathy was watching me. "I haven't seen the excuse from the Jones girl. If you don't have it tomorrow, she has detention."

I told Mattie again to tell her mother to write a note or she would have to stay after school the next day. The next morning, no note, so I told Mattie to go to Mrs. Lee's room at 3:00 p.m. Mattie lived five or six miles out and rode a bus to school, but she went for her detention. I went home.

The next morning Mr. Abernathy was waiting for me. "It's a good thing you weren't here after school yesterday. Mattie's daddy came up here—with his shotgun—looking 'for that sorry teacher who kept my girl from getting home on the bus and made her walk.' But don't worry about it. I covered for you. I explained that this is your first year as a teacher."

"What are you talking about, you 'covered' for me? I had nothing to do with it. I never wanted to keep her in at all. It was a stupid rule to start with, and this is the last time you'll get a name from me!" Still, in my heart I knew it was my fault, my responsibility. My daddy wouldn't have let them keep her in detention. Mama would have made Mr. Abernathy drive the girl home, or she would have stayed and done it herself. I had no excuse for letting it happen. My parents had taught me to think for myself and question rules, and here, when it mattered, I hadn't done either, just followed along like a sheep.

I had argued against every other thing I didn't like at that school, and they were far less important. Teachers' meetings! I certainly fought them! Teachers' meetings brought out the worst in me, and they confirmed some things about me. I wasn't a team player. I wasn't even a team member. Teams had meetings, and I hated meetings. Teachers' meetings were the worst part of my short teaching career. They were a succession of long-winded discussions on trivia. I sat there, miserable, as they dragged on and on, the tedium relieved only by near fist-fights when talk heated up on such crucial issues as which class should line up on which end of the hall for lunch, who was responsible for the messiness of the teachers' lounge, or the correct use of the copy machine.

The copy machine thing was huge, and the pet issue of Sharon, who taught senior high math. In my first teachers' meeting, she spent half of it ranting about the selfishness displayed by some of the staff regarding the copy machine. I'm not sure but I think she actually said, "You know who you are." (Over the years spent going to as few meetings as possible, I found there's one in every meeting.)

Mr. McKinsey, who taught social studies, was quick to come up with a solution. "I make the motion we set up a committee to draft a rule book for the copy machine and teachers' lounge etiquette."

I was drowning in a fish bowl. Was this the professional world? Did grown-up people really have nothing more important to get excited about than copy machine etiquette? And to then make an actual motion about it? And were there actually three people competing to second the motion? It was awful, but it got worse. I sat there imagining Sharon spontaneously combusting, and thinking, "I don't belong here." I was jolted back by someone saying my name.

"Ruthi, you haven't expressed your opinion. Why don't you be part of the committee?"

I really didn't want to have a copy machine rule book, let alone be involved in drafting one. This was my first meeting so I decided to be tactful. "I think it's a big responsibility and I'm just learning all it means to teach. Let me think about it."

I went to Mr. Abernathy the next morning to convince him I shouldn't be a part of the teachers' meetings. "I think I detract from the meetings. I worked with a team in a psych class and one person wasn't into the project. He brought the entire team down. I would hate to be the reason the meetings are less productive, so I think I should just not go." He didn't buy it.

Forced to attend dull meetings I couldn't talk my way out of, I acted like a spoiled brat. I'm not proud of it (but I'd probably do it again). Whenever anyone made a comment I thought was stupid, inane, or pointless, I'd let them know. I'd roll my eyes and say "Please" under my breath, or "You can't possibly care about that" out loud. Five minutes before the appointed end time, out came my jangling car keys and my toe started tapping the floor, which was code for "Time is up!"

Since I left teaching, I've avoided committees, with one short exception. I was asked to serve on the board of our church. I thought I should do my part, so I went to the meeting. If you think churches are supposed to be filled with love and goodwill, I can tell you that's not true in the board meetings. I thought teachers got overly excited about copiers, but I had never seen anything like this. I'm still fond of the minister, but he liked to run things his way. He grew more red-faced every time someone disagreed with him. The sweet old gentleman who always sat on the third pew on the left stood up and attacked some parking lot policy, and it started a screaming match. Battles over choir robes, where to put the new cross, or traditional versus modern hymns got loud and bloody.

The church meetings weren't boring, but they were too scary for me. I resigned the next week. "I can be on the board of this church, or I can go to church here, but I can't do both."

Back in Braselton, my second year teaching, I came upon another school rule that needed changing. The school auditorium (really, the cafeteria with a stage on one end) was not supposed to be used outside of school hours for anything other than PTA meetings and officially scheduled school programs. But that was a problem for me because I wanted to put on a play.

We were studying *Animal Farm*, and it was one of the few things all of the kids in my diverse class liked. I decided to read it out loud so even the half of the class who couldn't read enjoyed the story. I saw a couple of boys posturing like the pigs in the story and that gave me my great idea. We'd put on a play! I wrote a script and, while it wasn't Tony Award material, it had lines for every kid in my class. I asked one of the high school girls to type it. Then I broke a bunch of copy machine rules to print copies for everybody.

We did the play in our classroom. The kids loved it. Even the kids who sleepwalked through school were excited and having fun. We talked about why the animals behaved as they did, and how power changed them.

Then I had another idea, an even better one! We could put on the play for the whole school and hold a night performance for the families. Would I be able to convince the principal to let my class take over the auditorium to practice the play and put on performances, one during school for the students and one at night for the families? I didn't know because I didn't ask.

Knowing it's sometimes easier to get forgiveness than permission, I went forward with my plans. First we put it on for the other middle school classes. We didn't need the principal's permission for that. Parents volunteered to make dog and horse and pig costumes.

With the play a success in the middle school, I went to the principal. "Mr. Abernathy, we should put our play on for the whole school! The kids worked so hard, and did such a good job, and the middle school loved it. Come on. Let's put it on for the whole school. It will be easy. We'll decorate the cafeteria stage as a barnyard with hay bales and some old barn wood. We can even make a scarecrow. The parents can make more animal costumes. Every kid in the seventh grade can be in it."

But he wasn't nearly as excited as I'd expected him to be. "I've already told you we can't use the auditorium for things other than what is scheduled."

"I don't see why not. That old stage just sits there and never gets used at all. These kids don't get chances to shine every day."

"Ruthi, stop! There are more issues here. Other teachers would be impacted because they would have to give up a night. We'd need custodial help that wasn't put in the budget. A lot of these kids' parents never come to school events, and they don't have the money for costumes."

"It's no problem. I've already figured out all those things. The other teachers in my section are on board. And how much can it hurt to have the janitor set up chairs in the cafeteria the day of the play and take them down the next morning?"

He didn't give in right then, but I knew he would by the next day. We had our stage.

Mothers made more costumes, enough for every pig, dog, and horse. There was one skinny little strawberry-blonde girl who really didn't have much hope in life. Aggie couldn't read and she couldn't memorize lines. I decided she could be a rooster and sit front stage right while everybody else acted. I asked her if her mother could help her make a costume. Everybody said to forget it. Her parents were so poor they couldn't afford cloth. They probably wouldn't even show up for the play.

They had a point. Aggie was one of the poorest kids in the school, living on a worn-out dirt farm that was owned—as the town was owned—lock, stock, and post office by the Braselton family. Braselton's economy had been built on sharecropping. Many of the parents couldn't read or write. Every class had kids who were the products of incest. Child services didn't seem to exist. Whole families were inbred till the relationships—cousin, brother, father, mother—were blurred.

Families who didn't have the money to support one child had five, seven, or ten children. One morning two sisters came running into my class and up to my desk. They were breathless with joy. "We have a new baby sister. She's beautiful. Mama asked if you would stop at our house after school to see her. Can you come?" I went. It was a steamy September afternoon. The screen-less door was open to catch whatever breeze. As we walked down the center hall of the shotgun house, I saw there were two or three rickety beds in every room. The mother put her baby in my arms and beamed. She was a beautiful baby, all pink and sweet. I got it. The only things they ever got that were brand new, all their own and perfect, were babies, and they welcomed them.

I gave Aggie the part. She would show up or she wouldn't. I couldn't control that. The part was hers, and she did show up, and her parents too! No matter how tired, overworked, or poor they were, they came, and gave me one of the best memories of my life.

The lunchroom/auditorium was filled as parents and the community came out to see thirty of their children perform. Ralph, as "Napoleon," the pig dictator, strutted about the stage as belligerent as a Tammany Hall politician. Mark and Joe made a steadfast and sympathetic "Boxer," the horse. The A-group girls were wonderfully menacing as snarling, glowering attack dogs.

But the show-stealer of the evening was the one with not a single word to speak, Aggie the rooster, who came with both parents and Grandmama, and in a magnificent costume. Her mother made it from scraps of colored cloth. Aggie sat front stage right for the entire hour and forty-five minutes—being a rooster, craning her neck, crowing between lines. Her muscles had to hurt after so long, but she stayed on her roost, even during intermission, stretching her neck, ruffling her feathers, and flapping her wings, undoubtedly the best rooster there ever was.

My play had made a difference. I had made a difference! Wow! For the rest of her life that kid would know that for one night she was the best in the show! I saw joy in her face, the joy that comes with knowing you are awesome and you are a star. I felt it too. It was something they told me couldn't be done and I felt great. It was a feeling I knew I wanted to have again and again.

Teaching gave me a lot of chances to do things I wasn't supposed to do. I got a kick out of that. When something went wrong with the heat plant, sending the temperature in my room into the nineties in January, I complained day after day. But the rest of the school was fine, so I couldn't get much enthusiasm for fixing it until I took my class, bundled up, out onto the grass in front of the school where every passing car could see us. It was dreary and gray, a perfect day to read "Beowulf." They fixed the heat.

One of the last projects we did was produce a poetry book with every kid's poem. I have one of the poems framed and on the wall of my office, a trophy. Jeffrey, one of my favorite kids, wrote it about me.

Mrs. Holliman teaches us
all we should know.
She isn't hardly ever shy.
She's pretter [sic] than any rainbow
And if she was ugly
I think I would die.

The truth is, Jeffrey didn't write it. He paid George two dollars to write it. That made it even better. I was worth two dollars!

Gathering up my poems and my heightened attitude about authority and rules, along with a disdain for meetings and committees, I came to Washington and my job in the personnel agency, which, I was happy to find, had few to no committees.

Once I got into it, I discovered plenty of rules to break, and systems I would absolutely need to change. My new managers were as set in their ways as school principals and superintendents. I had no doubt I would end up with things my way, but it wouldn't happen overnight. Significant change takes time. Breaking rules was another thing. I could break rules on the spot. I broke my first rule within my first couple of weeks.

I'd only been on the job one full day when I got my very own applicant, and he was a great one. He was educated, well dressed, and professional. He was from Nigeria, had a degree in accounting, and had ritual tribal scars on either side of his face. Nigeria! Another first! Moving to Washington was going to be all I had thought it would be!

We had one job for accounting. It was with a company off the beltway near Springfield, Virginia. He lived in northeast Washington, and he didn't have a car. There was no Metro. I'd been in the area two weeks. The match seemed perfect to me, so I called the company and set up an interview. Somehow he got to the interview where they told him they needed a degree from a college in the United States, not from Africa. For the next week I called companies to find an accounting job for him. I called every day, but kept getting "no openings" or "no degree from Africa."

Finally I called the Hecht Company in Silver Spring, Maryland, and reached the business office. This was before computers centralized all accounting functions and eliminated the need for accountants in individual retail stores.

Yes. They needed an accounting person.

No. They didn't care where his degree was from.

Yes. They would interview him today, and if the interview went well, were ready to hire him.

But . . .

No. They wouldn't pay my fee.

I didn't spend a minute thinking about the fee I was supposed to charge. I didn't know if I would get in trouble for giving away my work for free, and I thought it best not to mention it. I set up the appointment and called him. "Go to the department store accounting office. Forget the fee. Just get the job."

I don't remember his name and I haven't spoken with him in thirty years, but he was my first—the first candidate I interviewed, the first I marketed, and the first I found a job for!

Actually, I did get paid a fee. It's hanging in my office today. A few weeks after he started his job, he stopped by my office with a package wrapped in brown paper—I've always loved packages wrapped in brown paper. I ripped it open to find a hand-woven scarf sent to me all the way from Africa by his mother. I'd never had anything from Africa before. This was exciting. I was in the capital of the country, and meeting people from all over the world, and getting presents too. So what if I'd missed the fee-charging point of the placement?

But if I was to build a future, or just keep my job, I had to get the fees coming in. Luckily, I found I loved selling and was good at it, so finding employers who were willing to pay me wasn't my problem. Cold-calling and selling to employers soon became my favorite part of the job.

I finally had a job and I loved it—except for most of it. I didn't like the recruiting, interviewing, testing, running references, and working with applicants, which was by all accounts 70 percent of the job. If I'd had my way, I would have been cold-calling and selling all day long, and letting others do the candidate recruiting-interviewing-testing part. But the company wouldn't let me—yet.

I thought about it and came up with the perfect answer. Of course it was the answer! It was clear as crystal. And so simple. So obvious. I went to my manager.

"Hey! I have a great idea. Most of the account executives don't like cold-calling and I do, so they can recruit the applicants, interview, test, and bring them to me when they're ready to market. I'll do all the cold-calling to find employers and get the jobs to fill, and then I'll screen everybody's applicants. It'll be great for everybody!"

It was the perfect plan, except they wouldn't let me do it. I couldn't imagine why they didn't see it too, but they thought things were working just fine as they were. "Don't reinvent the wheel," they told me. "We have a wheel, and it works."

I didn't think their wheel worked all that well. It was lumpy. But this was going to take time—and patience. I had never received the patience I had never prayed for. Instead of passive patience, I had active determination. Things needed to change and I'd change them. After all, this was the '70s, and wasn't it proving to be the decade for change? Things were changing so fast that by the time somebody could say, "That's not the way we do things," it was.

It was the decade of firsts: first Earth Day, first gay pride parade, and the first International Year of the Woman (declared by the United Nations). It was the decade that saw the end to gender-specific job ads that announced, "Young man needed," or "Girl wanted for clerical work."

In the '70s, females began to grow up. From being "girls" until they were grandmothers, they started being "women" as soon as they graduated high school. Things were changing and the world was accepting the changes. Wasn't Ms. starting to replace Miss or Mrs.? The best thing about Ms. was I didn't have to ask personal questions (i.e., Are you married?) before addressing a letter to a woman. Technology, as always, was changing faster than people. The '70s came in with manual-return typewriters and carbon paper and went out with machines that corrected their own mistakes.

If all those things could change, my business could change. And I was making progress in that direction every day. I had the strongest possible allies—the people who paid the fees. Increasingly, they were recognizing the value of agencies as resources and time savers, but there were problems. More and more agencies were opening and growing, and human resources people and office managers were becoming deluged with calls, and not just one call from each agency. They got calls from every individual account executive in every agency. They could, and often did, have calls from three or four people in one agency in a day. Then, when they gave the agency a job to fill, the calls didn't slow down.

Imagine you're an employer in 1974. You have no voicemail, no email, and no auto-attendants. Say you're an insurance agency with forty brokers, for instance. Your company is dependent on having a receptionist to answer the phone and deal with customers and your receptionist does more than answer your phones. She (Or he? In 1974? Don't be silly.) provides a vital link to your customers. She types letters and processes bills. Business is booming. And she just quit—with a one-week notice.

You have to find someone new right now so she can train them. The phones are crucial and your PBX (telephone switchboard) system is too complicated to learn in only a week. You must find someone who can hit the ground running, who has experience, and who can type at least 50 wpm to keep up with the work.

Out of the blue, you get a call from a woman at an agency who says she has an applicant with three years of experience in a one-girl office where she handled the PBX phone system for twenty doctors, did the billing, and types 50 wpm. You discuss salary and fee and set up the interview for this afternoon. This is too easy! Then the person at the agency says, "Okay. She'll be there at three. Hold on a sec and let me see if anyone else has an applicant for you."

Before you can say anything, you're on hold—ten—fifteen—thirty seconds. Then you hear this:

"Hi. This is Sara. I have a girl for your job. You'll just love her! She actually doesn't have PBX experience, but she answered the phones in her high school office both her junior and senior years. She types 50 wpm with three errors. She can be there at four."

"No. I need PBX experience."

"Okay. Just a sec."

"Hi! This is Trish. I have a clerk-typist you can't afford to pass up—50 accurate wpm typing and bookkeeping experience."

"No. I need a receptionist with clerical skills. Who was the person who called? Is she there?"

"Sure. I'll get her. There are just two more AEs who want to present to you first."

"This is Cherie . . . "

This went on until every person got to tell the employer about her candidate.

I went again to my manager. "I have another idea." (You might notice it was the same idea but on a new day.) "Clients have asked if they can just deal with me as the agency's only representative. Anybody who wants to send a candidate to these clients will get me to set up interviews. Jackie at Hill Company said she will call me with every job she has, if she can talk just to me."

"No" again. "It's not how we work. You need to convince Jackie to work our way. Let her know you don't know all of the applicants. It's not fair to the other account executives if they can't sell their own applicants."

"But we don't have to do that. I can tell her about them and she'll interview them."

"No. Other agencies are not going to stop calling her. What if you tell Donna not to call and some other agency calls and fills the job? No."

"But . . . "

"No."

I finally found the right formula: committed interview times plus exclusivity. My first personal client, and the man who changed agency history, was Fred Dixon. He was the vice president of Folger Nolan Fleming Douglas, one of the oldest and most prestigious investment firms in the city. It's still in its marble building on 14th Street, a building rich with history. It was in front of this building, in the late 1920s, that Mr. Hibbs, a firm partner, button-holed anyone he could talk with and said, "Don't buy. The market's going to crash!" I loved the history of it.

One day I called Mr. Dixon to find a place for a secretary I was marketing. Yes, he needed a secretary and she sounded good. He'd see her. We set up the appointment and I asked him to hold on for the group call.

"No." He stopped me. "I'll only work with you, no other agencies. I'll see three people. You pick your best three and send them. I'll hire one of them."

Sounds simple, doesn't it? It was revolutionary. I had to ask permission, so I put him on hold and asked my manager. Exclusive. Promise of hire. She said it seemed like a good idea to her. So that was the answer—to be my personal clients they had to be exclusive and let us control the interviews. Now I knew what to do.

Mr. Dixon hired his assistant from me that very day, and continued to hire from me until he died in 1984 (the last assistant I placed with him is still with the firm in a professional role). One of the dearest men I've ever known, he launched my career and I loved him, yet I never met him in person because we weren't allowed to leave the office to go out and meet the clients.

We had to match applicants to our clients' needs and explain the jobs with just the information we could get over the phone. That didn't make sense to me. But management was adamant. "Your job is to call, sell, write the job order, cover it, and move to the next call. You can't do the production we expect if you're spending too much time on a single client."

I argued. If I could meet with clients, I could get their loyalty. It was the best way to sell. I didn't think about it then, but the reason I knew it worked was because it had worked when I was in third grade. I spent time with the old ladies on Petain Street and they bought cards.

Until I convinced the manager to let me go meet clients in person, I made up for it on the phone. My calls lasted longer than was considered appropriate. "You're staying on a single call too long. Cut the length of the calls, and you will get more calls made."

What would be the fun in that?

For the moment, I gave up on the meetings, but I spent hours talking with managers, personnel people, owners, and lawyers. Maybe I wasted too much time in conversations that didn't bring in any money, but enough money came in so they didn't stop me.

Actually, it was during that time that I learned a lot more about how to engage people and how to sell. I didn't have expressions, physical gestures, or props to help me, so I developed skills at engaging, exciting, and winning people over with just my voice, my imagination, and my words. I'd found my Broadway—the phone!

I didn't just become better at entertaining people but also better at hearing them. Without distractions, I learned to focus all of my attention on the phone as though it was a live person. I learned to be totally with the person on the other end of the phone, to react, empathize, and show I cared with just my voice and words. Later, even my voicemail messages would sound as though I felt the presence of the person I was calling.

It was also a time when I was able to enjoy using my imagination. I talked with but never met face-to-face with some of my most memorable characters. In a way it was more fun—like radio. With no pictures, I was free to imagine the people any way I wanted. I gave them faces to fit my impressions. I created the faces to go with the words.

I can still see the face I created for one of the most interesting men I never met. Mr. Nikaido was a lawyer of Japanese ancestry. I knew that the first time I met him on a cold call. But he sounded as American as I did. He was the first Japanese person I ever met who spoke with an American accent. Actually, he was only the second Japanese person I'd ever met. The other I met when I was eight years old. Her name was Kazuko, and she only spoke Japanese. She came to live across the street from us in Prichard with her husband, Joe Bailey, who met her while he was in the army. All that summer, I spent every possible minute with her. She was learning English and I helped her. She taught me to write my name in Japanese.

Mr. Nikaido's unaccented voice, his direct, secure personality, and his sense of humor created a vivid and lasting impression. To this day, in my mind, he is an older Ken Watanabe (*The Last Samurai* and *Unforgiven*), but with hair salt-and-pepper at the temples and feathered back.

As we worked together to fill his secretarial position, I wanted to know more about him, so I asked. Where did he go to college? What was it like to be in the minority? What did it feel like to beat the people who were trying to hold him back? As I write these questions, I cringe that I asked things so personal, but it seems that twenty-three-year-olds with curiosity and "Oh, wow!" innocence can ask questions others can't, and get them answered. Mr. Nikaido gave time and thought to my questions.

He told me things that shocked me. He said some people still hated the Japanese—I couldn't imagine anyone disliking Kazuko—and still discriminated against them. He told me about universities (reputable universities—in the North!) having quotas to limit admission of people from all minority groups. I was young enough to be outraged—and ignorant enough to be shocked.

Ignorance was easier in the '70s. Those who weren't there or don't remember might think it odd that a woman with a degree in history from a respected university had never heard about the internment camps for Japanese Americans during World War II. But I hadn't. It wasn't talked about. Back then it was possible for guilty secrets to stay secret. We didn't have the web with YouTube to give us videos of every event, important or not. We didn't have docudramas on primetime, and even in the libraries there were few or no books on our more shameful events. I remember. It was in the '70s that I first heard about the death camps in Europe where Jews had been killed. I went to the public library in Bethesda to find books about the Holocaust. There were only two books on the subject in the entire library—two. As for the Japanese-Americans in camps, it would be twenty years before *Snow Falling on Cedars* became a bestseller.

The things Mr. Nikaido told me about were all new to me, and they were things I'd never have believed could happen in the United States—people ripped from their homes, possessions they couldn't carry in their arms lost forever. American people taken to live in camps of shacks. This wasn't Mississippi or Alabama where everybody knew horrible things had happened. It was California!

I told him about Kazuko and proclaimed, "I would have done something. I wouldn't have let them take Kazuko."

"Ten-year-olds are brave."

As we talked, I was struck with his calm, while I was outraged. "Why aren't you mad? How can you deal with people who did so much to your people?"

He didn't even sound emotional, or say anything sappy like, "We have to forgive and learn to live in peace." He said, "It's something we need to know we are capable of."

I ranted on and on. "How can you forgive them—they basically destroyed the lives of a generation!"

"They didn't destroy that generation. Even in the camps, they worked and built, they lived through it, and they came back stronger. Actually, because of the experience of the camps, the Japanese people were fully integrated in American society within a generation—more quickly than any other immigrant group." Every conversation taught me something new, gave me something new to think about. They continued until his job was filled. Then we moved on. I don't think we ever spoke again. I never met Mr. Nikaido face-to-face, but I'm still just a little in love with him.

By taking so much time for my talks with Mr. Nikaido and other employers, I was breaking rules. I assumed all those rules had been made for reasons. But I figured they hadn't been made for me anyway. I must have been right. My increasingly successful record proved it. My joy working in this business proved it. I liked winning the numbers contests but decided, so what if I didn't make the most calls? I had the most fun. Aside from Mr. Nikaido, I had relationships with hundreds of employers and spent hours listening to their stories. And, just like the old people on Petain Street, they bought.

9

THERE ARE LOTS *of* EXCITING PEOPLE *in the* WORLD

Magical Experiences

When I was ten years old, alone in my backyard, I played out stories in which I met all kinds of eminent people. I rode in my pretend limousine to pretend parties where I drank ginger ale-champagne from a crystal glass that hadn't come in a box of Crystal Wedding Oats (a cereal that came with a pressed glass bowl or glass or dish in every box). I glided around the glittery room, smiling and toasting people who were all beautiful, witty, and dressed in gowns and tuxedoes. Lots of them were famous too, like actors and senators. In the movies, senators and congressmen, even the bad ones, were silver-haired, elegant, and had deep voices. They also, or so it seemed to me, all had Southern accents, even the ones from Boston, but I suppose they couldn't have.

When I was eleven, I got to meet a real congressman! Daddy took me to Washington, DC, to see the capitol and meet the man he called "my congressman." I didn't think a man as important as Congressman Boykin would really talk to us, but Daddy didn't have even the tiniest doubt he would, and that's just what happened.

The capitol was big and white and marble, and everybody in it seemed important, but Daddy wasn't afraid at all. He went right up to a man behind a desk and asked for directions to Congressman Boykin's office. He found it, walked in, and then told the secretary who he was. "I'm Norvelle Simmons. I'm up here from Prichard, and I'd like to speak with my congressman." She said she was sorry, but he was in a lunch meeting in the congressional dining room. But wait! Let her call down there and let him know Norvelle Simmons wanted to see him. She picked up her phone and another assistant asked if I'd like to sit in the congressman's chair while we waited. In a few minutes, the secretary came in and told us to go right over to the congressional dining room. He would love to see us.

Congressman Boykin came out of the dining room, napkin in hand, to meet "my good friend, Norvelle Simmons," and grabbed his hand in a way that made it seem they really were good friends. He stayed there and talked to Daddy for long enough for me to get bored, then turned to me. "This must be your beautiful daughter. You'd better keep an eye on her with all these young fellows around here." He winked at me and the men laughed (like they always do when they say things that embarrass kids). Then, before I could duck, he kissed me on my face with a mouth that still had some of his mashed potatoes on it. I was sick and I stayed sick till I could get to a bathroom and wash it off.

I was surprised that a congressman would leave a meeting to talk with Daddy. Daddy wasn't rich or a political big shot. But I was more surprised by what happened the next time we met Congressman Boykin, four years later.

It was a Sunday. Mama, Daddy, and I took a picnic to old Fort Gaines, near Gulf Shores. Alabama was honoring one of Daddy's heroes, Seminole Chief Osceola. They picked Fort Gaines for the ceremony because that's where the white people kept the chief in prison before they banished him and his people from Alabama and Florida. Daddy was part Cherokee (the Seminoles were part of the Cherokee nation). He really was, but just about every person from below the Mason-Dixon Line claims the same thing. I told this to a friend from Scotland. I said, "It doesn't seem fair. First we massacred them, then we claimed to be one of them."

"No, no," she said quickly. "We refer to it as 'the unfortunate incident.'"

Anyway, Congressman Boykin was there to unveil a plaque honoring the chief. After the ceremony, we were standing off to the side of the large crowd. Then the congressman caught sight of Daddy and rushed toward us, his hand outstretched. "Why, if it isn't Norvelle Simmons. It's been too long. How are you?" I couldn't believe it. With all the people in south Alabama, how could he remember not only Daddy's face but his name after four years? That's before I read about the congressman and learned he made knowing south Alabama and its people his life's work. I was awed by the man. But I had learned my lesson. I moved back before he could kiss me again.

Congressman Boykin was the first "celebrity" I ever met, but I felt as though I knew another one because I was kin to him. Alabama Governor Big Jim Folsom was my cousin because Mama's mother was a Folsom and Big Jim was her cousin. He was one of the most famous people in the state for being governor and for his politicking to get there. I never met him, but heard people talk all about him. They said when he put on a rally, it was a show, with flags, barbeque, fish fries, ice cream, and country bands. Once he had a crowd gathered, he'd bring out a bucket of sudsy water and a scrub brush, and promise he was going to clean up Alabama.

A lot of the men in my family had that kind of big personality. Big Jim was a charmer, especially with the ladies. A lot of the men in my family were charmers too. And, like them, he is said to have been a womanizer. He got caught, but I imagine the women forgave him. The scoundrels I knew could usually smile and wink and get forgiveness for just about anything.

Until I went to college, that was it for my meeting people who were famous, unless you count the time when I was eight and stood in line at the fair to get an autographed picture from the Lone Ranger.

Once I was in college and dating Johnny, that changed. I got my chance to meet all the famous people I could want. Johnny and I went to concerts, talked with the performers in their dressing rooms, and ended up watching from seats backstage. The guys at WDOL joked about Johnny's talent for getting close to the stars.

At first it was fun to be places other people couldn't go. When we met Johnny Rivers ("Secret Agent Man"), I learned being *seen* with the stars was actually more fun than being with the stars. There was a mob of fans gathered at the door to Johnny's dressing room, but we were whisked in as part of his entourage. After sitting around the group of tired musicians for a while, we left, plowing back through the tangle of people. Then I realized I'd left my sweater inside, and we had to push back through the crush, to be greeted by a bodyguard, who clearly didn't remember us. Through a narrow crack in the door, I told him I had left the sweater. He pushed the door to make the crack even smaller, and called out to ask if anyone had seen a yellow sweater. We heard someone call back, "Here it is. Johnny's sitting on it." Then there were murmurs from the crowd, "Johnny was sitting on that sweater." We just barely escaped, sweater and all.

That was just in a dressing room. It would be different to have performers come to our apartment for a party—I thought. It happened, and it was one more event that turned out to be nothing like I had always imagined it would be.

The performer was a huge star, Jerry Butler, "The Ice Man," who was one of the greatest and most enduring talents ever. I loved his songs. "For Your Precious Love," "Let It Be Me," and "Make It Easy on Yourself" were in my top ten favorites.

After the concert, Johnny asked Mr. Butler if he would like to come to our apartment for drinks. He said yes! He came with his whole band. I couldn't believe it! Whatever I expected, and I suppose it was some kind of a jam session, it didn't happen. Instead, I ran around trying to put together enough food while Jerry and his crew played poker and drank beer.

So meeting the stars wasn't as I had dreamed it would be. They were there to perform and give autographs. The problem was I'd never dreamed of getting autographs. I didn't want to meet people just to say I'd met them. I wanted interesting, talented, exciting friends. The performers were in Athens for just a day and they were there to work.

After we graduated and were getting ready to leave Athens for Atlanta I just knew things would be different. Johnny was going to leave Top 40 radio to do the news at WSB, "The Voice of the South." I was partly right. Things were better—for Johnny. His job let him stretch and use his talents. I was still teaching school, and I didn't see anything more exciting coming down the road for me, except as a spectator at Johnny's career.

Even though I was just a spectator, there was a lot to see. Johnny was in the middle of everything that was interesting and exciting in the city. We had invitations to openings and fashion shows, complimentary tickets to all of the plays, and of course, backstage passes.

There was a certain high to being seen in these places, although there was one night I would have given anything to be invisible. It was at a fashion show, one of the big splashy affairs of Atlanta's social year. We had wonderful seats, so close to the runway we were almost on stage ourselves and bathed in the Klieg lights aimed at the models. I liked it. I knew I looked good that night. My hair, makeup . . . everything was perfect. I walked tall, sat tall, smiled, and was totally enjoying myself until I felt something strange happening to me.

The skin on my arms began to feel tight, then it started to tingle, then itch. Soon it wasn't just an ordinary itch. It was crazy itching, and I was in no position to scratch. When it was just on my arms, I tried to scratch it by rubbing against Johnny's jacket while pretending to whisper a comment on some model's outfit. But when it spread to my stomach, legs, back, then all over, I felt as though I'd been bitten by every mosquito in south Alabama, Mississippi, and Louisiana, and I couldn't do a thing about it.

By the end of the show, I wasn't even trying to hide my scratching. We passed up the cocktail party and I nearly ran out of the place. The next day I went to the doctor to find out I had one more thing I could blame on teaching. I had chicken pox. It was awful and it was embarrassing. I was twenty-one years old with chicken pox! By noon, everybody within two hundred miles of Atlanta knew it too, because Johnny sent a message of sympathy to me over the noon news broadcast.

Atlanta in the '70s was exciting on so many fronts. Hank Aaron was hitting home runs at Braves Stadium where we ate my favorite meal, Chick-fil-A. Underground Atlanta was newly opened, with roaming brass bands, peanut barrels, organ grinders, quirky stores, and theme bars.

Lester Maddox, ex-governor of Georgia, had a souvenir shop there. He had first hit the news in 1967 when, brandishing an ax handle, he chased black people from his Pickrick restaurant. When served with an order to integrate, he closed the restaurant rather than serve black diners. In his shop, he greeted and talked with shoppers. A parody of himself, he sold autographed ax handles. My favorite restaurant was the Burning of

Atlanta, where we ate dinner to the music of a torch singer, while electric flames licked at every window.

Of all the things Atlanta had to offer, the best was theater—real onstage theater with real actors! I had been waiting for this since I was in the chorus in junior high, singing songs from *Oklahoma!*, *Carousel*, and *South Pacific*. I knew the plays must be wonderful, but I had no way to see them. When I was in high school, I started reading them. I read *Fiddler on the Roof*, *Who's Afraid of Virginia Woolf?*, *A Funny Thing Happened on the Way to the Forum*, and *Tiny Alice*, waiting for the day when I would be able to see them performed live. In Atlanta, I finally got the chance and it was as magical as I'd thought it would be. I also enjoyed meeting actors I'd seen in old movies and on television more than I had enjoyed meeting rock stars, because the actors had stories to tell and many took the time to tell them.

One of the first plays I saw was *Carousel*. It was like meeting old friends, hearing the songs "June is Bustin' Out All Over" and "If I Loved You." I had sung them in chorus and still knew the lyrics by heart. Still on a high from the play, we went backstage to meet John Raitt, the star of the show. Mr. Raitt was a Broadway legend, but I couldn't know that because I had never yet been to a Broadway show and had seen very few movies. He had created the role of Billy Bigelow in *Carousel* on Broadway and introduced some of my favorite songs, including the song sung at every high school graduation for decades, "You'll Never Walk Alone."

I had a lot of backstage experiences I hardly remember, but one was significant. Mr. Raitt surprised me—he seemed to be as happy to have me there as I was to be there! And he talked so openly. He talked about Broadway the way it used to be, but he was angry and frustrated with things as they had become. The changes in the theater weren't for the better. It seemed to me he was saying Broadway had forgotten him. As he talked about touring, I could understand why he didn't like it—there was the constant travel, plus the audiences who didn't know who he was and theaters that might or might not have anything close to appropriate dressing rooms. We must have been there for over half an hour. Johnny was there too, but it felt as though Mr. Raitt was speaking only to me. He talked and I said little beyond, "Really?" or "What happened then?" or "How come?"

I was still a couple of years away from my job in the staffing business, and this was the first time I had this intense a conversation with a stranger. I felt something here I hadn't felt before. I was fascinated, of course, and amazed that he would tell me his feelings. I also felt a sense of responsibility. It wasn't that I had the power to do anything for him, but I felt I had a responsibility to him, and that responsibility was to listen. One thought kept going through my mind, not in so many words, but the essence was, "This man, talking to me, is important and famous, and he needs me to listen to him." So I listened. When he was finished talking, there was nothing more. No relationship came of it. We went on our way. I'm sure he never thought of me again but I thought about the experience many times over the years.

I had listened to the old people on Petain Street, and knew they appreciated the attention. But they were lonely. This was the first time I'd had a stranger tell me his story. And that was when I began to understand listening as a service, and somehow my duty, my avocation. In a couple of years, I would carry this forward to clients.

Stars of the theater weren't the only ones in Atlanta. There were other stars, political stars. The city was changing. It had its first Jewish mayor, Sam Massell, and first black vice mayor, Maynard Jackson. (The two were sworn in the same year the Confederate Memorial on Stone Mountain was finished.)

Sam Massell's birthday party was the best party I've ever attended to this day. My normal discomfort with parties didn't hold there. It was more show than party and I didn't want to miss a single act. The room, in the Hyatt Regency on Peachtree, was huge, with all kinds of food, including a non-kosher cake made of chopped liver with Mayor Sam's picture painted on it in cream cheese icing. Julian Bond and Andy Young were there. Everybody was there, from people in the media to people in the news.

I don't think Jimmy Carter was there, but it seemed to me he didn't fit into this crowd anyway. He certainly didn't seem to be as much fun as the rest of them. Either way, I didn't think much of him. I didn't understand how he was elected governor. He lost me with his campaign ads. In the ads he squatted in the middle of a field, holding a bunch of peanuts, letting the dusty dirt from them blow through his fingers. Why vote for a man whose ads just proved he could grow peanuts in Georgia? Who couldn't?

I continued to go with Johnny to plays and parties, but the initial excitement wore off. I wasn't really a part of anything. I was just a spectator at his career, while mine sat on a sidetrack in Jackson County. Finally I decided I had to make the move even if I wasn't sure where it would take me.

The day I quit teaching I was joyous. I felt free, released, almost euphoric. I had taken control.

That same day, as if it was meant to be, I met a woman who became my new hero. While I had just taken a baby step toward controlling my life, Mal Johnson had taken giant steps to control hers. By the time I met her, Mal was Senior Vice President of Cox Broadcasting, the first woman ever to hold the position. She had been a protégée of broadcasting legend J. Leonard Reinsch. She had been on President Nixon's first trip to China. This was the woman who came to dinner!

That was a night of surprises, when anything could have happened. I came home, newly jobless, to find my parents had driven up from Mobile to surprise us for the weekend and were waiting for me in my house, which I hadn't cleaned in a week, knowing I'd have plenty of time to catch up. After the hugging, I ran around gathering a few of the scattered pieces of clothes and newspapers, but they had already seen the mess.

I still didn't know we were going to have a dinner guest, and I didn't find it out until an hour before she got there. We were washing the dishes when Daddy said he had almost forgot to tell me, "Johnny called. He said he is bringing a friend home for dinner."

"Almost forgot?! When will they be here?" They were coming around six, expecting dinner, and I had little or no food in the house. I whirled around making the house suitable for company while Mama went in the kitchen. I don't know how, but she put together a feast from scraps.

At six, the door opened and guess who came to dinner? Johnny, with an attractive, stylish woman with an arresting presence—and she was black.

In a flash I took in the scene and thought of possibilities ahead. I couldn't believe this. Johnny knew my parents were there. He could have warned me, but that wouldn't have occurred to him, and it was one of the nicest things about him. He was colorblind. I raced forward to shake Mal's hand.

I knew Mama and Daddy weren't like the Southern people you saw in the news, the ones with sneering, ugly faces, shaking their fists at black children. They wouldn't do that. I never saw them show disrespect for anybody. Daddy had taken me to a black dentist once when my tooth broke while we were on vacation. But still, neither of them had ever had a friend who was black or had a black person to dinner. For most of my parents' lives black people wouldn't have been allowed to sit at the same lunch counter with them or even eat in the same café.

Now here was Mal, not only the first black woman, but the most famous person of any race they had ever entertained. But neither her position nor her color made the least bit of difference. Having dinner with Mal seemed to be the most natural thing in the world for them.

That evening ranks, along with my sixteenth birthday, as the most fun and memorable of my early life. I was spellbound by Mal's stories of the places she had been and the famous people she'd met. Mama was too. We went into the kitchen to get coffee, and Mama was almost bouncing up and down with excitement. She clapped her hands and said, "Just think! She goes all over the world and people pay her to talk. And she's here talking to us—for free!"

The one I had been worried about was Daddy. But I needn't have. As far as Daddy was concerned, Mal could have been anybody—anybody he deemed smart enough to argue with, that is. By dessert, he and Mal were arguing about politics and Georgia's Senator Russell. Daddy made his points with wild gestures and the occasional cuss word, and Mal gave as good as she got. Both of them had a grand time. I think Mal enjoyed baiting him. I could see she was entertained by Daddy, but she loved Mama. "Eva, if you get tired of this crotchety old man, you just leave him and come up to Washington and live in the Watergate with me." I believe she meant it.

On another level, meeting Mal made me mad. It was just as I had suspected when I was a kid in Alabama—there were people out there, intellectual, exciting, talented people, and they were hidden away from me, as hidden as if they were behind some kind of giant wall. It wasn't fair! But at that time, I thought it was just because I lived in the South. Later I learned it wasn't. The wall was everywhere. I desperately wanted to crash through it, and Mal was my first crack in it.

With all of her glamorous friends, I didn't know why, but Mal befriended us. I think she must have collected people the way some collect coins or shoes. Mama wasn't planning to leave Daddy, so Mal invited Johnny and me to visit her at her apartment in Washington instead.

The Watergate was a long, long way from Petain Street, but when I walked into her apartment, I recognized it. I recognized everything. I'd seen it in old movies and built my dreams on it. I'd drawn it on paper. I'd created it out of sawhorses in my backyard. But this apartment was real, and Mal was real, and that evening, unlike the evenings I played out in my backyard, was real. Two of Mal's friends came for dinner. They were interesting, creative people—intellectuals—and the conversation was witty and sparkling, just as I knew it would be.

These people knew everybody in Washington, and their personal stories were about people who were in the news every day. Why was it different from Atlanta? It was an intimate group and we were part of it, not just spectators. Mal made me feel that I belonged.

The more I knew of Mal, the more I was in awe of her. So far, all I'd done to create the life I wanted was to draw the Yellow-Haired Girl living it on paper. Mal had drawn her life in reality. She made things come out her way. I so wanted to do that too.

With every story she told, I was more inspired. If Mal could do all of the things she did, I could too. If she had the courage to face any obstacle and say, "No problem," so could I. . . . At least I hoped so. Mal had faced problems in her life that made what I had done seem minor.

When I didn't know where my money would come from, I got married. Mal was already married when she faced a money crisis. Her husband was in the military and they were sent from the East Coast, where Mal had a teaching position, to a base in California where there was a glut of teachers and no jobs. She was far from her family, living was expensive, and they weren't making ends meet on his salary. Mal had the same problem I was still grappling with at the time I met her—she didn't know how to do anything except teach school. But she made short work of her problems—she picked up the help-wanted ads and told her husband she would find a job.

He said, "But you don't know how to do anything."

"Don't worry about it," she told him, "I'll find a job. Here, look at this one." It was an ad for a chef at a private estate. "I can do that."

"What are you talking about? You can't boil water!"

"Don't you worry about it. I'll learn."

Mal got the job. It was for an heiress—I always remember her as the "Sinclair heiress." That wasn't right, as Mal corrected me every time I brought up the story, but my memory was too strong to switch. Anyway, Mal went out and invested in a gourmet cookbook, and started her job. I wondered if I had that kind of courage.

First she stashed the cookbook in the servant's powder room off the kitchen. When Miss "Sinclair" told her what she wanted for dinner, Mal slipped into the powder room, wrote the recipes on three-by-five cards, and returned to the kitchen. It went smooth as clockwork—until the day the lady brought in a bag of things Mal had never seen before. "Mal, I have a guest coming for dinner tonight. This is his favorite. I know you have the menu planned, but please cook these as well."

Mal looked at the things. She had no idea what they were. But she never allowed for the possibility of defeat. No problem; she would figure it out.

"No problem" was a sentence that reverberated through Mal's stories. It definitely makes the top ten list of the best things ever said—and it's my favorite lie. Of course it was a problem, but that wouldn't stop her. Could she cook these ugly green things that didn't even look edible? "No problem." She just needed to figure out what they were.

She telephoned her husband at the base, described the things, and asked him to go to the base library and look through books until he could find something that looked like them. "You're going to get caught now for sure," he said.

"Don't worry about it. Just find it and tell me what it is."

That was another one of the best things ever said: "Don't worry about it." I thought of it as, "Don't present reasons why I can't, because I'm going to." And she did.

He called half an hour later. "I think I have it. It's an artichoke. Mal, you've never heard of these things. How can you cook them? This is the end!"

"No, it's not. I'll do it. It'll be fine. Don't worry."

It was better than fine. Mal served the dish to the artichoke connoisseur and he loved them. He came back to the kitchen after dinner and told her, "I've never had artichokes anywhere as good as yours. I'd love to get your recipe."

No problem. "I'm so happy you like them, and I'd love to give you the recipe, but I can't. I'm so sorry, but you see, it was my grandmother's recipe, and she made me promise I'd never let it out of the family. But I'll cook them for you anytime you want them."

How could you not be inspired by that story? I wanted to be just like her. I wanted to prove I had that never-say-uncle backbone too.

Over the next couple of days, I learned more about just how victorious Mal Johnson had been over life's circumstances. Her husband died young, leaving her without some of the tools we consider basic for life. For one thing, she had never learned to drive. She had a new car her husband had bought shortly before his death. Friends said she should sell it. It was of no use to her and she could use the money. She wouldn't hear of it. When Mal told the car story, she got a little glint in her eye that reminded me of Mama when she did something somebody had told her she couldn't do.

Mal said, "I looked at that brand new automobile sitting out front, and I made up my mind I would learn to drive it, and I'd learn it by myself. I went out and bought a book." Mal Johnson is the only person I've ever known who learned to drive from a book. I stopped her and said I didn't even know there was a book on how to drive. "Of course there is. There's a book on how to do anything you want to learn."

"But didn't you have to practice? How did you do that without help?"

"I learned to drive at four o'clock in the morning. I studied my book until I was pretty sure I knew what to do. Then I was ready to practice and I couldn't do that with traffic around, so I set my clock for four a.m. and went out driving. I kept it up until I was good enough to take my test. That could have been a problem. When you go to take your driving test, you still don't have a license, so you're supposed to have someone drive you. I didn't have anyone, so I drove myself and parked the car way off in the back corner of the parking lot where you couldn't see it from the front door. Everything went fine until after I passed, got my license, and was about to leave. The policeman who had given me the test asked where my driver was. I said, 'Oh, didn't you see him wave when we were getting in the car? He was going over to the diner down the street to get something to eat while he waited.'"

Over the years, I lost touch with Mal. She had moved from the Watergate and I didn't know where she was. I finally found her phone number and called her. I was lucky to have found her in time because she died the next year.

We met at Café Milano for dinner. In her eighties, Mal breezed in, still stylish, funny, and all about planning her next venture with the organization American Women in Radio and Television. It's funny, all the stories Mal had told me were about her personal victories. I knew she was a great woman. I knew she was my hero. I knew bits and pieces about her extraordinary life, but she had never dropped names or talked about her public life.

After dinner, we went to my house where the conversation remained vibrant. I asked her to tell me about some of the exciting adventures she'd had working in radio and television. Her answer took me by surprise.

"I was the first person to know Secretary of State Rogers was on his way out to be replaced by Henry Kissinger."

It took me a minute to compute what she had said. "Really? President Nixon told you that?"

"He didn't have to. It was on his first trip to China." I never even knew Mal had been on President Nixon's trip to China.

"I was with the press corps. We were all standing on the airfield waiting for the cars to pick us up, and I was standing near Mr. Rogers and the president. President Nixon walked over to me and put his arm around my shoulder and said to Mr. Rogers, 'I want you to make sure our Mal is taken care of.' I knew it right then. No president would tell a Secretary of State to take care of a reporter unless he was on his way out."

It was a wonderful final story from a woman who had been so important to me because she showed me that the world I'd dreamed about was possible. There *were* fabulous apartments and women who, by their own efforts, got themselves there. When we made the move from Atlanta to Washington the next year, I was on fire with anticipation. I was actually here, in the capital of the United States. Every place I went held some piece of history, some landmark, such as Ford's Theatre. For some reason I got a particular thrill when I walked down 16th Street toward the White House and passed the Russian Embassy.

Now I was here and it was my turn! I still didn't know where I was going, but I was inspired to believe it would be exciting, it would be filled with interesting people, and I would find it in Washington. I did, and it was even more exciting than I'd hoped. The staffing business gave me a career and a front-row view of some of the most fascinating people I would ever meet. And I was able to approach these people without the same fears I had in social settings because I had a job to do for them.

That job gave me the chance to see a few of the rich and famous up close. You learn a lot about a person when you are matching him or her with an executive assistant. I was allowed into private offices, even homes, and saw things the public didn't.

I remember when I was in the car on my way to meet Eunice Kennedy Shriver. Wow! I was going to meet the sister of President Kennedy, the woman who had founded Special Olympics. I don't know what I expected to see in Mrs. Shriver's office, but what I saw wasn't it. There was nothing impressive about it. It was small and oddly shaped with a large column that stood off-center and didn't fit the room. Mrs. Shriver's desk, which was pushed against one side of the column, was piled with books and papers. Actually, every piece of furniture was stacked high. With all of the art she must have owned, none of it adorned the walls. Instead, her life story papered them. Newspaper and magazine clippings about her children hung in layers on walls and all sides of the column. Photos of family were taped up as well. Every inch of wall space, column space, and desk space was dedicated to her family.

As I started trying to get her to talk about the job, I knew she was going to be an almost impossible client—and boss—because she expected me to know, without her telling me, exactly what she wanted and needed. I could not get her to focus on my questions, but I kept trying. She didn't seem irritated by them, just unimpressed as she gave vague answers and leafed through correspondence on her desk. Then she said, "Are you familiar with Special Olympics?" When I answered that I thought it was a wonderful organization, Mrs. Shriver showed me the fire and the passion she had to make a difference, and the reasons we loved the Kennedys. All conversation about the assistant position was over. I'd have to guess the rest of the details. Special Olympics was what she cared about. I should get involved. Every child should have the opportunity.

I walked out energized but well aware that finding her assistant was going to be tough. Actually, top-level executive assistants are almost always hard to deliver. They are the people who have to make huge decisions for their bosses, and mistakes are costly. I think of them as higher life forms.

One famous client called me after he fired his assistant for failing to give him a message, costing him an important appointment. This would bother any boss, but while the owner of an insurance agency whose assistant cost her an appointment may regret her loss as much, it just doesn't have the sex appeal of, "My assistant has to stay aware of people in the news because they may be part of my life. When I was at the Cape, Lucy took a call from [not the actual name] Joyce Mason. She should have known the name. Joyce has been in the news every day for a project she's setting up in conjunction with the United Nations. Lucy didn't think or connect the dots. She didn't even get a full message. If she had called me or emailed me, I wouldn't be here today because I would have spent the last four days at Ted Turner's Montana ranch working out the details for a project he would sponsor."

So it's simple mathematics. The higher you go, the fewer executives there are and the equally fewer candidates who fit them. And Mrs. Shriver was a mountaintop. I don't even know how many candidates I interviewed before finding the one needle-in-a-haystack. When I met her, I knew instantly she was the one. Mrs. Shriver hired her on the spot.

Several years later, I got a call from Mrs. Shriver's business office. Could I find someone for her executive assistant position again? I thought about the amount of energy it took before and said I was afraid I couldn't give it the time it needed. What I was thinking was, "I'm only allowed one miracle per client."

The rich have their problems too, as I learned, but theirs are real different from ours. A Green Book socialite set up a meeting with me because she needed a new assistant. I went to her northwest Washington home. It was the home of someone with old money and a love for beautiful things—lots and lots of beautiful things. They covered every inch of wall space in the foyer and as far as I could see up the staircase—paintings, etchings, and drawings by artists whose names I recognized. There were more in the living room, where antique tables held marble and bronze sculptures, a grand piano was covered with sheet music, and an enormous easel held an oil portrait of a woman in a gold gown.

Mrs. C motioned me to the sofa. She picked up a stack of brochures from a gilt chair across from me and sat down.

I took out my legal pad and pen, ready to work, but before I could ask the first question on the subject of her assistant, she thrust the bunch of brochures at me. "I need to make a decision on this." I took a quick look at them. They were all advertising jet airplanes.

"We've been thinking about buying a private jet. We have to travel so much—and commercial travel has gotten so troublesome. Your own plane is so much cleaner and you aren't locked to an airline's schedule. You travel when you want. We had almost decided to buy, but some of our friends have gone with co-ops, and they say they are just as nice as the private jets and certainly much nicer than commercial. Well, of course they would be. And you needn't worry about maintenance as you would if you owned. What do you think?"

It took me a minute to realize she was serious. The answer was, I didn't think. I had never thought about private jets once in my life. So I told her, "You know, I've never thought about it."

"Well think about it! Look at the brochures and tell me what you think," she snapped. "Which one would you choose?" She looked at me as though this was a simple service that I shouldn't have considered unusual.

I turned the thick, glossy pages and looked at the pictures of jet airplanes. They were all beautiful, with white leather seats that turned into beds, white carpeting, and one even had a dining table with fresh flowers. And they each cost . . . I don't know. There were no prices listed. The price didn't seem to matter.

As I dutifully studied the brochures, Mrs. C cataloged the benefits and detriments associated with the different co-op plans according to her friends.

Much of it was lost on me, but apparently even though co-owners wouldn't have total control of scheduling, they were guaranteed a takeoff window within a certain number of hours. Once I looked through the last brochure, she stopped and looked at me. She really wanted me to give her an answer.

I thought about it and reasoned, "I hate dealing with maintenance on my car. So I guess I'd prefer the co-ops."

"Good. I'll tell my husband that's what we've agreed on. Now, do you want to talk about filling my job?"

All that and I got paid, too!

There was something about the fame and power of Washington's celebrities that seemed to spread, like light, and give the illusion of fame and celebrity to those people nearby. I certainly felt it. Sometimes all it took was to be in a place where power walked to make everybody there appear to be a somebody. It's funny to say, but it made me feel important just being there. The Mayflower Hotel bar did that for me.

It seemed to me everybody who was important went to lunch there, and everybody I saw there seemed important. When I saw men in suits with earpieces, I knew it meant somebody really big was in the building, or about to be. Those men were usually as close as I came to seeing the people they were protecting, except for the time I saw Dan Quayle. (Who's he?) Once, Mayor Marion Barry walked right past me as he came into the building wearing a pinstriped suit with kente scarf and matching kufi hat (African scarf and hat).

The Mayflower took me back to Petain Street and the girl who was afraid she didn't belong. Before I got the courage to go in, I passed it a hundred times, afraid if I went in I'd be spotted as an impostor. Even if they didn't throw me out, they would know. One day I gathered my courage and walked through the lobby, all the way from Connecticut Avenue to 17th Street.

Then came the day I took a client there for lunch. It's hard to express how high I felt. It was the kind of high you only get when you're young. I felt like a big shot. I was there and I belonged! I can still see the scene. We sat at one of the dark velvet banquettes. I looked around the dimly lit room, and my imagination ran wild. I saw foreign agents and congressmen, a spy with his handler, a CIA operative with his source, and a future president of the United States.

Over the next twenty or so years, the Mayflower became as familiar to me as my backyard had been. I also started viewing Washington in a different light. In so many ways, it was more of a small town than city, and the Mayflower was its local diner (but with big-city prices and a breakfast menu that included miso soup).

Back in Prichard, we'd had our local heroes and dignitaries too, even if they weren't on television and magazine covers all over the world. In Washington, instead of Mayor Dismukes eating just down at the Kress's lunch counter, Ted Koppel, Leslie Stahl, or Madeleine Albright might be at the next table at the Mayflower. Or, Mike Wallace might be ahead of me in line and turning around to chat about the city being unusually crowded for August.

The Mayflower's waiters could have been plucked out of a small-town diner. Once they knew you, they might drop by your table to share a bit of gossip just as they did in Prichard, except for the subjects of their gossip. "You're having the brioche. That's John Kennedy Jr.'s favorite breakfast. He was in yesterday for some meetings about his new magazine—left before breakfast today." Or they might just have a gripe to get off their chest. "This is going to be a long week. The DAR convention is in town, and most of the little ladies are in my station. Watch. I'll give them the bill, they'll take out their coin purses, and insist on splitting it to the penny. 'Here. The shrimp was mine . . . ,' 'I didn't have an appetizer.'"

If you hadn't been in for a while, it was only polite for the waiter to stop by your table, even if it wasn't his station, and ask about the family or where you've been since he hadn't seen you in so long. It didn't matter if you were alone, with friends, or trying to sell to a new client, as I was when my friend Peter came to our table with menus and questions about mutual friends. "I haven't seen Ron in here lately. Hope he's doing okay." An answer was expected, so I told him Ron had been traveling. It was also expected that I introduce him to my client, whom Peter then included in the conversation. "I haven't seen you in here before. Are you from out of town?" My client said he was from Florida. "That's where I want to live. I'm going to Tampa next week. Ruthi, don't you be surprised when you come in one day and find out I've moved." Just like Kress's lunch counter!

When people moved away from the Mayflower neighborhood, it was just as if they had moved away from Petain Street—somebody always stayed in touch and kept the rest of us up on news of them. Last year, I was discussing strategic plans for the company over lunch with my business partner. One of the waitresses saw me and interrupted us with the latest news on Peter and his life in Tampa. Of course she did! She knew I would want to know.

There was one character at the Mayflower who was worthy of any Southern diner. At somewhere around ninety years old, she was Washington's oldest waitress, and had worked there for longer than I had been in DC. A little woman with gray braids wrapped tightly around her head, she zipped around the restaurant like a hummingbird with attitude, snapping at undecided diners.

"Take your order?"

"Um, I'm thinking about the baked chicken . . . or . . . or . . . maybe the steamed vegetable basket, or . . . "

"I'm busy. I'll come back when you know what you want. I have other customers."

She was terrifying, and I'd go early just to make sure to get her table.

One lunchtime when I was dieting and having a hard time finding something that was both legal and appetizing, I asked hopefully, "Is the shrimp casserole done with oil?"

"Yes."

I was disappointed. "Oh. Gee. I can't have oil."

"Don't order it then," she snapped.

After that lady, meeting other famous people of Washington, DC, didn't seem so scary.

The city had one thing found in no other place in the world: the Hill. Of course, I'd been there before, but as I attended receptions with Johnny, I got a different impression of the Hill from the one I got when I came here with Daddy. I came to the conclusion this congress was a long way from the congress of Daddy and Congressman Boykin. The personal touch wasn't possible because senators and members of congress were constantly surrounded by aides who worked to push the followers and favor-seekers through. Meeting these congressmen meant nothing more than a move-them-down-the-line handshake. I couldn't imagine any of them as someone a blue-collar voter would call "my congressman."

A lot of the people who were close to those in power assumed they were powerful too. It was as though power and greatness were things they could catch, like a cold, just by being near the great ones. With all their puffing and posturing, they needed those people who kept their feet at least close to the ground. I met a seventy-year-old executive assistant to an association president who had been doing that for her boss for many years. Now she was retiring and I was there to get information to refill her position. She started with a tour. "I suppose we should start by letting you see his office. That'll tell you something. Then I'll tell you about the job."

The room was designed to be impressive, with dark wood, overstuffed chairs, a small glass conference table, and a wall with more framed pictures than I had ever seen. I stared and picked out two presidents, a vice president, and a large number of men who looked important, even if I didn't recognize them. "Wow!"

She snorted dismissively. "Oh . . . those. They're the 'me-and' pictures."

I looked at her and it was clear I didn't know what she was talking about. She said, "You know. Me-and-the-senator. Me-and-the-president. All executives have them."

I decided I didn't want any "me-and" pictures. As we continued to attend events, I stayed in the background, out of the handshake lines, so I didn't meet a lot of people. One I regret that I didn't meet was Hubert Humphrey. It was only a year or so before he died. Johnny and I were going to some dinner. As people arrived, we were herded into a small room to wait for seating. We were early so we had chairs, but the room quickly filled to leave only standing room. Senator Humphrey sat one chair away from me, graciously saying a few words each to person after person who squeezed past the crowd to reach him. He looked tired. One of the senator's aides leaned over and whispered to me, "Would you like to go over and be introduced to Senator Humphrey?" I considered for a minute walking the length of an armchair to meet this man who was old, tired, and bombarded with people. Maybe he needed to talk with some of them, but he didn't have the slightest need to meet me.

I thanked the aide, and said no. I couldn't understand why the aide was noticeably insulted. I thought about something Mama told me: "If a person wants to give you something, take it. You're doing it for him more than for you." I was wrong. I had just refused the aide's gift and scorned his influence. The man is probably still out there somewhere and I'm sure he has never forgiven me.

There was one hand I did shake, however, and it was an experience I'm glad I didn't miss. The hand belonged to Senator Strom Thurmond. He was close to a hundred years old at the time, and looked every day of it, in spite of his hair, which was still the color of Carrot Top's. His face was what carried the mark of his age, looking as though it might disintegrate in front of my eyes. But there was nothing old or weak about his handshake. When he took my hand, I was stunned. I never knew a handshake could be so intimate. It took ten seconds, and it was pure sex.

If I was insecure about approaching people, Johnny was just the opposite. He approached anyone with wide-eyed enthusiasm, no matter how big they were. Even the most casual encounters don't feel casual when they're with the most powerful man in the world. Johnny came home one night all excited because he had met the president.

"I interviewed the president today. Can you believe that? I interviewed the president today! I was walking out of the press room at the White House and ran right into him."

"Tell me about the interview."

"I said, 'Hello, Mr. President. How are you?' And he said, 'Fine, thank you, and you?'"

Maybe I would have met more of the famous people in the world if I'd just recognized them. It's bad enough I don't remember names, but I don't remember faces either. I learned from experience there are some famous people who want to be recognized and they don't like it when you don't. One such person was Ron Ziegler. A lot of people may not know his name today, but when I met him he had been in the news every day for years as press secretary to President Nixon. Mr. Ziegler had been on the plane with him when the newly resigned president left the White House for good. I met him in an elevator, one I nearly missed, and it would have been less embarrassing if I did. I was running toward the closing door when one of the two men in suits held it for me. I thanked him.

He smiled and chatted with me, "You seemed to be in a hurry. You late for a meeting?"

"Yes. No. I think my natural state is frantic." I stuck out my hand. "I'm Ruthi Postow. I'm with the personnel firm here on the seventh floor." (Who knew? He might be a client.)

He took it. "I'm Ron Ziegler."

"It's nice to meet you," I said. "What do you do?"

He didn't say a word—just looked at me for a minute and turned away. When the door opened, he got off without his earlier display of chivalry.

In the early '80s, I met a man any baseball fan would have given a month's salary to meet, and I had no idea who he was. I met Bill Veeck as I sat in the lobby of a resort, waiting for Johnny to come out of a meeting. When I looked at him, I saw an older man with a wooden leg just sitting there, and I thought he must be lonely, so I started a conversation with him. He was very nice, and seemed eager to chat. I decided it was because he was lonely. So I listened to him. He talked about running a baseball team, which I thought was an administrative role. He said something about owning a team I'd never heard of and assumed was a minor league team that he had a small percentage of.

It soon became clear to him that not only did I not know *who* he was, I didn't know enough about baseball to understand *what* he was. He got up and walked away, obviously disgusted with my ignorance. Later I Googled him and discovered just what a huge opportunity I lost that day. I could have listened to one of the legends of baseball tell me the best stories I would ever get to hear, and to be able to brag to my baseball-fan friends about meeting him.

There was one man I did recognize, and he changed my life—for a moment. I met Michael Caine in an elevator in a hotel in New York City. I got on the elevator and there he was, the sexiest man on the planet, in an ankle-length, creamy linen coat. He smiled and spoke to me in his forever-Alfie accent. "You look beautiful and breezy for such a steamy day."

I smiled (I'm pretty sure I didn't giggle) and said, "Thank you."

He continued the conversation, asking if I was in New York for business or pleasure. I managed to tell him I was there for both.

"Do you visit New York often?"

"As often as I can. I love New York."

"And where is home?"

"Washington, DC."

"I was there a few months ago—another beautiful city."

The elevator stopped on my floor and, as much as I didn't want to, I got off. I never saw him again, but I know, for a few seconds, we shared something special—something magical. Any woman who doesn't believe in love at first sight has never shared an elevator with Michael Caine.

So I learned. There are some people who, just to be near them, even if only for minutes, is a magical experience. For Johnny it was on the White House lawn when he "interviewed the president today." For me, it was New York City, an elevator, and Michael Caine.

10

"BEAUTY'S ONLY SKIN DEEP—
UGLY'S *to the* BONE"

Prejudice Hurts and It's Not Fair

Fall was coming and I was excited because I was going to start first grade at Turnerville Elementary School in Prichard. Then Daddy's job changed and we moved to Houston. But in Texas, they said I wasn't old enough for first grade, because my birthday was three weeks after the cut-off date. Mama said that was just silly. She went up to the school and when she came home, I was enrolled in Wharton Elementary School. My teacher, Mrs. Thompson, didn't like it one bit—although I didn't know it then.

I woke up that first day and was ready to go an hour early—new dress, new shoes, new socks, even new underwear. I was so excited. The first time I saw my teacher I was in love. I thought she was beautiful. As we filed in, I watched her smile and welcome every child. But when it was my turn, she changed. She didn't smile or say anything nice as she had to the others. She just said, "Oh, yes. You're here. Take a seat over there."

I didn't understand. Didn't she like me? I had never experienced anything like that before. The baby of my family by many years and one of only five children in the kind of blue-collar neighborhood where every adult is your parent, I had gotten in trouble and been scolded, but I knew everybody loved me and they all said how smart I was.

Now here was a person, an important person, who didn't love me. She didn't even like me. And I quickly found out she didn't even think I was smart. I've been thinking back, trying to remember what I felt. I didn't feel mad. I felt confused and ashamed, even if I didn't know what I was ashamed of. I wanted more than anything to please her and make her like me. I wanted to be as good as the other children.

The second day, Mrs. Thompson put us in groups according to how smart we were. She didn't say that, but I knew that was what she was doing. I got put in the lowest group. I knew that too. There were four of us. We sat with our desks facing each other in a corner of the room that seemed to be far away from the other children. All the other groups got workbooks and readers. We didn't. We worked with word/picture cards.

I was embarrassed to be there, even though Inez was in that group too and she became my best friend. She was from Mexico, and she knew good songs and could talk in Spanish *and* in English. The other two children weren't any fun. They never talked or told riddles, and they couldn't even play the same games, and we always had to wait for them to finish the assignment before we could do something new. My other friends were all in the second group. I even had a boyfriend. He had freckles and wore glasses. The top group of children didn't play with anyone outside of their own group.

When the better-group children did good work Mrs. Thompson hung it on the wall. I worked hard because I wanted to show Mrs. Thompson I was smart. Coloring was something I was really good at—my kindergarten teacher always said so. It was my favorite, next to finger-painting. So when Mrs. Thompson gave us pictures of Little Red Riding Hood to color, I knew I could do it, and she'd be proud of me and hang my picture on the wall.

I leaned over the paper, bearing down, coloring with all my might, till I used up the point of my new red Crayola, and my Red Riding Hood's cape was as neat and shiny and dark red as I could make it.

Then I heard Mrs. Thompson say to make sure we made the cape "bright" red. No! I'd messed up again. I didn't know what "bright" meant. I was afraid to ask. I knew dark red. I thought about it. Bright was like the sun. So was light. Bright red must mean the same as light red. So I had done it all wrong! I didn't want my picture to be wrong. I used my fingernails to scrape off every bit of the shiny red. When I finished, the picture was a washed-out mess with a tear in it. I tried to color over it—coloring easy to make it "bright" (or light).

Mrs. Thompson came by my desk and saw the picture. Her face turned mad. "What are you doing?" I kept my head down but peered around the room. The other children were looking at me, and Mrs. Thompson kept talking. "This is NOT what I said to do! I told you to make the cape bright! Don't you ever listen? What a mess!"

But I had listened! I was too ashamed to tell her I didn't know what "bright" meant. I didn't say anything.

I never thought about it being connected to first grade, but to this day, if I feel accused without being heard, I react childishly. Even if I manage to control it, I want to cry or throw a tantrum. It's odd because I don't mind admitting mistakes. I even take responsibility for the mistakes others make if it ends the argument. It's when I'm accused or somebody attributes motives to me without first giving me the chance to explain that it happens.

The strangest thing—and something I've wondered about from time to time—is how I felt about Mrs. Thompson. I loved her. I was distraught when, in the middle of the year, she suddenly left. Years later I found out she had quit because she was going to have a baby. They had to do that back then and, of course, they didn't tell the children she was pregnant. That was a subject we shouldn't know about. We shouldn't even hear the word before we were grown, which was the cause of one of Mama's more embarrassing moments.

I was seven or eight and still didn't know what the word "pregnant" meant, when I overheard my Sunday school teacher say one of the other teachers had gone home to rest because she was pregnant. Mama and I were sitting in church in the quiet moments as the service was about to start. I announced in the kind of child voice that could be heard to the back of the church, "I have a headache. I think I must be pregnant."

Back at elementary school, a new teacher came to replace Mrs. Thompson, and Inez and I decided to hate her. We walked home together, giggling and making up stories about her. "I'll bet she's a witch and she made a spell to make Mrs. Thompson have to leave, and she lives in a haunted house. She puts spells on trees, too, so they can walk, and she rides to school in walking trees." Our stories got sillier every day. Then I suppose we got bored and found a new game.

While I was making up my stories about her, the new teacher was moving me into the higher groups. Mama noticed the difference. "Thank goodness Mrs. Thompson left. I ran into your teacher today and she told me you are doing well."

"Well, I still don't like her, and I miss Mrs. Thompson."

"Well you shouldn't. She never wanted you in her class. She said you were too young. This teacher is taking an interest in you and she's teaching you."

Mrs. Thompson didn't want me in her class? I was surprised. My chest felt tight and my throat felt as though it was closing up. I wanted to cry, but I couldn't. She hadn't liked me! I didn't know it wasn't all my fault. Children don't know that. I learned from Mrs. Thompson that there must be something wrong with me. I learned I wasn't as good as the other children whom she did like.

I went on and finished the year in one of the higher groups and with the new teacher. I don't even remember her name. But why should I? She's not the one who taught me the big lessons. Mrs. Thompson did that. I just didn't know what they were yet.

As I grew up and learned about such things, I realized Mrs. Thompson had given me my first lessons on prejudice and discrimination. By making decisions about me based on only a statistic, and without knowing me or giving me a chance, she helped me understand what being the object of prejudice feels like. Being in authority and holding me back without testing me, she taught me about discrimination and prepared me to rage against things I thought were unfair to me or others. Mrs. Thompson was to be of great value to me.

At the end of that year, we moved back to the loving world of Petain Street, Turnerville Elementary School, my friends, and Grandmama. Grandmama was the best playmate I ever had. I think I spent more time playing with her than my friends. As we played, she taught me more of the lessons that would come back to me and be valuable later. Grandmama's view of right and wrong was simple. People who do mean and bad things are ugly.

People who hurt other people on purpose are ugly. People who are kind and sweet are pretty, and . . .

> Beauty's only skin deep
> Ugly's to the bone;
> Beauty goes away
> But ugly holds its own.
> —Amanda Thomas Simmons, my Grandmama

That summed it up—that and Mr. Jack Dobie. Grandmama said he was a man who would come and take away the bad children to . . . I don't know where, but it surely wasn't a good place. "Ruthi's being bad. Come get her, Jack Dobie, and take her where the bad girls go." I'd jump on her bed and hide my head under her pillow, screaming, "No! Don't call him!"

"Well, all right this time, but don't be bad anymore." I knew it was a game, but I'd just as soon she would not call his name anyway.

Over the years, the lessons all came together for me. By the time I was in a position to do something about it, I knew what discrimination was. I knew how it felt. I knew it was a mean thing, and people who did it were ugly. Mrs. Thompson had not been fair to make assumptions about me, and I was enraged by it! It wasn't fair to make assumptions about other people based on their skin or their age, and it was mean and ugly. I knew it, and eventually I got the chance to do something about it.

When I came to Washington, I brought an invisible army with me. Daddy's wit and sayings, Mama's strength and determination, Grandmama and Jack Dobie—all came right along, although I wasn't aware of them until situations came up in which they were needed. They answered questions of right or wrong, fair or unfair, ugly or pretty for me in a place where I was close to people and saw, first-hand, people doing things that were fair and things that were unfair, things nice and things not nice.

I was meeting all kinds of people. I was getting people jobs. And I was laughing because people are funny. The weird things people do in interviews are funny. Arrogant bosses are funny. I'm funny. With all the merriment, the unfunny things stood out in contrast. Discrimination is one of the most not-funny things I can imagine, and I was shocked to find it in Washington, DC.

I was thinking about this a couple of years ago. The truth is, I was silently patting myself on the back for my part in opening the workplace to people who hadn't had access. I had watched the progress and knew we were better than we were forty, thirty, twenty, even ten years ago. It had been years since I confronted overt discrimination. The last time any employer asked me to discriminate was back in 1980. I hadn't thought about it in years because it was an uncomfortable memory for me.

The market was tough in 1980. When the receptionist buzzed me to say I had a call from the office manager of Aetna's government affairs office, I knocked over my coffee cup jumping to grab the phone. It was great news. Polly was calling to ask my help in placing an executive assistant to their lobbyists. I felt such relief as I took notes. Finally, I had a job order to fill, and it was "hot." Polly said she wanted to interview and hire immediately. I started thinking through the candidates who fit the job. One popped into my mind who was a standout. I was tasting the placement. Then Polly added, "Just one more thing. This is a busy time for me. I don't have time to waste so don't send me any minority [read: black] candidates."

I stopped breathing. "What?" I don't know if I screamed it or just thought the word, because I was dumbfounded. I felt sick. I remember how I felt as if it happened yesterday, and this is the part I'm not proud of. I was only thinking about myself, about what she was doing *to me*. We were in a recession, and I needed that piece of business. I felt so sorry for myself. I didn't even think of the person being deprived of his rights and the opportunity for a job.

I reminded myself to breathe and knew I had to say something—I searched my memory for the scripted line I'd been taught and hadn't had to use in so long: "I *can't* discriminate based on race, religion, or sex, but I will screen each candidate to meet your every other qualification. We will search every sector of the market to get the best person. Polly, wouldn't your executives want to hire a person who is smart, polished, and qualified regardless of race? That's the only candidate I would send." Why did I say "can't" as opposed to "won't"?

My voice was strained. I know I sounded desperate, and I was. I was so hoping she would change her mind and say of course she would hire a quality candidate of any race. But she didn't.

"Look, I'm working with two other agencies who understand our problem. I do not have the time to interview people we won't hire. But think of the candidate. If you want to send a minority candidate, fine, but all you're doing is wasting her time. I wouldn't want you to waste my time if I were looking for a job."

"But how can a company as big as yours refuse to hire a minority candidate in your government affairs office?"

"It's not that we don't hire minorities. We have over our quota, but this is a high-visibility position. Appearance matters." Finally! I heard what she was saying. A black employee was a quota, not a person. I could just picture their quota—in the huge central office mailroom or on the loading dock. It was wrong.

I said, "I'm so sorry," and I wasn't lying. I really was sorry. "I can't do it. I can't even work with you. Even if I don't discriminate, I'd still be discriminating. It's illegal. This is the only job I know how to do, and I need to keep doing it." It was still about me. It's pretty clear why I wanted to forget.

It was the very last time anyone asked me to discriminate—until "yesterday" came, twenty-eight years later, and crumpled my vision of our city as inching along toward the "promised land." I call it "yesterday" because I want to remember how close we are to where we were.

"Yesterday" was 2008, during the presidential campaign, and the call was from the office of the campaign manager for a United States presidential candidate. I was in a meeting with Erin, a senior member of my staff, when Ronda called to ask us to find an administrative assistant for an immediate opening. The person would be working closely with the campaign manager, handle administrative duties, back up phones, and drive him to rallies and meetings.

Except for the driving, this was a job I had filled so many times. I was sure we had candidates. Would she be available to interview tomorrow?

"Yes. But one more thing," Ronda said. "The candidate has to be white."

Erin told me later she had never seen my face change so abruptly—as though I'd seen a ghost. She was right.

"What?" I said. That seems to be the only word that comes to my mind in these cases. As I tried to do the nondiscrimination speech, I stammered. "I can't do that. We—I don't discriminate. It's illegal." I had forgotten the script but I finally got the message across.

Ronda was adamant. "You have to understand. It matters how things look. This is a national presidential campaign. What if people saw him?"

I was reeling, trying to come up with some rationale—something that would make this make sense. I couldn't.

I said, "Of course people would see him. Why would that be a problem? We only represent smart, educated, professional people. Minority candidates are just as polished as white candidates." I started out inarticulate and degenerated to babbling.

Everything she said made it worse. "Do you think he could do it?"

What was she talking about? Do what? Answer a phone? File? Type something in the most user-friendly software ever invented? I've never wanted off a phone so much. I said something spineless and inane about having to get back to my meeting. I'd get back with her.

My head wasn't in any other meeting that afternoon. This job was to work for the confidant and advisor to a man who could end up being the most powerful person in the world. Ronda, who apparently spoke for him, was openly discriminating. It was hard for me to imagine people in such public positions, even if they didn't have better ethics, wouldn't have better sense.

I drafted a high-handed email rejecting their business and informing them that discrimination is illegal and wrong, and . . . Cooler heads persuaded me to delete it and simply say, "Given the parameters of your position, I regret we are not going to be able to assist you with it." I liked my email better.

I couldn't get my mind off of the Ronda situation for days. I would be in a meeting and realize my mind wasn't there but was puzzling over how there were still some people who based their hiring decisions on race. I found myself ranting, "And these people aren't in whatever places skinheads come from. They're just across the river from the capitol. And they're powerful. And they actually thought I'd help them!" That made me mad and worried me too. I thought I had built a better reputation. But I also thought as a community we had progressed more than this. Maybe we hadn't come all that far after all.

I finally realized there was one sign of progress—the fact that these requests shocked me. In the '70s, it wasn't shocking to have an employer demand only white applicants. But now it was. I was shocked. Everybody I told was shocked. Shock was progress.

When I first entered the staffing business it was the 1970s. I assumed discrimination didn't happen outside of the Deep South. I found out I was so wrong, but until I learned that, my assumption proved to be an advantage for me.

I knew about prejudice and discrimination. I had grown up with segregation. I'd seen the newscasts. Selma. Dr. King. James Meredith at Ole Miss. I'd seen the pictures of Little Rock and a pretty girl in a crisp white dress and sunglasses walking into a school past a crowd of distorted faces. I had seen the pictures of Lester Maddox and the ax handles he handed out in front of his restaurant, the symbol of his right to keep black Americans away from his white food. As a teacher, I knew and worked with the third grade teacher who I later learned had told one of my black students he didn't need an education. After all, what would he do with it?

But this was Washington! I knew those things wouldn't happen here! I was wrong, but I acted on what I assumed was true, and it worked.

When I was working with my very first candidate, the young man from Africa, and found employers refusing to hire or interview him, it didn't occur to me that it might be because he was African. I assumed they just needed different training and skills. I kept calling companies to market him. And it happened. I found the woman at the Hecht Company who didn't care where he came from or his color. She just needed to get a job done.

It all happened so fast. I found him the job before somebody told me, "Nobody is going to hire an accountant who is black and from Africa." But somebody had and I had my first placement—even if I didn't get paid for it with money. Then it happened again—another placement.

With my third placement, I discovered another erroneous assumption I had made—that blacks were the only people who were discriminated against.

When I met the woman who was to be my third placement, I thought she was one of the most beautiful women I had ever seen. From my first conversation with her on the phone, I knew she was going to be the next applicant I would place in a job. She had a great British accent that sounded elegant *and* she was from Pakistan—I had never met anybody from Pakistan before! After meeting her I was even more excited. She was polished, poised, and gorgeous with long raven hair. I don't remember anything about her experience, but she must have had the right kind of experience to make me think she would be right for a teller trainee position, and we had plenty of those with Perpetual Federal Savings and Loan Association. They would hire her. I was sure of it. "Look at her!" I thought. "Who could turn her down?"

There was just one little thing to fix about her. She came to my interview wearing pants instead of a dress or a skirt, something else that was hard to imagine if you weren't there in that era. It was not acceptable for a woman to wear pants to an interview or to work, even if it was a tailored and elegant pantsuit of creamy ivory silk. I arranged an interview for her with Mr. W., the human resources director of Perpetual, for the next day. Then I told her to wear a dress, not pants to the interview. She had no problem with that.

Just as I knew she would, Ravinder got the job! When I called the company to confirm her salary and start date, I could sense Mr. W., who was always a little stiff, was uncomfortable.

"Yes. We are pleased to have Ravinder join us. Yes. She is hired at an annual salary of $5,000. But I need you to do something. Can you call her and ask her to wear pantsuits to work?" That was odd.

"You want her to wear pantsuits? She wore a pantsuit to my interview, but I told her to wear a dress to yours."

"She did. She wore a sari. We certainly can't have tellers wearing saris on the platform [the teller line]. In her religion, she has to cover her legs, so please tell her to wear pantsuits to work." I didn't realize till then that this was a first for him. Ravinder was the first person of color to work in their main branch—as long as she didn't wear a sari. That was the '70s. Have you been in a bank lately?

I was getting an education. Washington, DC, discriminated. But I didn't get it from the owner of San-D or from Karen. I'm certain they never told me to screen for any client based on race. My education came from the marketplace and from the people who have always been a primary source of information for new people in any organization, the coworkers. The more experienced account executives jumped in to teach us the ropes management hadn't taught us. They warned us about the companies where we shouldn't send black applicants—and they did it right out loud. They weren't even embarrassed about it. After all, they thought they were doing us, and the candidates too, a favor. Marcia came to the company shortly after I did and with the same assumptions I had.

One day we were standing at the Xerox machine while Marcia was making copies. A black woman sat at Marcia's desk waiting for her. Susan, who had been with the company a few months, came over and pulled Marcia out of the room. "I heard you talking with that applicant about the Creek Company. Don't waste her time or gas money going to interview there. They won't hire a black applicant."

Marcia was mad. She held up the letter that had just been copied. "They just hired one. She's just here to pick up her employment verification letter."

Making the wrong assumption had worked again. The problem was Marcia and I weren't the only ones making assumptions, and most assumptions did not lead to positive outcomes. Susan wasn't alone in assuming employers would prefer one race, age, or gender over another. She was in the majority. It was an easy mental leap to make because most employers did discriminate in some way or other. Until the early '70s, newspaper advertisements regularly specified, "Girl needed for secretarial position." Another ad might have specified, "Man [often young man] sought for position," especially when the job was either a "professional position" or otherwise deemed more fitting for a man than a woman. Employers requested young, old, pretty (I don't remember one ever asking for ugly), thin, married, unmarried, past baby age, or Asian (code for not black) because, "They work harder."

Mr. Meil, the owner of San-D, had a policy against discrimination, but it was one thing to have a policy and another to hold people to it. My manager certainly worked at it. She was constantly on the lookout for it. I know that because one day I got in trouble with her for discriminating—or rather for writing discriminatory comments on an application.

She happened to notice an application I'd thrown into the out-box to be filed, an application on which I had scrawled "hippy and dirty" across the top. She grabbed it and came straight to me with the paper held in her fist, and dropped it onto my desk. I looked at it and back at her. I could see she was mad, but mad wasn't the only reaction I could see on her face. She was confounded that I could be so stupid.

"What were you thinking? You can't write this on an application. The Labor Board could come in here and shut us down."

I had a good defense. "But she's not black."

"I don't care. You can't write this kind of thing on an application."

"But she *was* hippy and dirty."

The look she gave me was one I learned to dread. Then she turned her back on me and said over her shoulder, "Just don't ever write anything like that about any person on an application—nothing personal—not ever."

But discrimination happened anyway, even in our company where there was a policy against it. A vocabulary even developed to support it. When "they won't hire black candidates" became something people were embarrassed to say out loud, they came up with new ways to say it. First, "they won't hire black applicants" was softened to, "they have a problem hiring minority applicants." That was eventually shortened to, "they have a problem." Finally just one code word was said, and usually in a whisper: "problem." It lasted well into the '80s.

It didn't matter that a lot of the "problems," maybe most, were in the heads of the account executives. A job request would come in from a new client, and with no history to base it on, you would hear that word whispered around, "Do you think they have a problem?" or "I don't know if we should send her. They might have a problem."

The first time Karen heard it, she snapped, "That word is more disgusting than saying you aren't sending black applicants out loud." She was tough. The word was banned. It figures if discrimination happened in our company, it happened even more in others where management didn't share the same principles—or weren't so scary.

Change happened in tiny steps. Thinking back, I remember how monumental each step of progress felt then. In comparison, they seem so pitiful and empty now. Even the embarrassment that led to code words was a kind of progress. It meant people knew it was wrong—or illegal.

For every San-D or Les Meil or Karen Towers in town, there were a dozen agency owners and managers who were fine with discrimination, as long as they didn't get caught. It wasn't easy to create change. Our management knew we were in a competitive business. Account executives were afraid they would lose the business of employers whose demands weren't met. Employers could sound so reasonable, so logical, even magnanimous in their requests. They were only doing this *for* the applicant. "She [he] wouldn't be comfortable here. We don't want to waste her time or bus money." But we at the agency *did* want to "waste her time," and let her have the chance to compete—even if she lost. And if she got the job, we could handle letting her suffer a little discomfort.

Mr. Meil didn't stop at telling us not to discriminate. He invested time and money in training us to deal with the employers we faced every day who were comfortable with all-white offices and didn't want to change.

"You're in sales. Change their minds. Sell them on the idea that our service is superior to those agencies that are willing to discriminate. We cast a wider net and give them access to the best of the best candidates in the whole marketplace, as opposed to one small segment." The first time I heard that I thought, wow, what a great presentation!

In the '80s, somebody developed new screening criteria, BOQs, or "bona fide occupational qualifications," and we were among the first to be trained on them. By the time they came into general use, we had already been using them for a year or more.

Thinking back to BOQs after so many years, I can't believe how silly they seem. Back then, we were wowed by them. They were revolutionary. They covered not only race but gender, age, and marital status. I can imagine people today would wonder why it was such a big deal to have a BOQ that addressed the hiring of young women. Fortunately things have changed and many of the people reading this never worked in a time when it was common for employers to refuse to interview a woman because she "might get pregnant." The BOQ rules said employers could apply any restrictions as long as they were applied universally. They could refuse to hire a woman who might need six weeks off to have a baby if they also wouldn't hire a man who would require an equal amount of time off for major surgery. So the question was not, "Will you hire a pregnant woman?" but, "If we have a candidate qualified for your job who needs to take off six weeks in about seven months, can you afford to give that employee the time off?" It was amazing the things that we considered progress.

While we were learning how to win clients over to the idea of ignoring race and hiring on qualifications, there were personnel firms out there that still openly discriminated. Based on how much trouble I got in for writing "hippy" on an application, I was shocked to learn people in other agencies coded their applications. "P" meant "problem" and that meant "don't send this candidate to employers you assume won't hire them." It struck me as so much more work, and more work was something I didn't want. Finding people who could pass the typing tests was hard enough.

Come to think of it, maybe we weren't all that good. Maybe we were just lazy, and adding race as one more qualification was more than we wanted to do. The whole placement process was hard enough when we only had to match skills. But the market changed, and every year matching people with jobs became more complicated. Employers didn't just want fast typing anymore, but personality matches, culture matches, and interest matches. It was like putting together a jigsaw puzzle. Finding the talent was the biggest and most important part of the process. The recruiting staff might have talked with a hundred people just to whittle it down to twenty to interview, and that twenty would be screened down to maybe a dozen for me to meet. Putting the puzzle together would have been exhausting if we had to toss out all of the pieces of one color, one size, or one shape.

In the 1990s, Channel 5 television did an exposé on discrimination in the staffing business. It was the first time the news had done anything aimed this directly at our business. We didn't hear about it until after it had aired, but we were able to get a copy of the newscast. We put a TV in the conference room and gathered around to watch. A few firms were named but the focus was on the one firm found to be guiltiest. We saw the candidates as they entered the offices, and heard the audio of their interviews. One was an unqualified white candidate and the other was a qualified black candidate who was skilled, professional, and poised—somebody our recruiters would beg for. But the account executives in the video promised the white woman a job and went to work to build up her resume and her skills. They blew off the black candidate.

Afterwards, we sat there staring at each other. It just didn't make sense why they would do it. "This is Washington. Are they crazy?" "Why aren't they caught? How can they stay in business?" "Don't they care about making money?" "Do you think Channel 5 would give me the black applicant's phone number?"

It was right after we saw that exposé that I interviewed Sheila, a candidate who had actually been to that agency, although I wasn't aware of that at first. If I had one talent that helped me make the more complex matches, it was the ability to see people, to see past the resume to the real skills and traits that might never show on paper. That's what let me get past the words to see Sheila. She was terrific—good education, judgment, communications skills, but a job history that had nothing to recommend her as an executive assistant. She was in my office looking to change her career path from some kind of management to the right arm of an executive. She knew what a great assistant should be because she had had assistants herself.

I had a brand new client I wanted to impress. She was number two in a big-name, powerful organization, so high-level that their president was soon to be appointed to a cabinet post. I had gotten in because the executive at her firm had been through two bad experiences with assistants. She was frustrated and gave me a long list of requirements. I had to find a one-in-a-million candidate and I had better send in a winner the first time. Actually, that was my favorite kind of client. If I hit a home run, the client was mine for life! I loved the pressure.

As I went through the interview with Sheila, I got excited. Before I was even finished, I knew. She was perfect. She was exactly the person who would make this woman happy. In fact, she was going to seal this client for me. I got positively bubbly as I started telling her about the job.

She looked at me for a long time. "Are you sure I fit the job? They won't mind that I don't have an executive assistant background?"

"Absolutely! She needs brains and judgment. You clearly have those. And you've done the things she needs, just wearing a different hat. All we have to do is go through your resume, job by job, and break down the steps that show your experience."

I thought she was going to cry. I didn't do well with crying, so I was glad she didn't. That's when she told me about her experience with the owner of the agency that had been the subject of the exposé.

"You can't know what this means to me. I went to another agency and it was awful. The owner told me there was no way I could get this kind of job. I left there feeling I had no value at all. It took me a week to get the courage to call your firm."

She said the owner had also told her nobody was going to hire her because of how she looked. I sat back and looked at her. She was big boned and tall, but certainly professional in a crisp black suit and neat brown pageboy hairstyle. She looked fine to me. I couldn't see the problem. Sheila said the owner had told her she looked like "Darth Vader in drag." That one took my breath away.

I opened my mouth to say something but closed it again. Finally I said, "Well, whatever 'Darth Vader in drag' looks like must be the 'in' look for today, because I'm sending you to get hired at the one client I most want to impress."

She got the job. I got paid. That's what I could never understand. What did being mean do for that woman? I don't think I'm all that nice. I think I'm selfish, but being mean doesn't do a thing for me. That agency owner was ugly to the bone.

I don't know what happened to the woman who owned *that* agency—the one in the exposé, the one so cruel to Sheila. Maybe Grandmama was right. Maybe "Jack Dobie" got her.

However small the steps, we have come a long way. Today, people of color are more likely to get in the door. But prejudice doesn't stop at the screening process. Sometimes making it past that first wall just means you've won the right to get in the ring and fight for equal—or at least humane—treatment.

Not long ago, I had a lunch meeting with Donna, an African-American office administrator of a huge company. Over lobster at Morton's, our conversation trailed off to stories about goofy interviewing experiences we had, mistakes we made, bizarre situations with employees, and difficult bosses.

"Who was the most difficult boss you ever had?" I asked, expecting another story about a boss asking her to help him hide an affair from his wife or to do his kid's homework.

"I don't know that I've ever had a boss I couldn't work with," she told me. Before I could prod her, she went on. "Well, there was one, but I handled him, and we were able to work together."

I was ready for the punch line. "Tell me."

"I worked for this man at Georgetown University. He asked me to do something that was against the university's policy, and I told him I couldn't do it. He didn't like that answer and snapped, 'You report to me, and I told you to do it.'"

As she continued to explain that it was against university policy, the VP's answers went from demanding to mean. "Are you stupid or something?"

She actually answered him! "No. I'm not stupid. I'm a college graduate with two degrees, and I've read the policy manual."

"Where did you get your degree? A junior college? I suppose you went on scholarship?" (I thought it was a good thing to get a scholarship. Donna explained he was suggesting she hadn't earned her right to attend Rutgers.)

"No. I was a regular student. I worked my way through. I'm going back to my office now. And you owe me an apology."

He didn't move, and she went into her office and closed the door. He opened it. "This isn't over."

"No, it isn't. You still owe me an apology."

She told me the story dispassionately, as if this were just an everyday occurrence instead of outrageous. I certainly didn't feel dispassionate. I felt rage. Who raised that man? How dare he! Nobody had ever talked to me like that. I couldn't imagine what I would have done. The insults Donna dealt with—that a lot of people dealt with—were beyond me. How did they control themselves? I wanted to tear his face off.

"How did you do that? How did you control yourself?"

"I knew where I had to draw the line. I was a manager. I had information that I knew he would need eventually, and I'd deal with it then. He did and I did. He didn't speak to me for weeks. Then the day came. He came in and started hemming and hawing, then said he thought we should put the bad feelings behind us and move on."

"I told him I'd put it behind me weeks ago and hadn't thought of it for a second since. 'But you still owe me an apology.' He apologized."

Okay, I know Donna handled it with dignity, but dignity just didn't feel like enough to me. I couldn't stop thinking about it. She said she had to pick her fights. She said she decided where she would draw the line. No! All I was sure of was I didn't want to handle him with dignity. I didn't want to pick my fights. And I wanted to draw the line at the point before he got to open his mouth.

But he kept opening that mouth. When he learned Donna's daughter had received a special commendation on her job, he paid Donna what he took to be a compliment—on the good job she had done as a "single parent."

"Single parent? Did you think I wasn't married?"

"Well, you don't have a husband."

"That's because I'm a widow."

"Oh. Was your husband killed?"

"Killed? My husband wasn't a drug dealer or in a street gang. He died of a heart attack."

I was enraged. I've never been in a racial minority. Nobody ever told me I couldn't do something because of my color or my ethnicity. Everything in me rebelled against that executive. I came from a place that seemed to breed tough women, and the women in my family always seemed to me to be among the strongest. My favorite cousin joined FEMA when she was a great-grandmother and received accolades for her work in disaster areas.

The women who raised me just hated the word "no," and they brought me up to understand that there was nothing outside of myself that could hold me back. I couldn't imagine them tolerating the prejudice and insults Donna and so many others lived with. They wouldn't have taken it. But they wouldn't have ever had to, at least not for their race.

Of course, race wasn't the only basis for discrimination in the workplace, but racial discrimination was the only kind we thought much about or took action on before the 1980s. If the client didn't want a man, well, we didn't have many male candidates for admin anyway. But that changed, and I got to be part of the change and bumble my way through my part in it. Nelson Janes, an executive with the Society of Industrial and Office Realtors, was one of the nicest, and most long-suffering clients I ever had. At the time he was hiring a secretary, I had my first male secretarial candidate and sent him to interview for the job. Afterwards when Nelson said he had chosen a different candidate, I attacked with, "Was it because he is a man?!! It's not fair!"

When I shut up, Nelson said coolly, "Ruthi, I hired a man."

Would we try to place a pregnant woman? Not for years, yet . . .

Men weren't supposed to be secretaries. Men were supposed to be executives. They were supposed to make more money. On this count, I was lucky for a lot of things. One was where I came from and how I was raised. Another was I landed in a career in which my income was not in salary but the commission based on what I produced. That let me compete with men on an equal footing. If I was better than a man, I made more money. If money was equality, I was equal—or even superior to most men. I was lucky, too, that I came along in the era of the baby-boomer women who were with me in demanding the right to "have it all."

Sex discrimination applied to men as well as women. There were jobs men weren't supposed to have. I remember the first man I ever represented in his search for a secretarial job. I remember the first gay man I placed. They stand out in my memory because they were rare. Today, neither would stand out at all.

I admit it. I didn't try to fight all forms of prejudice. But age discrimination was different for me. I just didn't understand the problem. I had grown up with old people. Discriminating against age has probably been around forever because no matter where we're from, we get older—although it didn't seem that way to us in the '70s when more than half of the country was under thirty-five. We were young and we were in the majority. I know I thought anyone over thirty-five was a senior citizen, but I was okay with them because I had always loved "old people."

Pauline was one of my favorite candidates. She was upbeat, energetic, and maybe sixty years old with years of experience on Capitol Hill. I threw myself into her job search.

I found a possible job for her with an octogenarian lawyer (and certified curmudgeon) whose secretary had quit abruptly. Pauline had the right background. He had the right job. I got them together.

My phone call with him after her interview was a comedy routine.

"I don't want her."

"Why?"

"She's no good."

"Yes she is. She has the skills you need and the experience."

"Well . . . she's too old. She's going to die."

"She's not old. She's younger than you are."

"That's not saying anything—everybody's younger than I am."

"Mr. F, she has the skills and she'll work for you, and—"

I was stopped by a commotion on his end of the phone, and what sounded like sirens, then scuffling and Mr. F yelling, "Stop that! I don't need you here. It's just a little smoke. Leave that alone! Get on out of here!"

When it quieted, I asked, "What is going on? Are you all right?"

"Yes. Of course, I'm all right. Those stupid firemen. They came bursting in here. It's just a little smoke from my toaster. There was no need for them to come in here."

"Mr. F, you need Pauline. She's starting tomorrow. I'll send you my bill."

Pauline started. And she did not die. She not only worked with him for years, but she started the firm's bowling league!

Getting Pauline that job was fun. Breaking down doors was fun. That's been possibly the best part of my career—breaking rules and winning. The truth is, prejudice is easy. Discrimination is easy. Fairness is hard. You have to think. You have to question. Sometimes you have to fight—and sometimes just showing up for the fight is enough.

A couple of years ago during an "economic downturn" I met Mark, an executive assistant. Mark admitted he was not an easy man to place. He was very expensive for the market. He was also middle-aged, black, a towering six-foot-six, and gay. I knew all that. I also knew he was one of the finest executive assistants I'd ever met. I selfishly committed every minute of every day to searching for the right job for him until he had it.

Mark asked me how I came to be me. I wasn't what he would have expected as someone who grew up in segregated south Alabama. The answer was I got my views where most people get theirs—at home. But I don't think I'm unique. There are many people in the Deep South who believe in equality and in treating all people as equals.

Mama was a born-again liberal. She was a feminist even before the word was coined. She taught me segregation wasn't fair, then she had an experience that made her realize that it was not only unfair to African-Americans, but it was also not fair to *her*!

My cousin gave me her hand-me-down school clothes, and Mama took me to a seamstress to fit them. We met the woman at her home. She was black. I had never been in a black person's home before, but Mama was as comfortable in her living room as she was in Aunt Pauline's. After the clothes were fitted, the two women sat and talked and talked way past the time when I got bored. They talked about grocery prices, the Bible, and segregation. The seamstress was Catholic and she told Mama the Catholic Church was integrated (the other churches weren't, of course). I thought they would talk forever, but we finally left.

We got in the car and I complained that the whole afternoon was practically gone and I hadn't played at all. Mama said, "You get to play all the time, but I don't get the chance every day to just sit and talk to such an interesting person. I was enjoying myself."

I could tell Mama was thinking about the situation and getting madder by the minute. Finally she said, "You know, the people in that Catholic Church get to talk with her any time they want to, and we can't. It's not right."

When I was in the sixth grade, talk of desegregation swept through the schools. Kids would bluster and boast, "If they come here, I'll [fill in the blank]." Some kids said their parents would put them in private school, but I was pretty sure those parents didn't have the money for that.

I went home and asked Mama what I would do if we integrated. "You'll have to study and try to keep up! Do you think these people are stupid?"

She taught me to accept people who don't agree with me. Most born-again Protestants worried about the souls of Catholics and vice versa. My best friend, a member of the Holiness Church, told me all Catholics were going to hell. I didn't see how that could be, so I asked Mama. "Even nuns and priests? But they live their whole lives and never get to have any fun at all."

She said, "That is not true. It says it right in the Bible. If you accept Jesus as your Savior, you are saved. There'll be just as many Catholics in Heaven as people from her church!"

I asked, "What about Jews? God was always getting mad at the Israelites."

She sat up and looked a warning at me. "Don't you worry about the Jews. And don't you ever say anything bad about them either, or hurt one. God will take care of them. The Bible says they're God's chosen people. Do you think he's changed his mind?"

Mama exposed me to ideas about work, opportunity, and fair wages. She was one of the leaders who started the union in the grocery store where she was head cashier. Then she was the shop steward. She was a mix of liberal ideas and born-again Christian. When one of the union leaders was about to go to jail for stealing union funds, she marched right up to him. "It just makes me sick inside to know you did that, and now you won't be around to raise that sweet son of yours. I want you to know, though, that I'll be praying for you every day you're in prison, that you'll turn your life back around."

Mama didn't like the things people did, but she allowed for the possibility of finding something of value in each person. She prepared me for my career and for the twenty-first century, because she left room for everybody. Of course Mama's "everybody" was limited to people she knew about. Mama wouldn't have believed some of the people I've been able to meet.

11

BUILDING *a* BUSINESS IS JUST LIKE BUILDING *a* PIANO BENCH

Just Find the Next Right Step

The piano bench wasn't the only thing Daddy ever built that he didn't know how to do. When he needed to build on a room for Grandmama so her bed didn't have to be in the living room anymore, he got two of my uncles and they built the room in a week—and not one of them had ever done it before. I watched them—they started at the bottom and kept building until they had a room.

With Grandmama's bed out, Daddy redid the living room. He did it mostly by himself, except he made me stand on boards to steady them when he sawed them. It was tiring just standing there, being still. I whined about it until he let me bring in a kitchen chair and sit on the board.

Just as when he built the piano bench and Grandmama's bedroom, Daddy learned to redo the living room by doing it. That meant doing more things he had never done before, and he made plenty of mistakes along the way. When he made a mistake, I'd hear him cuss all the way out in the backyard. I asked why he didn't get somebody to teach him. He said he didn't need to be taught what to do when the next step was the only thing that made sense and when you learned from your mistakes. He said it figured that he had to take off the old walls first. Then he had to get two-by-fours to build a frame to hang the sheetrock on.

But Daddy wouldn't settle for second-rate walls. He didn't put the sheet-rock directly on the frame. He put up plywood first. He might not have known how to build a wall, but my daddy knew what a quality wall meant. "You can't drive a nail in sheetrock. These are walls you can hang pictures on." If we ever got any pictures . . .

As my daddy's daughter, when I set out to build my own business, his model was what I had to work with. I knew about as much about building a company as he had known about building a piano bench or redoing living room walls. Like Daddy, I knew I wanted it to be a quality business—and I knew I wanted walls I could hang pictures on. I also knew there had to be a beginning, then a next step, and then another next step until I had a company.

The first thing I had to do was leave my old employer to avoid any possible conflicts. I quit the job I'd had for a quarter of a century. That brought me to a question of money—you have to have money to start a business! I didn't have any, and now I didn't have a job either, plus I had three boys to support. So my next step was pretty clear. I had to get money, which meant I had to convince a banker to give it to me. To do that I was told I had to write a convincing business plan, which would also be a blueprint for my company. Not knowing how to write a business plan, I jumped right in.

There are some hard facts I didn't know about starting and building a successful business. As I wrote my business plan, I started learning them. I had to provide proof to the bankers that I could make money at my planned endeavor. This requirement presented me with fact #1: Be confident you have something, know something, or are able to do something people are willing to pay for, and be sure you can prove it.

After all those years in staffing, it was clear that I knew things and could do things people were willing to pay for. I knew how to attract clients and gain their trust and their loyalty. I knew how to get inside people's heads, figure out who they were, and match them with jobs. I had a reputation and clients who would follow me to my new company. Those were my assets—no products, no inventory, no property to sell, just me. I created a spreadsheet to show the bankers my client base and the track record of revenues I had produced over the last five years. I wrote a plan for building on established client relationships, hiring a staff of recruiters, and setting up an office that would carry out my brand as an upscale staffing firm.

Now I needed to find a banker to whom I could present my plan. I didn't know any, and learned the value of fact #2: You will need to ask other people for help because you can't do it alone. When you build a business "all on your own," expect to encounter plenty of occasions when you will have to go back to someone and say, "Thank you."

The first person I went to for help was a man who started out as my client, then became my supporter, partner, best friend, and finally my husband. Ron Birch was and is the most fascinating character I ever met—and it was another meeting in an elevator.

This is an elevator story with a perfect ending. Ron and I had been working in the same building and riding in the same elevators for five years and had never noticed each other until one day . . .

I was riding the elevator and looking down at the floor, avoiding eye contact with strangers, when I first became aware of Ron. The first thing I noticed were his shoes, which were the nicest I'd ever seen on any man. Then I looked up and saw a distinguished man in a sharp tailored suit. But his shoulders and posture were what made the clothes stand out.

I suppose I stared at him for so long that it became obvious, because he started a conversation. His firm was on the twelfth floor. I told him I was with the staffing firm on the eighth floor. When his secretary left a few weeks later, he hired me to do the search.

Once we started talking, I discovered Ron wasn't just a pretty face. He had the best stories I'd ever heard and had spent his life doing amazing things— he graduated from Columbia Law School when he was just twenty-two and was offered jobs in Wall Street firms. He chose instead to go to Alaska to clerk for the State Supreme Court Justice Jay Rabinowitz as the state's future was still being created. From there he came to DC as the chief of staff for Senator Ted Stevens. He went back to Anchorage to build the largest law firm in Alaska, then here to open the Washington office.

That life history had to be filled with unique anecdotes, and I didn't have to wait long to start hearing them. It's impossible to stop Ron Birch from telling them—everybody who knows him will tell you that.

In the process of placing Ron's secretary, we became friends. He saw that I wasn't satisfied with my job anymore and encouraged me to build my own business. He said he was certain I would be successful beyond what I could even imagine.

Once I decided to move and I had my business plan in hand, I asked Ron to read it. He then helped with the next crucial step—he took me to his own bank and smoothed the way for me to get started in the process of getting the money I needed. Ron introduced me to Horacio, the loan officer who would be one of my best friends for the next couple of years. Horacio also saw the merits of my plan, and we started the application process.

After Horacio and I had all of the paperwork in order, I found out there were actually two "bankers" in the mix. Horacio was the easy one. He clearly wanted me to succeed. The other "banker" was a body called the loan committee. It wanted to prove I couldn't. I never saw the loan committee, and I came to think of it as an apparition ensconced somewhere in the bowels of the bank, uttering the howls that could be heard throughout the bank on quiet days: "Nooooo." I imagined them commanding Horacio, in icy voices, "Give her more forms to do." I was no less afraid of forms than I'd ever been. The forms made the next fact, which would have been important anyway, an imperative for me. Fact #3: Find a good accountant and a great attorney to keep up with the numbers and read the fine print. Luckily I had both. They produced or reviewed the mountains of financial statements, projections, and contracts.

The loan committee wasn't done yet. "You ran out of forms? Okay, give her a credit check back to the cradle." Once that was done, we were on to the collateral I'd have to put up. But I was all ready for that one—or I thought I was. I had a 401k plan that contained a third more money than I was asking for. Nope. They couldn't take a 401k as collateral because . . . I don't know why. I owned my house. What about using that? No, Horacio warned me, because if I put up my house, I couldn't sell it or refinance it if I needed additional money later—which I did. Then I remembered some money that I had invested twenty years earlier. I had entrusted it to Mr. Bellamah, my stockbroker, and pretty much forgotten about it. He had tripled it over the years.

Yes, the committee agreed the stocks would do fine as collateral, and added, "Just let your broker know you are using your portfolio as collateral for a loan, and he needs to contact us before trading the stock."

Mr. Bellamah was another one of the wonderful characters I've lucked into over the years. Irascible and a bit eccentric, he never came into his office before 2:00 p.m., and he returned only the calls he deemed worth returning. I hadn't spoken with him more than once or twice over the twenty years that he managed my account. My only regular communications with him were quarterly statements I never read and his annual Christmas card, which I looked forward to every year. It was one of those bargain box cards like the ones I sold to the old ladies on Petain Street, except I didn't remember mine having the printing faded and slightly askew on the page. But better than that was his signature, which was not written but rubberstamped. This from the man who had more than tripled my money.

No way was I telling Mr. Bellamah he had to get permission to do anything. I said, "I'll tell him the loan committee will be contacting him. They can tell him what they want." So they called.

Horacio called me later that week—after Mr. Bellamah had finally gotten around to returning the calls. As he told me about the conversation between the vice president and the broker, I thought I could actually hear him smiling over the phone. It had taken four days and a half-dozen messages, but Mr. Bellamah finally returned the banker's calls, to hear what the bank vice president told him he would "have to do." He would have to contact the bank for permission before making any trades. Mr. Bellamah's answer was pithy. "No."

I imagine the banker's face reddening and his voice showing his strained patience as the conversation went forward. "Sir, you don't understand. We are holding Ms. Postow's portfolio as collateral for a business loan."

Mr. Bellamah said, "That's fine. You can do that."

"Good. You understand then that you can't buy or sell stock without contacting us first."

"No. I won't do that," he said, in the nicest possible tone.

"You have to."

"No, I don't. Now, here is what we are going to do. After I make a trade, I'll send you a notice." I love that man—he has now retired and I still haven't found anyone to fill his shoes. The committee backed down to Mr. Bella-mah, but they had another joke to pull on me.

I picture evil grins on their decaying faces as they told Horacio, "Go ahead and give her the loan—but give her only half of what it will take to make this business successful. Keep us posted on her progress. This should be fun to watch." I had my loan, and learned fact #4: Be prepared to get by on less money than you thought possible because the bank will lend you only enough money to see the promised land, not to get there. Start thinking of a back-up plan.

Money in hand, I was ready to learn another one of those lessons they don't put in business books, fact #5: Having money doesn't mean you can buy things, because, in the business world, nobody wants to be your first.

I needed a computer, copiers, printers, furniture, and office space. I wanted to lease the equipment so I could upgrade as necessary. But the companies that sold computers and copiers wouldn't take my money. They wouldn't lease their equipment to me because I didn't have a track record. I didn't have credit, just money. Like Julia Roberts's character in *Pretty Woman*, I was saying, "I have money to spend here."

The same was true when it came to finding office space. I had visions of a beautiful office on K Street, but I could forget that location. In fact, I could forget class-A buildings altogether. Even if I could afford them, they didn't want me.

Another friend came to my aid, my real estate broker, Duke Brannock. Duke took me to building after building. The first was an aged medical building on I Street (since torn down). The walls were green, an appropriate color for a building that had the smell of old medicine and maybe rotting body parts.

The next office was in a small building on 15th Street. This one too had seen better days, although the owners didn't seem to realize it. They were sure their building was way too good for my business. The schoolmarmish property manager, who possessed the kind of nose that was made for looking down, asked, "And what business are you in?"

"Professional services . . . we do administrative staffing."

Her seemingly bloodless face paled even more, and she took a step back as though afraid she would get dirty. "Does that mean you will be having people come in here to interview?"

"Yes. We hope we will."

"That means they will come in through our lobby." It wasn't a question.

Before I could say, "No. We expect our candidates to grow wings and fly up through the windows," my real estate broker grabbed my arm and swept me from the building, and yes, we went right through the lobby.

In spite of my lack of appeal, my broker finally found a building that would take me and, if it wasn't K Street, it was at least without noticeable odor. Lawyer, accountant, broker, and property manager passed forms and contracts back and forth until, finally, I had an office.

Next I had to decorate my new space. I would learn later that buildings gave new tenants something called a build-out allowance, but there was no mention of that for me. (Fact #6: Expect to do your own hauling, painting, and heavy lifting.) So I had to create a designer office on a shoestring budget.

I could do that! If there were two things at which I excelled, they were shopping and decorating. I went to every estate sale and consignment shop in upscale Bethesda. I bought silk overstuffed chairs for the lobby that had been in a barely used private office, enough matching desks for a staff of six, an antique conference table, and the heart of my lobby, a rolltop desk that the receptionists would complain about forever. The office would be warmed by indigo blue accent walls—the painting of which cost more than all of the furnishings put together. Now I needed art for the walls, and I had just the art I needed. I found the sketchbooks from my term in art school, cut my favorite drawings from them, and framed them myself. We added carpet, in my signature red, of course. (I added my mark to the building. Before the carpets were installed, I took the can of red spray paint I was using to redo some old tables, and painted RuthiPostowStaffing, Inc. the full length of the cement floor of the bull pen.)

My office was ready for business! It was beautiful and in a building on M Street that had a nice lobby and housed other professional companies. It was also right across from several of DC's most prestigious strip clubs including the famous Camelot Gentleman's Club, which is touted on the web as the "only strip club in Washington that's worth checking out." I came to appreciate the proximity of the clubs, which brings me to the sleeper sofa and fact #7: When you're building your own business, it's not a bad idea to buy a sleeper couch for your office.

When I worked for someone else, I went home at 5:00 p.m. without a care. Now five o'clock just meant everybody else would go home and I would be able to work in peace. First I finished the work the young staff I hired hadn't done or been able to do—I redid their candidates' resumes, called candidates to be sure they were confirmed for interviews, and so on. Then I created brochures, wrote ads and marketing pieces, made lists of things I would do tomorrow, checked billing files, and read those pesky P & Ls (profit and loss statements). This went on till ten o'clock . . . eleven o'clock . . . midnight. That's when I went into the extra office, opened the sofa, and slept. It was safer than driving when it had been weeks since I slept five hours in one day.

I can imagine what my daddy would say about me sleeping all alone in an empty office building in downtown Washington, DC. Was I crazy? Was I trying to get myself killed? Or worse? But my building was safer than my house. It was on the best lit and best police-patrolled block in all of Washington, DC. After 9/11, while people fled the city in a crawl of traffic, I stayed and avoided the frustration because I knew I was safe. For months, I had seen the men who went in and out of the clubs and I knew there was no way they were going to let anything happen to the beauties they came every night to watch. I enjoyed the economy of my office space plus the security of the strip clubs for five years before I was well enough established to make the move to a class–A building on K Street.

But back to the beginning. With money, computers, three new employees, and an office to put them in, I had a business to run. That was the next step, managing the business—a long-term step—that I didn't know how to do. Fact #8: Look at your weaknesses as well as your strengths and partner with someone who can fill in your blanks.

Early in my career, I had the opportunity to go to management training classes. I was a dropout—three times. San-D had a policy of developing its people and offered a management training program. The training covered everything from organizational planning to behavior modification and rivaled university business courses that cost thousands of dollars. All of the senior account executives in every office vied for acceptance into the program—all except one.

Whenever they came around talking about the opportunity to grow, I kept my head down. I didn't want to grow. In fact, I never trusted the very idea of growing a person. The word didn't mean anything. Almost every candidate I interviewed told me they wanted a job with growth. What did they want to grow into or do more of?

Most had no idea. I liked what I was doing and wanted to keep doing it.

One of the managers said I couldn't stay an account executive my whole life. I had to continue to grow to be successful. It took me back to the boy in college who said I had to join a sorority or I wouldn't have any cool dates. I still wasn't going to let anybody tell me what it meant for me to succeed.

They were relentless. "You're the top producer in the company. You could have the top office in the city." They wore me down, and I went to the first session of the management training class—on the difference between a leader and a manager. What I learned was a leader is charismatic and makes people want to follow while a manager manages.

The leader encouraged open discussion of the material. It was teachers' meetings all over again. Two or three of the trainees pontificated about leadership. Then there was the one who asked questions that had been answered hours ago. In the end, I didn't care who led and who managed as long as they all left me alone to work with my clients. That night was drop out number one.

I was talked into trying it again. This time they had me at lesson number three even though I missed the first two. I came into a three-hour session on how to create budgets and read P & Ls—more forms! Creating budgets made no sense to me at all.

Here is what I understand them to have said: To create a budget, I had to guess how much of something, for example copy paper, I would use in a year and write that down. Then I was supposed to guess how much it would cost and write that down. Then I was supposed to make myself spend that amount. I was once again a dropout and swore I'd never do it again. After all, I thought, maybe management couldn't be taught.

"You didn't give management training a chance. If you give it one more try, a sincere try, and still don't like it, I won't mention it again." Okay. This time they were teaching behavior mod (behavior modification—it was very "in" then). Behavior mod methodology seemed to be rooted in the verbs. In dealing with employees you should use active verbs such as "did" ("You did a bad thing and that hurt my feelings"), instead of passive verbs such as "are" ("You are a jerk"). That made sense. I'd always felt that way, although I wasn't a fanatic about it. Some people are jerks. Anyway, if that was their point, I got it and I was ready to go put it into practice. But they didn't stop there. They went on until I was drowning in a sea of wordy words—empirical data, operant variability, positive punishment, and respondent conditioning. An hour of that and I was gone again.

A few years later I was "behavior modified," and happily so. I smoked. I didn't want to anymore. I didn't like to think anything could control me, but I also didn't think anything could help me quit. Someone told me about a b-mod program called SmokEnders. I don't know if it was the "operant variability" or the "respondent conditioning" that did it, but it worked.

After my management training, I decided I would never be a manager under any conditions. It had to be an awful job. It was a demotion. I couldn't imagine why I would voluntarily stop being the best at what I was to become the worst at what I didn't want to be. Instead of being on the front line, having fun with my clients, and getting recognition (and money) for it, I would be stuck off in the background where I'd spend my days guessing how much copier paper I'd need and reading, or trying to change other people into me.

Then, after all my bobbing and weaving, the company gave up on the training phase and made me a manager anyway. They just could not believe I wouldn't translate the success I had as an account executive into success as the manager of one of their offices. They were wrong. I never mastered the smoke and mirrors of budgets. I hated trying to modify the behavior of the people I managed to make them make the cold calls I wanted to make but wasn't supposed to anymore. And my employees picked on me. It was awful. They complained about everything, from the changes in the market to the weather, as though they were all my fault. I was miserable.

In trying to grow me, the company had broken the Procrustean rule: Don't try to grow good employees into misshapen and unhappy forms.

Procrustes, according to Greek mythology, was a man who kept a house by the side of the road. This was in a time before Ritz-Carltons and there were few inns where weary travelers could find rest. Procrustes offered his home and hospitality to passing strangers, inviting them to come in, dine with him, and rest the night in a bed that, he promised, had the mystical power to fit any man who lay upon it. Whatever the man's height, the bed would be an exact fit. The travelers who accepted the invitation enjoyed a fine dinner, and then were shown to a bed, which appeared to be just ordinary. But Procrustes had promised a fit, and a fit he would make. Those who were too short were stretched on the rack. Those too tall had their legs chopped off. The bed fit, but the guest was left dead or maimed.

After a year and a half, I wasn't maimed, but I was determined. I talked them into letting me drop out of management and I went back to the job I loved. It was nearly two decades before I took the leap again by starting my own company. But even when I launched my company, I held on to the hope of avoiding management by hiring a manager who would do all of the things I didn't want to do while I kept doing what I did best. That's fact #9: Know which things you don't know and find a partner who does know them.

It took me over a year to find that partner. When I found Jenni O'Toole, I knew intuitively and immediately she was the one. It took nine months for me to convince Jenni I was right.

Jenni not only grew the business, she grew me. She had enough foresight to know things were different now that I was an owner. She wasn't okay with my idea of staying in the job I had for decades. She did what no management course was able to do thus far—she made me learn to read our financial statements, pay attention to our business affairs, and step back so our employees could take on the work I used to do.

We were ready to grow the company. I had managed to survive the two-year hurdle Horacio warned me about and 9/11, and keep the business on an upward track, meeting the payrolls and making the bank payments. Now that Jenni had joined me, we were ready to build something. But we needed capital to do that.

I didn't want to keep borrowing money, so I started looking for a financial partner to buy into the business. I quickly learned facts #10 and #11.

Fact #10: Never do business with a "friend" or bring one into your business. Fact #11: Look at your books, and your back, every day, and be quick to rid yourself of people who threaten you or bring you down.

The financial partner I found was one I had known for several years. He went to my church (big red flag). I knew he had built several successful businesses and sold them. They were in the technical field, but we didn't need him to run the business. We talked and I offered to bring him in as a 40 percent partner if he brought the funds we needed to keep going till our revenues could carry us.

It was another one of those times I needed fact #12: Always listen to the little voice inside your head warning you of danger! From day one, this "friend" came in making changes. He took over our conference room and started accessing all of our computer records. Then he changed one vendor after another, hiring his friends to handle our insurances and database development, and talked about replacing our accountant with another of his friends (bigger red flag!). At least I said "no" to that one.

His ideas became more and more alarming. We should change banks to one with whom he had a relationship. Then we should cut overhead by firing the receptionist—and Jenni. When he said to fire the only person who was bringing in money besides me, I tried to give him the benefit of the doubt. I hoped it was only because he had no idea how the business worked, and maybe I could teach him. But all of those intuitive pieces of me were by now sending off rockets.

Then I found out he was trying to take control of my company; but he had never signed the contract, avoiding my attorney's calls about our agreement, and had failed to bring the promised funds.

At about that same time I grew concerned about his relationship with our bookkeeper—they were excluding me from important discussions, it seemed. Then I saw him driving out of the garage with her one night. They didn't live near each other. The next day, I found out he had put her on as signatory of our new bank account. They hadn't told me. I only found out when I asked for the checks I needed to sign. He was nonchalant, "Oh, MJ already signed them."

"She can sign my company's checks?"

"I decided to have her on it when we changed banks."

I didn't need any more signs. I fired him on the spot, walked him out of the building, and told the guards he could never come back. He was there not even three months, but for the first time since I started my business, I was in serious financial trouble—and I didn't even know how serious yet.

I discovered things about myself. I had courage and the ability to make quick and bold decisions. You have to be brave to own a business. That's fact #13: There will come a time when you are in a crisis, and you have to be prepared, at that moment, to put everything you have on the line. If you're not prepared to do that, there is no use starting.

I remember the exact time and place I was when I realized I was at that crisis point. It was eight o'clock on a Friday night in mid-July 2003. I sat at my desk, feeling like a poor kid, nose pressed against the toy store window. Everything I had been working for and dreaming of my whole life was right in front of me. In spite of everything, Jenni and I had the company poised to take off and grow. I could see it, but I couldn't quite reach it, and I faced the real possibility that I never would.

I sat hunched over, as though pinned under the enormous weight of my problems, problems that had been mounting all that year but had exploded into an overwhelming mass that summer. We were in a recession that hit the permanent staffing business hard. Payroll was due. Rent was due. College tuition was due for two of my sons. There was no money in the bank. I'd been too distracted by business to create business, so there were no new revenues in sight. That night I felt I might be too exhausted to go out and build a business again. I'd started my business and nurtured it for nearly two years, even after 9/11. But in the last few months of a bad market, I had been pulling money from my personal savings to keep us afloat. I felt powerless to save the business to which I felt I'd given all I could give.

I didn't sob, but tears streamed down my face. I had neither the energy nor the inclination to stop them or wipe them away, so they rolled on until they dried on my skin or landed on the spreadsheet in front of me. My eyes didn't focus or appraise, but roamed around to stare first at one spot then another in this office that I was once excited to decorate all by myself, from the cobalt blue accent walls hung with my own drawings to the window beside my desk. I was so proud to have that window, even if it only had the flat view of another office building just six feet away and into the window of a gynecologist's office when his blinds weren't drawn.

All summer, everywhere I turned, people were telling me how bad times were. The sympathetic ones could be the worst, "I don't see how you'll make it." Each one added just that much more to the weight I was already carrying. Advisors were no help. "Cut back," they said.

"You should close that expensive office and get rid of the employees. You can do your business by yourself from home."

"You are going to ruin your future if you take any more money out of your 401k plan. You won't have anything to live on."

"What if you get hurt or you're too sick to work?"

"The market isn't going to get better any time soon."

The voices I was listening to that night belonged to other people—not to me, not to Mama, not to Daddy.

Then all of a sudden, I heard another voice. It was mine. It sounded as demanding and impatient as I had sounded when I was a child and was determined to get my way, glaring straight ahead and stomping my foot.

"I can too do this! I want it, and nobody is going to keep me from getting it!" Once I listened to my own voice, I was not powerless. I didn't have to tell the other voices to stop. They were gone.

The mountains of problems were gone too, along with the confusion. Everything was clear. It was suddenly so simple. All I had to do was make a plan. My dream was right in front of me, ready to happen. I knew it. I saw it, and I knew I could make it come true! Instead of the pile of problems I had minutes before, I had only one—I needed money. Okay. So I'd get more money.

The next week was all action. The first thing was to solve the problem, and I did what some people would deem the unthinkable. I took everything I owned and bet it on my dream. I called the woman who managed my 401k, the one who had been giving me dire warnings that I would end up living out my old age on a grate. I wouldn't hear her anymore. "Move $75,000 dollars to the company account today, and be ready to move that much more next month." She did it, but she didn't speak to me again for years. I took money I'd saved for my boys' educations. I refinanced my house—again.

The money problem was handled. Now I didn't have to decide what to do. All I had to do was work. I knew how to make money in this business. Jenni and I got on the phone to employers and found jobs we would fill and candidates to fill them.

It was simple, but it wasn't easy. All through August, I made more cold sales calls than I'd made in years to get not one positive result, no new client, no job to fill, and very few pleasant people on the other end of my calls. It was rough work, but it wasn't a problem, because I was able to work. I knew all I had to do was keep going and somebody would give me business. Finally, in September, business started coming in just a little at a time; but it was a start.

Now, only weeks past looking disaster in the face, I decided to take another step. I would build. Saving the company wasn't enough. I would grow it. We would create a new division to staff temporary positions, not next year, but now. There were naysayers still who would tempt me into negativity and failure. "This is insane. How long do you think your money will hold out? You can't carry this company forever."

I had one answer for them all: "This company is poised to soar. I'm sure of it. It deserves to live and I'm going to make that happen." I felt the truth of that to my core.

While my mid-July crisis was the most dramatic, it was not the only one I've had in my career. I've faced down recessions, changing markets, and lost clients, and never stopped believing I'd win. Optimism doesn't mean you will never have a crisis. It just gives you what you need to refuse to turn back or even settle for halfway there. It lets you get up and get on with it.

I was right. We soared. Within months we were showing a profit and the trend continued. We started getting recognized in the business media for our growth, then in the *Washington Business Journal* as one of the best places to work in Washington. We grew and I finally got my office on K Street.

What a difference that negotiation was! I was negotiating for things I could now afford! No more loan committees because my line of credit was paid off. Copier companies stood in line to lease equipment to me. Instead of the cold reception and shoestring budget on which I'd built and decorated the M Street office, my new landlord introduced me to a build-out allowance. I had walls moved and painted whatever colors I chose, the kitchen updated, and wires pulled, and I didn't have to pay a penny. *They* were paying for everything, including architects and designers, custom build-outs, and the five coats of paint to achieve the deep blue I selected, plus twelve-inch crown molding in the lobby!

K Street and crown moldings! Could it be more perfect than this? Yes, and it could get worse too. Hence fact #14: Things that should be easy aren't—when you're up against an illogical yet all-powerful adversary. Our move to the new building was only three blocks. We mapped out the logical steps to getting it accomplished like clockwork. But I didn't anticipate this roadblock. I never even knew that there are dictators with absolute power right here in the United States, and they are called Verizon. One snap of their fingers and business shuts down. They are also the nation's single largest employer of people who don't know the answer but will transfer you to someone who does if you just follow the prompts.

Our work is connecting with people and to do that we have to have computer and phone service. We thought we had taken every step necessary to avoid any break in that service. Six months before the move, we arranged for Verizon to move the phone and computer lines. We confirmed the arrangements monthly, then a week before the move. Then we moved, and no phones. After hours of following the prompts of the tape-people, we finally got through to an actual human being who had an answer for us. It was, "We can have half of your phone lines in by a week from Wednesday, but we won't have the computer lines up until the middle of next month."

I must have sounded like a seven-year-old when I whined, "But you promised!"

Actually, all of this isn't quite accurate. I did say, "But they promised," but I said it to the woman who was in charge, Marcia Wheatley, my business manager—and the answer to fact #15: Invest in a trustworthy and long-suffering business manager to make sure every detail is handled.

Most of the packing, moving, phone calling, holding the line, and arguing was not done by me, because during the move, I went on vacation and let Marcia whine and plead with the phone company, the movers, the computer people, and the painters who were still painting as we moved in (as the seventh coat of cobalt blue went up on the accent walls). I like to think of it as getting out of Marcia's way to allow her to handle the whole move. I think she likes doing that sort of thing, and there has to be some payback for all of those nights I slept on the couch.

Finally we were in this beautiful office and doing business—and it's been easy street ever since. Wrong! There have been more facts to discover, more problems to fix, and more things to do that I didn't know how to do.

One of the hardest facts to face in this business was fact #16: People leave. When we moved to the new office I was secure with my staff of well-trained, sharp business professionals who had been with me for years. Then within a couple of years they all moved on, some to different states and some to different careers. I had made one of the biggest mistakes a business owner can make. I had stopped recruiting for my own company. Ever since that time, my most important job is finding, hiring, and developing the people who are the company's only real assets.

A year after we moved, a new recession started. Recession! It was all you heard about on the news. I turned off the newscasts. I'd learned many recessions ago to avoid the news reports of doom and gloom because, no matter what else was happening in the world, I was going to keep the business going.

Recently I was a guest on a business radio show. The host asked me: "You left a lucrative career to start your business. Didn't you realize that 80 percent of businesses fail in the first two years?"

The answer to that is no. And the most important advice I can give the person starting a business is this: *Don't look down!* When I was a kid starting out I had nothing on the line. I could afford fear. It even helped me in a way, because the feeling that I was always running from failure kept me moving up. But when I started this business, I had everything on the line. Failure was unthinkable so I didn't let myself think about it. Actually, the first year, I was euphoric. Every little step was new. Every small accomplishment was a great victory. Problems were inevitable, but no matter what happened, I could fall back on the lessons that had brought me this far.

This year the company is fifteen years old. I owe its success and all the success I had in my career to the things I was taught by the working-class people on Petain Street. Don't complicate things. Live in the moment. Don't borrow tomorrow's problem—if it can't be solved now, put it away until it can be. Don't let one failure slide on to cause another one. Deal with it. Mourn it if I need to, then stop and plan my next step; and go to bed and get some sleep, so I can get up and go to work in the morning.

LEFTOVERS

I have more blue-collar lessons than I can fit into one book, so I have leftovers. They, like Mama's leftover fried chicken, are too good to waste. So here they are.

PETAIN STREET LESSONS FOR SUCCESS:

- Waste time dreaming.
- Worrying is useless. Plan and move on.
- Take time to listen to people. You'll be surprised at the people who have an interesting story or two.
- Collect good stories. They will make your life more interesting.
- Time is the most valuable thing you have to share with people. Share some with people who can't give you anything.

DADDY'S LESSONS FOR SUCCESS IN BUSINESS AND IN LIFE:

- "If it's the other guy's fault, you can't fix it. Don't blame other people for your problems. That gives them all the power. Own up to your mistakes."
- "If you don't want people minding your business for you, keep your mouth shut about it."
- "When you get mad at your boss, don't go home telling your husband about it. For one thing, your job is your job. For the other, tomorrow you'll be over it and your husband will still be mad."
- "Ask questions. Never be embarrassed that you don't know something or afraid of what other people will think. When I was a little boy in school, I didn't understand a lesson so I asked questions. Some boys laughed at me. I didn't care. I learned."

- "If you don't speak correctly, people won't respect what you have to say. Don't say 'ain't.' It is not a word. People will know you're ignorant."
- "If you don't know what a word means, don't use it. It's a sure way to make yourself sound ignorant."
- "When you're talking to folks, don't jump in too soon with what you think. Stay back and wait. You might learn something."
- "Don't follow the crowd until you are sure you want to be where they're going."

MAMA'S LESSONS ON INTEGRITY, WORK ETHIC, AND HOW TO TREAT PEOPLE:

- "If you don't have the money to buy the real thing, don't buy a fake thinking you're going to impress people. You won't."
- On getting up and going to church or work when she wasn't feeling well: "I won't feel a bit worse at church (or work) than I'd feel if I stayed home."
- "If someone wants you to admire them, go ahead and do it. It won't hurt you and it may help them."
- "Don't ask for anything but if someone wants to give you something, take it. It will mean more to them than it does to you."
- "Your shoes are the first and last things people will notice about you. Never go out of the house with shoes that are scuffed and run down at the heel."

AND FROM MAMA AND DADDY: LESSONS ON CHARACTER

- "Whatever you've got can go. In the end, all you've got is your character" (which Daddy pronounced kay'-rek-tor).
- "You're going to meet people in this world who are fine, quality people. They'll build your character, and you want to hang around with them. Then there are the ones who don't do right. They will tear you down. Be nice to them—never hurt anybody—but don't hang with them."

- "When somebody tries to look big you can see just how small they are. If you want to know a person's character, don't bother about what they tell you. It's what they do and how they act that count. Pay attention and you'll learn who they are."
- "You show who you are by how you talk and dress and carry yourself."
- "You should never be ashamed if your clothes aren't as good as somebody else's when they are the best you can do and they are clean and neat."

————

The clothes my parents wore to work were uniforms. They were plain and cheap, but Mama and Daddy took pride in how they looked. Daddy's uniform was a khaki shirt and pants, just like Mr. Webb's and Mr. Farley's and just about every other man's on Petain Street.

Once, Daddy took me with him to Merchant's National Bank in Mobile where he met with Mr. Dison, his banker. Mr. Dison had on a suit and tie. Daddy had on his khakis. I got embarrassed. It seemed to me that khakis were all Daddy owned. From there we went to J.C. Penney's in Prichard so Daddy could buy himself some new clothes. They had all kinds of things, but he picked out the same old khaki shirts and pants.

"Daddy, those are what you always get. Why don't you get blue pants and a white shirt like Mr. Dison?"

He looked at me and at the Penney's salesman. I knew I had embarrassed him. I looked at the floor. He waited till we were in the car.

He didn't yell. "I need to tell you some things. You can't be shamed by the cost of your clothes if you're doing the best you can and they're clean and neat. I'd sooner trust a man in clean khakis than one in a dirty suit.

"Always be proud of what you are. It never works to try to be something you're not. My clothes are the right things to wear for the work I do at Brookley [Air Force Base]. It would be just as wrong for me to wear a suit and tie to work as it would be for Mr. Dison to wear this. If I wore a suit, I couldn't work for fear I'd get diesel fuel or oil on it. The men I work with would think I was putting on airs. If Mr. Dison wore khakis, I wouldn't trust him to bank my money."

ACKNOWLEDGMENTS

To all of the people from Petain Street who live on in my heart and in my book, thank you for teaching me the lessons for success in life and in business that brought me here.

To Mama, who had the integrity to stand up for what she believed, thank you for teaching me a woman can do anything a man can do and to live my life without excuses.

To Daddy, thank you for pushing me to "get off Petain Street and be somebody," and for being there with common sense advice to keep me on track.

To my sons, thank you for the time with me that you gave up as I built my business and for becoming the accomplished, interesting people you are.

To Mr. Les Meil, the founder and CEO of the staffing firm where I started, thank you for your commitment to training and for setting the industry's standards for ethics and equal opportunity.

To all of my clients, thank you for your trust and loyalty and for sharing your stories with me.

To my partner, Jenni O'Toole, thank you for adding your talents, creativity, and drive to building our business. And thank you for reading the drafts of my book and constantly telling me to "edit it down and keep it simple."

To my editors, thank you for all of the care you put into helping me to be clear and say what I wanted to say.

Finally, to my husband, Ron Birch, thank you for believing I'm the smartest, funniest, and most beautiful woman on earth and for giving my story a happier ending than I ever could have dreamed possible.

QUESTIONS *for* DISCUSSION

1. The author dedicates the book to "people with dreams that will take them far from where they started." Do you believe the author went far from where she started on humble Petain Street? Or can you describe ways in which she actually never left?

2. Ruthi says she learned "everything I needed to know to succeed in life and in business" on her humble childhood street in south Alabama in the 1950s. Can you describe some of what she learned? Do you think everyone would have learned those lessons, or did young Ruthi have some qualities that enabled her to be a good learner?

3. What lessons from your own childhood were you reminded of as you read this book? How did you learn them? Do you think you were a more willing learner when you were young, or are you better at it now?

4. The famous poem "My Heart Leaps Up" by William Wordsworth (written in 1802) includes the line "The Child is father of the Man." While readers over the years have interpreted this differently, one reading is that our younger selves ("Child") actually guide and teach our older selves ("Man"). In what ways does Ruthi's story reflect this truism? In what ways does your own life reflect it?

5. What was your favorite part of the book? Why? Who were some of your favorite characters from the author's life? Did they remind you of some from your own?

6. Did reading this memoir give you a new view of the world? In what way?

7. Often we hear adults extoll the virtues of growing up in blue-collar towns

or in families of limited means. But it seems many of those same folks move away from those roots as they pursue education and careers, which means they end up raising their own children in more privileged circumstances. Do you think those children can learn the same lessons their parents did? Why, or why not?

8. Ruthi's rise from the clay-baked streets that colored the poverty of this south Alabama town to the glinting offices of Washington, DC, seems to follow the American dream. Yet everything comes with a price, as the author is quick to point out. What are some of the downsides to Ruthi's upward climb? Do you believe the outcome is worth the cost?

9. There is quite a bit of understated humor in this memoir. What did you find funny, and why? How did the author bring this to life for the reader?

10. It's clear that Ruthi looks at herself, her life, and her experiences with a sense of humor. She seems to look for what's funny in most every experience, including her own mistakes. What difference do you think that has made for her?

11. Can you imagine this book, *How to Build a Piano Bench*, as a film? Who would you imagine in the starring role of Ruthi? How about other characters?

12. If you could have a cup of coffee with Ruthi—at any of the ages she describes in the book (little girl, awkward teen, wannabe beauty queen, struggling career seeker, driven career woman, panicked mother, successful business owner)—which one would you choose? What would you ask her, or what advice would you give?

13. Ruthi has had more than her share of folks who confided deep secrets in her. She writes: "I had people talk to me about serious problems. There were some who told me stories so painful I wondered if they didn't have friends who would be better confidants. . . . But I realized there are some things we can only tell strangers because we don't want our friends to know." Have you been on the telling or listening end of such secrets? Why do you think it's easier to share secrets with strangers than with our closest friends?

14. One of Ruthi's worst moments came when she worried she was spending so much time building her career that she was shortchanging her children. Have you felt the same way—as a mother or a father? Were you, or would you be, willing to let someone help raise your children as you pursued a career? At what point do you think you'd need to pull back and give more time to your children?

15. As Ruthi relates her life story, she doesn't hesitate to share her struggles, failures, and personality flaws—even if that means readers might disapprove of her behavior. Would you prefer to read a memoir of a person who didn't admit her flaws, or did you appreciate this author's honesty? Would you have the courage to reveal your shortcomings as this author does?

16. If you could spend an evening with one character from this book, whom would you choose, and why? What activity would you like to do with her or him?

17. If you could spend an evening with the author, Ruthi Postow Birch, what questions would you want to ask or what would you want to tell her?

18. If you could ask the author for more details about one of the events of this story, which would you choose, and why?

AUTHOR Q & A

Q: It's quite an accomplishment to write a memoir, Ruthi. How do you feel now that it's done?

A: *My exact feeling: I actually did it! Hooray! I've wanted to write as far back as I can remember but was stopped by thinking I wasn't good enough, or even if I wrote something it would never get published. I'm very results oriented!*

I'm excited to picture people reading my stories and laughing or thinking about how it affects them, or just feeling better about themselves because they can see they're not alone.

Q: Did you discover anything new in the process of writing this? As you sifted through past memories, did anything surprise you? Perhaps causing you to make connections you hadn't made before, or seeing elements of your life in a new light?

A: *I don't think I discovered anything new in writing the book. But when it came to selling it to an agent, I experienced a new kind of pain and learned how terribly shy I am when it comes to selling myself.*

That shouldn't be true. Sales has been my life and I thought of myself as fearless. I'm not. I have lots of fears but I've made a habit of pushing them into a closed box in my mind and refusing to look at them. That's what I did with my book. After a dozen rejection letters from agents, I decided it hurt too much. I hid the book in a folder in my computer so I wouldn't see it. Then, instead of pushing to get it published, I started revising it, over and over— hoping, I suppose, that revising it would create some kind of magic.

Q: Do you find yourself feeling any differently about your past, or has this been more of a process of solidifying what you already believed?

A: *I don't feel different. I've carried my impressions and these people with me my whole life. I was always proud of where I came from—maybe because I knew where I was going. How could I not be proud of a daddy who was a tugboat captain and a mama who was a liberal-feminist-Bible-scholar-Christian who helped start the first Retail Clerks Federated Union in Mobile and fought for fair wages for workers? (I still have her union pin.)*

Q: You portray your interactions with the humble folk of Petain Street with love and compassion. Yet you were determined to become successful and move away from that blue-collar neighborhood, and you ended up raising your own children in an area that was far removed from those homespun roots. Do you think your children have missed out on some of the benefits you got back in south Alabama?

A: *I passed on my stories to my boys, and they were able to get to know Sister and Daddy and to hear their stories for themselves.*

What broke my heart is that they missed out on knowing Mama, who died three years before Joe was born. There was no way stories about her could fill the hole she left.

But they had their own impressions and memories to make, and there were other people in their lives to help them.

They had much of the same freedom to explore and dream because I was working. I think it allowed them to develop their independence and resourcefulness.

Q: What do you hope readers take away from this book?

A: *I hope they laugh when they read the stories, then remember them from time to time and laugh again. I think the most important message I'd like readers to take away is to accept yourself and appreciate what makes you special—even your flaws. I hope the book gives people permission to lighten up and laugh at themselves. And of course I want to spread the down-home advice from Petain Street.*

Q: A lot of would-be and accomplished memoir writers believe they need to portray themselves in only positive ways. Yet your memoir is honest in areas where you found yourself coming up short—whether it was the way you worried that you were letting your children down as you built your business, or the way you fretted in your teen years. Was it hard to reveal your flaws so publicly? What might a reader—or writer, even—miss out on if the story told is always one of unblemished success?

A: *I'd be dead boring. As my twelfth grade teacher, Mr. Wallace, wrote on my term paper about a woman I admired: "C. Perfect people are rarely true and never interesting."*

The mistakes I made are the fun parts of the book. Anyway, if all I told were the sweet and nice things about me, the book would be a pamphlet.

Q: Can you tell us something of your writing schedule? Obviously you're a busy person with daily work demands. How did you fit writing into your routine?

A: *Writing and building a business are both energy-consuming commitments. I couldn't take on both at once. I had almost finished a novel when I started my business, but I realized I had to put my energy into the business. Once that was going well and I could afford the time to write, I decided it was* *more important for me to write this book. Structure is imperative for me. To fit writing into my life, I had to have a committed place as well as time. My office was for business. I worked in there every day until two, and then I went home to write.*

Q: Speaking of writing habits, can you tell us yours? Did you outline first? Write by hand, dictate, or type it yourself on a computer? How many drafts did this take you? How many months/years? Have you learned anything that will make the process easier for your next memoir—and will there be a sequel?

A: *I wrote on the computer. I actually started in the '90s by writing poetry about my childhood impressions of Petain Street and Mama, Daddy, Grandmama, Aunt Pauline, and the other people there. Gradually I realized this was a story—a book—and I rewrote the poems as prose. That was the beginning. Some of my favorite lines came directly from the poems.*

> *I love Grandmama*
> *but I think she's going to Hell*
> *because she won't go to Church with Mama and me.*

As chapters developed, I put each one in its own Microsoft Word document to keep myself focused—an ADD thing. At first I intended to tell the story in a straight timeline, but one early reader suggested I start each chapter in my early life, then connect those experiences to my business life and career.

How many drafts? Ten? Twenty? I saved many of them and will have to count them someday.

I'm not planning a sequel but I have an almost-finished novel I plan to follow up with.

Q: We're glad to know there really is a Ruthi Postow behind the eponymous company, Ruthi Postow Staffing. What's next for you—in business, life, or literature?

A: *My husband really did give my story a happy ending. Now I spend half of my time traveling with him or just "wasting time" at home enjoying him.*

I enjoy speaking, telling the stories of Petain Street, and hope to do more. I believe these are messages many people need to hear.

I also plan to finish my novel, which is based in a place similar to Petain Street.

Q: What was the most difficult part of this process? The easiest?

A: *The easiest was writing it. Petain Street is so visible in my mind. I see it in color and hear the people. Events from all of the parts of my life roll by as though I am watching them on YouTube. The hardest was organizing it to answer the so-what questions, to make it relevant to other people. And, of course, getting past my fears to sell it.*

Once it was finally done I was too insecure to stick my neck out and sell it to agents and publishers, so it sat in my computer for nearly ten years. I'm grateful to my husband for giving me the courage to go on. Seeing it become real is a great feeling.

Q: You built up a successful business in an era—the 1970s and '80s—when it was much harder for women to gain a foothold in the male-dominated world of business. Do you think the business climate has changed significantly, or is it still hard for women to be taken seriously as leaders?

A: *It has changed. When my husband graduated from Columbia Law School in 1965, there were six women in a class of 320—and those women had to* *have fortitude to put up with the abuse. In 2016 there are 551 women to 616 men, according to the Columbia website.*

In my world, women have been leaders for a long time. I see the most significant improvements in the successes of women like Shonda Rhimes, who would have been discouraged or blocked from bringing her talent to light years ago. Other women still wait to get their fair share. They still earn far less than men in the same jobs—e.g., our women's hockey team.

Q: If you could meet your younger selves—the little girl on Petain Street, the nervous pre-teen in junior high, and the college co-ed at the University of Georgia—what would you say to them? Do you think they'd listen?

A: *I think I'd listen to their thoughts more than I'd try to tell them things. I don't think my child self could hear me if I told her she was okay as she was and didn't have to change or be like anybody else.*

I might want to tell my high school self that plane geometry would never, ever matter in her life, but I'm pretty sure she already knew that.

ABOUT *the* AUTHOR

RUTHI POSTOW BIRCH started life in deep-south Alabama in a town that straddled the poverty line. She rose to be one of the most respected members of the Washington, DC, business community, guided by the uncomplicated common-sense principles she learned from the working-class people who raised her.

After graduating from college, she taught middle school for two years in Braselton, Georgia, but her dream was of a career in business. Moving to Washington, Ruthi joined a staffing firm and launched her business career. But she entered the job market at a time when men were the professionals and women were "girls," expected to settle for second place. She broke through the limits to become the company's top producer and remained there throughout her career. She was also active in business organizations and served on committees with the Greater Washington Board of Trade.

In 2001, she founded Ruthi Postow Staffing, recruiting temporary and permanent employees for businesses in the DC area. The company has won several awards, including *Washington Business Journal*'s "Best Places to Work," and "Future Fifty" by *SmartCEO* magazine. In 2005 she established an annual scholarship dedicated to helping others succeed through education.

Ruthi wrote a column for *The Washington Business Journal* for two years. She created two blogs, *Three O'clock in the Morning* and *I Hate Interviewing. How to Build a Piano Bench* is Ruthi's first book.

Ruthi is the mother of three boys, each on his own path to success. She lives in Old Town Alexandria, Virginia, with her husband, Ron Birch; their Wheaten terrier, Mr. Magoo; and a family of chimney swifts that return every spring to nest in their 18th-century chimney.

I am Ruthi and I am real!

There was a time when I thought that should be taken for granted. But that ended soon after I started a business and gave it my name. The better known the company became, the more I faded away until the day I heard a staff member say to a client, "No. There really is a Ruthi! She comes into the office every day." I wondered, was that the only proof I was still a person—and if I stopped coming to the office, would I disappear entirely?

Made in the USA
San Bernardino, CA
08 November 2017